W9-BWK-351

THE BIG BOOK OF
INSTANT POT® RECIPES

THE BIG BOOK OF
INSTANT POT®
RECIPES

240 MUST-TRY DISHES
FOR YOUR MULTI-FUNCTION COOKER

**KRISTY BERNARDO, EMILY SUNWELL-VIDAURRI,
AMY RAINS AND STEFANIE BUNDALO**

PAGE STREET
PUBLISHING CO.

PAGE STREET
PUBLISHING CO.

Copyright © 2019 Kristy Bernardo, Emily Sunwell-Vidaurri, Amy Rains and Stefanie Bundalo

First published in 2019 by

Page Street Publishing Co.

27 Congress Street, Suite 105

Salem, MA 01970

www.pagestreetpublishing.com

All rights reserved. No part of this book may be reproduced or used, in any form or by any means, electronic or mechanical, without prior permission in writing from the publisher.

Distributed by Macmillan, sales in Canada by The Canadian Manda Group.

23   22   21   20   19   1   2   3   4   5

ISBN-13: 978-1-62414-882-8

ISBN-10: 1-62414-882-4

Library of Congress Control Number: 2019935117

Cover and book design by Ashley Tenn for Page Street Publishing Co.

Photography by Emily Sunwell-Vidaurri, Amy Rains, Stefanie Bundalo and Donna Crous

Cover image by Donna Crous

Printed and bound in China

Instant Pot® is a registered trademark of Double Insight, Inc., which was not involved in the creation of this book.

Page Street Publishing protects our planet by donating to nonprofits like The Trustees, which focuses on local land conservation.

CONTENTS

INTRODUCTION

Light, fresh, hearty and common ingredients all thrown into one pot and magically transformed into a complete meal in under an hour . . . SIGN ME UP! I am sure those were your first thoughts upon purchasing an Instant Pot. The Instant Pot has become a worldwide sensation, and for good reason! We've become a culture obsessed with getting our meals made quickly, and without a sink full of dishes. The Instant Pot continues to prove that fantastic tasting meals prepared at home can still be attainable in our busy lives.

In this book, we explore a variety of flavors and dishes from breakfast to dinner, and sides to dessert, all using wholesome ingredients in the process. The majority of the recipes found in this book can be made in less than 45 minutes, and are truly one-pot meals. Dishes and clean-up have never been so easy!

Why use an Instant Pot? Pressure cooking can cut traditional cook times by up to 70%, making it a great choice for a busy weeknight. With little more to do than dumping all ingredients into the pot and securing the lid, we're redefining the true meaning of "one-pot" cooking! From a nutrition standpoint, the Instant Pot method preserves more nutrients in your food because of the shorter cook time and lower temperature than traditional cooking methods. Found yourself in a situation without a stove or oven? Instant Pot to the rescue! A college student in a dorm room, a family on a camping trip or anyone who has found themselves living through a kitchen renovation can still have a complete home-cooked meal.

The Instant Pot allows us to simulate the effects of long braises, boils and simmers in a fraction of the time. Whether it be an authentic ethnic dish (like Chicken Tikka Masala, page 302), a hearty soup or stew (Lobster Bisque, anyone? page 174) or even dessert (hello, Mini Cinnamon Crunch Monkey Breads! page 455), you will soon find that the Instant Pot can do it all! Looking for an easy breakfast or brunch idea for the weekend? Breakfast Enchilada Casserole (page 28) is calling your name!

Whether you're an Instant Pot guru, amateur or rookie, you've picked up the right book. You might be a tad late to the trend, or already in a long-term committed relationship. Either way, we're so glad you are trusting us with your meals!

JALAPEÑO-CHEDDAR BAGEL CASSEROLE

While I was growing up, my dad used to always get jalapeño-studded, cheddar cheese–coated bagels from our local bagel joint. I always made a face at the bagels. Now, I am a grown-up and know better. Jalapeño and cheddar were meant to be together. Especially on a bagel with fluffy eggs and even more cheese. The Instant Pot takes your leftover jalapeño-cheddar bagels and transforms them into the fluffiest breakfast casserole. **SB**

SERVES: 4

1 cup (237 ml) water

6 large eggs

¼ cup (60 ml) heavy cream

Salt

Freshly ground black pepper

1 jalapeño pepper, thinly sliced

1½ jalapeño-cheddar bagels, cut into ½" (1.3-cm) pieces

½ cup (58 g) shredded cheddar cheese

1 tbsp (9 g) feta cheese crumbles

Unsalted butter, for baking dish

Chopped fresh cilantro, for garnish

Pour the water into the Instant Pot and insert the steam trivet.

In a bowl, combine the eggs, cream, salt and black pepper to taste and the jalapeño and mix until the eggs are beaten. Stir in the bagel pieces and cheeses. Let sit for 3 minutes.

Butter a 7-inch (18.5-cm) round baking dish. Pour the egg mixture into the prepared baking dish. Carefully insert the baking dish into the Instant Pot on top of the steam trivet.

Secure the lid with the steam vent in the sealed position. Press pressure cook until the display light is beneath high pressure. Use the plus and minus buttons to adjust the time until the display reads "20 minutes."

When the timer sounds, quick release the pressure and carefully remove the lid.

Use the steam trivet handles to lift the trivet and baking dish out of the pot.

Let the casserole cool for 5 minutes and then garnish with chopped fresh cilantro.

DAIRY-FREE GRAIN-FREE PALEO

CHOCOLATE-SPICED PUMPKIN BREAD

Spiced pumpkin bread is such a treat during the colder months when pumpkin is in season. The sweet winter squash adds a nice texture and flavor to this easy quick bread that's spiced with cinnamon, ginger and allspice plus lots of chocolate, because you can't go wrong with chocolate. **ESV**

SERVES: 8 to 10

8 tbsp (112 g) grass-fed butter, ghee or avocado oil, melted, plus more for casserole dish

½ cup (120 ml) pure maple syrup

1 cup (245 g) pure pumpkin puree

2 large eggs, at room temperature

1 tsp pure vanilla extract

1 cup (120 g) cassava flour

¼ cup (28 g) unsweetened cocoa powder

¼ cup (28 g) grass-fed hydrolyzed collagen powder

2 tsp (5 g) ground cinnamon

¼ tsp ground ginger

¼ tsp ground allspice

1 tsp baking soda

½ tsp sea salt

1 cup (175 g) chopped quality chocolate

1 cup (237 ml) water

NOTES: Use quality chocolate bars for the chocolate, preferably fair trade. Lots of Paleo versions of chocolate are available in natural food stores and online.

Sustainably sourced grass-fed collagen is sold at most natural food stores and widely available online.

Use your healthy fat of choice to grease a 1½-quart (1.5-L) casserole dish that fits inside the Instant Pot. Line the bottom of the casserole dish with a circle of parchment paper. Set aside.

In a blender, in the order listed, combine all the ingredients, except the chopped chocolate and water. Process on low speed until smooth and fully blended, about 20 seconds, scraping down the sides, if needed. Add the chopped chocolate and give it a stir with a spatula to fold in. Pour the batter into the prepared casserole dish. Cover the casserole dish with its glass lid. If your casserole dish doesn't come with a glass lid, you can cover the top of the dish with unbleached parchment paper, then top it with foil and secure it around the edges.

Pour the water into the Instant Pot and insert the steam trivet. Carefully set the covered casserole dish on top of the trivet. Secure the lid with the steam vent in the sealed position. Press manual and set on high pressure for 55 minutes.

Once the timer sounds, press keep warm/cancel. Allow the Instant Pot to release pressure naturally for 20 minutes. Using an oven mitt, do a quick release. If there is any steam left over, allow it to release until the silver dial drops, then carefully open the lid.

Carefully lift the trivet and the casserole dish out of the Instant Pot. Use oven mitts or towels because the Instant Pot and dish will be extremely hot. Carefully remove the hot lid from the dish, taking care not to drip any of the condensation on the top of the bread. Test with a toothpick to make sure the center is fully cooked; no more than a few moist crumbs should be on the toothpick. If it needs more time, re-cover with the lid (make sure to wipe off any condensation first) and return the dish to the Instant Pot to cook on manual for another 5 minutes, then do a quick pressure release.

Allow the bread to cool at room temperature sitting on top of the trivet (as a cooling rack) for 45 minutes. Gently run a knife around the edges of the bread to loosen it when you're ready to remove it from the dish. Turn the dish upside down on a plate to release the bread. Cut the bread into thick slices and serve immediately.

GF

GLUTEN-FREE

GINGERBREAD FRENCH TOAST CASSEROLE

Say hello to your new favorite holiday breakfast! You'll love this cozy "bake" on Christmas morning or just for a weekend breakfast. The Instant Pot can make anything happen, and this simple French toast is no exception! The bread gets extra toasty by sautéing with butter, eliminating the need for an oven. **AR**

SERVES: 4

2 tbsp (28 g) unsalted butter

½ loaf French bread or sourdough bread, cut into 1" (2.5-cm) chunks (about 3 cups [150 g]) (see note)

Nonstick cooking spray, for bowl or pan

3 large eggs

¾ cup (175 ml) whole milk or nut milk

¼ cup (60 ml) molasses

2 tbsp (30 g) coconut sugar or dark brown sugar

1 tsp ground ginger

1 tsp ground cinnamon

¼ tsp ground cloves

Pinch of salt

1 cup (237 ml) water

Pure maple syrup, for serving

Select sauté on the Instant Pot. Once the pot is hot, melt the butter, then add the bread cubes. Cook, tossing them around a bit, so all the bread cubes become lightly browned and toasty, 6 to 7 minutes. Select cancel.

Lightly spray a 6- or 7-inch (15- or 18.5-cm) glass bowl or springform pan with nonstick cooking spray. Place the bread cubes in the bowl and set aside.

In a separate bowl, whisk together the eggs, milk, molasses, coconut sugar, ginger, cinnamon, cloves and salt. Pour the egg mixture on top of the bread and gently toss. Cover the bowl with foil.

Place the water in the bottom of the Instant Pot and insert the steam trivet. Place the casserole bowl on top of the trivet.

Secure the lid with the steam vent in the sealed position. Select manual or pressure, and cook on high pressure for 15 minutes.

Use a quick release, and be sure to release all of the steam before opening the lid. Gently remove the bowl, using pot holders. Serve the casserole hot with warm maple syrup.

NOTE: You can easily substitute a gluten-free bread or your favorite bread of choice.

DOUBLE CHOCOLATE BANANA BREAD

For breakfast, brunch or snacking, this chocolaty banana bread is meant to be savored. The Instant Pot helps give this bread a soft texture—it's perfect gently warmed and even toasted. Go ahead and slather a slice with some grass-fed butter for an extra-special treat. **ESV**

SERVES: 8 to 10

8 tbsp (112 g) grass-fed butter, ghee or avocado oil, melted, plus more for casserole dish

½ cup (120 ml) pure maple syrup

3 small ripe bananas, quartered

2 large eggs, at room temperature

1 tsp pure vanilla extract

1 cup (120 g) cassava flour

¼ cup (28 g) unsweetened cocoa powder

¼ cup (28 g) grass-fed hydrolyzed collagen

1 tsp baking soda

½ tsp sea salt

1 cup (175 g) chopped quality chocolate

1 cup (237 ml) water

NOTE: Use quality chocolate bars for the chocolate, preferably fair trade. There are lots of Paleo versions of chocolate available in natural food stores and online—everything from stevia to coconut sugar to maple or honey sweetened.

Use your healthy fat of choice to grease a 1½-quart (1.5-L) casserole dish that fits inside the Instant Pot. Line the bottom of the casserole dish with a circle of parchment paper. Set aside.

In a blender, in the order listed, place all the ingredients, except the chopped chocolate and water. Mix on low speed until smooth and fully combined, about 20 seconds, scraping down the sides, if needed. Add the chopped chocolate to the blender and give it a stir with a spatula to fold in. Pour the batter into the prepared casserole dish. Cover the casserole dish with its glass lid. If your casserole dish doesn't come with a glass lid, you can cover the top of the dish with unbleached parchment paper, then top it with foil and secure it around the edges.

Pour the water into the Instant Pot and insert the steam trivet. Carefully set the covered casserole dish on top of the trivet. Secure the lid with the steam vent in the sealed position. Press manual and set on high pressure for 55 minutes.

Once the timer sounds, press keep warm/cancel. Allow the Instant Pot to release pressure naturally for 20 minutes. Using an oven mitt, do a quick release. If there is any steam left over, allow it to release until the silver dial drops, then carefully open the lid.

Carefully lift the trivet and the casserole dish out of the Instant Pot. Use oven mitts or towels because the Instant Pot and dish will be extremely hot. Carefully remove the hot lid, taking care not to drip any of the condensation on the top of the bread. Test with a toothpick to make sure the center is fully cooked; no more than a few moist crumbs should be on the toothpick. If it needs more time, re-cover with the lid (make sure to wipe off any condensation first) and return to the Instant Pot to cook on manual for another 5 minutes, then do a quick pressure release.

Allow the bread to cool at room temperature sitting on top of the trivet (as a cooling rack) for 45 minutes. Gently run a knife around the edges of the bread to loosen it when you're ready to remove it from the dish. Turn the dish upside down on a plate to release the banana bread. Cut the banana bread into thick slices and serve immediately.

DAIRY-FREE GLUTEN-FREE

EVERYTHING BAGEL CONGEE BREAKFAST BOWL

You might be reading that recipe title and thinking to yourself, What in the world is congee? Congee is an Asian porridge made from rice. Plain and simple. I came across it late in my life and got hooked. On days when I have an upset tummy or am feeling sick, congee is right up there with chicken noodle soup now. It is cozy and comforting and, thanks to the Instant Pot, it is a fuss-free creation. **SB**

SERVES: 4 to 6

1 cup (195 g) uncooked jasmine rice

7 cups (1.7 L) water

1 cup (150 g) stemmed and sliced shiitake mushrooms

¼ tsp sesame oil

½ tsp dried minced garlic

½ tsp dried minced onion

½ tsp salt

3 large slices peeled fresh ginger

1 tsp everything bagel seasoning mix

Optional toppings: soft-boiled egg, sriracha sauce, soy sauce, sliced green onions

In the Instant Pot, combine the rice, water, mushrooms, sesame oil, garlic, onion, salt and ginger.

Secure the lid with the steam vent in the sealed position. Press porridge; the time display will read "20 minutes."

Once the timer sounds, allow the pressure to naturally release. When the float valve falls, remove the lid. Taste the congee and adjust the salt, if needed.

Place equal portions of congee in individual bowls. Top each with ¼ to ½ teaspoon of everything bagel seasoning, plus an egg, sriracha, soy sauce and/or sliced green onions (if using).

DAIRY-FREE GLUTEN-FREE GRAIN-FREE

MEXICAN EGGS IN PURGATORY
WITH CHORIZO

When I was pregnant with each of my children, there was one thing, aside from Taco Bell, that I craved . . . eggs in purgatory, or shakshuka. Whatever you call it, I wanted it. Runny yolk eggs cooked in a spicy sauce with a side of toast to sop everything up. Yes! This version cooks quickly, thanks to the Instant Pot. It uses salsa verde as the base and has potatoes, chorizo and tomatillos to bulk up the recipe and make it more filling. Pregnant or not, you are going to be craving this, too! **SB**

SERVES: 4 to 6

1 tbsp (15 ml) extra-virgin olive oil

1 small russet potato, diced

2 tomatillos, husked, washed and diced

1 yellow onion, diced

1 jalapeño pepper, minced

8 oz (225 g) ground pork chorizo

½ tsp ground cumin

½ tsp smoked paprika

Salt

Freshly ground black pepper

1 cup (237 ml) salsa verde

1 cup (237 ml) low-sodium chicken stock

4 to 6 large eggs

Place the olive oil in the Instant Pot. Press sauté. Wait 1 minute for the oil to heat up and then add the potato, tomatillos, onion, jalapeño and chorizo. Sauté for 5 minutes, stirring occasionally.

Stir in the cumin, paprika and salt and black pepper to taste. Sauté for an additional minute.

Press cancel. Stir in the salsa verde and stock and be sure to scrape up any browned bits from the bottom of the pot.

Secure the lid with the steam vent in the sealed position. Press pressure cook and use the plus and minus buttons to adjust the time until the display reads "4 minutes" on high pressure.

When the timer sounds, quick release the pressure. Remove the lid.

Give the mixture a quick stir. Press sauté until the display light is beneath normal.

Crack the eggs into the salsa verde mixture, leaving about an inch (2.5 cm) between each egg. Season the top of each egg with a little bit of salt and pepper. Sauté for about 10 minutes, or until the white part of the egg is no longer translucent.

GF GLUTEN-FREE **GRAIN-FREE**

SHAKSHUKA

Shakshuka is a traditional Middle Eastern dish with poached eggs in a slightly spicy tomato sauce. Basically, my perfect meal! I have always made this on the stovetop, and only recently played around with preparing it in the Instant Pot. This fantastically delicious sauce gets even tastier when pressure cooked. Serve plain or with some crumbled feta and bread. **AR**

SERVES: 2

2 tbsp (30 ml) avocado oil or olive oil

1 small yellow onion, diced

1 green bell pepper, seeded and diced

1 clove garlic, minced

¼ cup (60 ml) water

1 (28-oz [800-g]) can whole tomatoes, with juices

1½ tsp (3.5 g) smoked paprika

½ tsp ground cumin

½ tsp sea salt

4 large eggs

¼ cup (15 g) chopped fresh parsley or (10 g) cilantro, for serving

3 tbsp (28 g) crumbled feta cheese, for serving (optional)

Select sauté on the Instant Pot. Once the pot is hot, coat the bottom with the oil and add the onion and bell pepper. Sauté for 2 to 3 minutes, then add the garlic. Cook for another minute, or until the vegetables are softened and fragrant. Select cancel.

Deglaze the pot with the water. Now, add the tomatoes with their juices, paprika, cumin and salt.

Secure the lid with the steam vent in the sealed position and select manual or pressure. Cook on high pressure for 6 minutes, then use a quick release and remove the lid.

Gently crack each egg into a ladle or large wooden spoon and slowly lower into the tomato sauce. Secure the lid once again, and select manual or pressure and zero minutes (yes, zero).

Use a quick release and remove the lid. You can leave the lid on longer for a more cooked egg (see note).

Serve hot with fresh parsley or cilantro, and feta cheese.

NOTE: If you prefer a more cooked yolk, keep the lid on after the cook time is complete, for another 3 to 4 minutes.

BREAKFAST ENCHILADA CASSEROLE

I had the idea to make an almost lasagna-like enchilada casserole for this book and knew it would be a hit. Not only is this breakfast great for a crowd, it is flexible, and the leftover slices reheat so nicely. The ingredients can be totally customizable. If you don't like meat, add more veggies. Switch out the cheeses or even add cooked ground chorizo instead of breakfast sausage. If you are like me and can eat Mexican food for every meal, every day, you will never tire of this fun breakfast recipe. **SB**

SERVES: 4 to 6

1 cup (237 ml) water

1 tbsp (15 ml) extra-virgin olive oil

20 small flour tortillas

6 oz (170 g) cooked breakfast sausage links, diced

1 red bell pepper, seeded and stemmed and thinly sliced

½ yellow onion, thinly sliced

½ cup (86 g) drained and rinsed canned black beans

¾ cup (175 ml) canned red enchilada sauce

4 large eggs

1 tsp heavy cream

¼ tsp dried oregano

¼ tsp crushed red pepper flakes

Salt

Freshly ground black pepper

1½ cups (173 g) shredded Mexican-blend cheese

Pour the water into the Instant Pot and insert the steam trivet.

Oil a 7-inch (18.5-cm) round baking dish or leakproof springform pan with the olive oil.

Layer 2 or 3 tortillas on the bottom of the dish, enough to cover the bottom. Place one-third of the sausage, one-third of the sliced red bell pepper, one-third of the sliced onion and one-third of the black beans on top of the tortillas. Top with 2 to 3 tablespoons (30 to 45 ml) of the enchilada sauce.

In a small bowl, mix together the eggs, cream, oregano, red pepper flakes, salt and black pepper.

Pour one-third of the egg mixture over the veggie- and bean-topped tortilla. Sprinkle a big pinch of cheese over the eggs and then top with 2 or 3 more tortillas. Do the same with the next two layers, ending with tortillas.

When the layers of tortillas and fillings have just about reached the edge of the dish, add the remaining ⅛ to ¼ cup (30 to 60 ml) of enchilada sauce and the remaining cheese to the top of the tortillas.

Cover the dish with foil and carefully insert into the Instant Pot on top of the steam trivet.

Secure the lid with the steam vent in the sealed position. Press pressure cook and use the plus and minus buttons to adjust the time until the display reads "25 minutes."

When the timer sounds, quick release the pressure. Remove the lid and use the steam trivet handles to lift the trivet and baking dish out of the pot. Remove the foil and let the casserole sit for at least 10 minutes before slicing.

GF GLUTEN-FREE GRAIN-FREE

ZESTY EGG WHITE BITES

You know those popular little sous vide egg bites from a very popular coffee shop chain that cost close to five dollars? You can make those at home for way less if you just buy a handy-dandy little silicone egg bite mold. The silicone mold makes seven egg bites—that's a week's worth of a bite of breakfast on the go, for a fraction of the cost. Plus, the added caramelized onion, ham and cheese will make you forget those other egg bites even exist. **SB**

MAKES: 7 egg bites

1 tbsp (14 g) unsalted butter

½ yellow onion, sliced

Salt

Freshly ground black pepper

3 oz (85 g) thick-cut ham, diced

1 cup (237 ml) water

½ cup (55 g) shredded Swiss and Gruyère cheese blend

6 large egg whites

1 tbsp (15 ml) heavy cream

½ tsp prepared ground horseradish

¼ tsp dried thyme

Press sauté until the display light is beneath less. Once the pot is hot, add the butter. When the butter melts, add the onion. Sauté for about 10 minutes, or until caramelized, stirring occasionally.

Season with salt and pepper to taste. Stir in the diced ham and sauté for 5 more minutes.

Transfer the ham and caramelized onion to a plate to cool. Clean out the inside of the Instant Pot and return it to the device.

Place the water in the Instant Pot and insert the steam trivet.

Place some caramelized onion and ham along with cheese in the bottom of each well of a silicone egg bite mold.

In a small bowl, whisk together the egg whites, cream, horseradish, salt, pepper and thyme. Pour the egg mixture over the ham mixture, filling each mold about three-quarters of the way full.

Carefully insert the silicone egg bite mold into the Instant Pot on top of the steam trivet. Secure the lid with the steam vent in the sealed position. Press steam and then use the plus and minus buttons to adjust the time until the display reads "8 minutes."

When the timer sounds, let the pressure naturally release for 10 minutes. Quick release any remaining pressure.

Remove the lid and, using the steam trivet handles, carefully lift the trivet and egg bite mold out of the pot.

Use a butter knife to cut around the edges and release the egg bites from the mold. Flip the egg bites out onto a plate. Season with more salt and pepper, if needed.

GF GLUTEN-FREE   **GRAIN-FREE**

TOMATO & OLIVE CRUSTLESS MINI QUICHE BITES

I love to add unexpected ingredients to breakfast dishes. It keeps it interesting and gussies up an otherwise ordinary dish. The tomatoes and green olives in these quiches complement the creamy eggs and goat cheese. We are using the little silicone egg bite mold here because we are going for a poppable yet slightly fancy breakfast. If you want, you can use four small soufflé ramekins and make it really fancy. **SB**

SERVES: 4

1 tsp extra-virgin olive oil

5 large eggs

½ tsp onion salt

½ tsp dried basil

½ tsp chopped fresh dill

½ tsp chopped fresh parsley

½ cup (75 g) sliced cherry tomatoes

¼ cup (25 g) chopped pitted green olives

¼ cup (75 g) crumbled goat cheese

1 cup (237 ml) water

Place the olive oil on a paper towel and then use the paper towel to oil each well of the egg bite mold.

In a medium bowl, whisk together the eggs, onion salt, basil, dill and parsley.

Add ¼ to ½ teaspoon each of the tomatoes, olives and goat cheese to the bottom of each well in the mold. Pour the egg mixture over the toppings to fill each well about three-quarters of the way up. Add the remaining tomatoes, olives and cheese on top of the egg mixture.

Place the water in the Instant Pot and insert the steam trivet. Carefully insert the egg mold into the Instant Pot on top of the steam trivet.

Secure the lid with the steam vent in the sealed position. Press steam. Use the plus and minus buttons to adjust the time until the display reads "8 minutes."

Once the timer sounds, allow the pressure to naturally release for 10 minutes. Quick release any remaining pressure.

Remove the egg bite mold. Flip the mini quiches out onto a serving dish. If any sticks to the mold, use a butter knife to go around the quiche and remove it that way.

GF GLUTEN-FREE GRAIN-FREE

BACON & GRUYÈRE CRUSTLESS QUICHE

This quiche reheats very well, so I like to make it and keep it in the fridge so we can just heat up a quick slice when hunger strikes. It's a wonderful dish for weekend brunches with a light salad, too. **KB**

SERVES: 4

6 slices bacon

1½ cups (355 ml) water

Nonstick cooking spray, for pan

6 large eggs

¾ cup (175 ml) heavy cream

½ cup (55 g) shredded Gruyère cheese

1 tbsp (4 g) chopped fresh parsley

½ tsp coarse salt

Freshly ground black pepper

Press sauté to preheat the Instant Pot. When the word "hot" appears on the display, add the bacon. Cook until the bacon is browned and crispy, then remove it with a slotted spoon and place on paper towels to drain any excess fat. Discard the drippings without wiping clean.

Add the water to the pot, taking care to scrape up any browned bits from the bottom of the pot. Insert the steam trivet. Press cancel to turn off the Instant Pot.

Spray a 7-inch (18.5-cm) round cake pan with nonstick cooking spray.

In a medium bowl, whisk together the eggs and cream until frothy. Crumble the bacon and stir it in along with the shredded cheese, parsley, salt and pepper. Pour the mixture into the prepared cake pan and place the pan on the trivet.

Secure the lid with the steam vent in the sealed position. Press manual and immediately adjust the timer to 30 minutes. Check that the display light is beneath high pressure.

When the timer sounds, quick release the pressure and carefully remove the lid. Carefully remove the cake pan from the pot. Slice the quiche and serve immediately.

BACON & VEGGIE-PACKED MINI BREAKFAST FRITTATAS

GF GLUTEN-FREE GRAIN-FREE

These protein-packed mini breakfast frittatas are so fun and especially helpful for on-the-go breakfasts, lunches or snacks. When cooked in little half-pint (250-ml) Mason jars, these frittatas can be packed to go with you on busy mornings or stashed in your bag for lunch. **ESV**

SERVES: 4

2 tbsp (28 g) grass-fed butter or ghee, plus more for jars

½ cup (35 g) cleaned and thinly sliced white button or cremini mushrooms

1 large celery rib, thinly sliced

½ cup (15 g) prewashed finely chopped fresh spinach

6 large eggs

¼ cup (60 ml) milk of choice

½ tsp sea salt

½ tsp garlic granules or garlic powder

¼ tsp onion powder

¼ tsp dried thyme

2 tbsp (8 g) chopped fresh flat-leaf parsley, plus more for garnish

½ cup (58 g) shredded sharp or mild cheddar cheese

¼ cup (20 g) shredded Parmesan, provolone or Gruyère cheese

4 slices cooked crispy bacon, crumbled

1½ cups (355 ml) water

Place your healthy fat of choice in the Instant Pot and press sauté. Once the fat has melted, add the mushrooms and celery and sauté, stirring occasionally, for 7 minutes, or until lightly caramelized. Add the spinach and sauté, stirring occasionally, for 2 minutes, or just until wilted. Press the keep warm/cancel button.

Butter 4 half-pint (250-ml) wide-mouth Mason jars or ramekins (my preference is the Mason jars because they come with lids). Set them aside.

In a large bowl, whisk together the eggs and your milk of choice until the eggs are fully incorporated. Add the sautéed veggies, salt, garlic granules, onion powder, thyme, parsley, shredded cheeses and crumbled bacon. Evenly pour the mixture into the prepared jars. Secure the metal lids on top of the Mason jars, or if you're using ramekins, cover the tops of the ramekins with unbleached parchment paper, then top them with foil and secure it around the edges.

Pour the water into the Instant Pot and insert the steam trivet. Carefully transfer the jars into the Instant Pot on top of the trivet.

Secure the lid with the steam vent in the sealed position. Press manual and set on high pressure for 5 minutes.

Once the timer sounds, press keep warm/cancel. Using an oven mitt, do a quick release. When the steam venting stops and the silver dial drops, carefully open the lid.

Carefully remove the jars from the Instant Pot and remove the lid from each jar. If the flat part of the metal lid has sealed, you may need to release the suction with the side of a can opener.

Allow the frittatas to rest for 5 minutes before serving.

NOTE: Mini bok choy or kale can be substituted for the spinach.

CUBANO STRATA

Everybody has a trusty standby sandwich. The sandwich you can always order when you're having trouble picking something new. The Cubano, or Cuban, sandwich is that sandwich for me. It's shredded pork, ham, pickles, mustard and Swiss cheese. You can't really mess it up. Those flavors translate well into an egg, cheese and bread–based strata. The little bites of pickle really cut through the richness from the meats and cheeses. Twenty minutes in the Instant Pot is all it takes to make my number one crowd-pleasing brunch strata! **SB**

SERVES: 4

1 tbsp (14 g) unsalted butter

1 cup (237 ml) water

6 large eggs

¼ tsp ground cumin

¼ tsp mustard powder

⅓ cup (80 ml) heavy cream

Salt

Freshly ground black pepper

½ cup (95 g) leftover Mole Carnitas (page 322) or store-bought cooked pulled pork

½ cup (75 g) cubed ham

¾ cup (83 g) shredded Swiss cheese

2 cups (100 g) cubed French bread

1 small to medium kosher dill pickle, thinly sliced

Butter a 7-inch (18.5-cm) round baking dish. Pour the water into the Instant Pot and insert the steam trivet.

In a medium bowl, mix together the eggs, cumin, mustard powder, cream, salt and pepper.

Stir in the mole carnitas, ham, Swiss, bread and pickle. Let the mixture sit for 2 minutes before transferring to the prepared baking dish.

Carefully insert the baking dish into the Instant Pot on top of the steam trivet.

Secure the lid with the steam vent in the sealed position. Press pressure cook until the display light is beneath high pressure. Use the plus and minus buttons to adjust the time until the display reads "20 minutes."

When the timer sounds, quick release the pressure. Remove the lid and, using the trivet handles, carefully lift the trivet and baking dish out of the pot. Let the strata cool slightly before slicing.

NOTE: The strata can be prepared, placed in the baking dish, covered with plastic wrap and then stored in the fridge the night before serving.

GF
GLUTEN-FREE

CARAMELIZED ONION, MUSHROOM & SPINACH STRATA

Savory stratas are an egg and cheese–based bread casserole. They're perfect to serve for breakfast or brunch. This stellar gluten-free strata is brimming with caramelized onions and mushrooms, with herby aromatics, spinach and a hint of lemon. **ESV**

SERVES: 6 to 8

3 tbsp (43 g) grass-fed butter or ghee, plus more for casserole

1 large yellow onion, thinly sliced

8 oz (225 g) cleaned white button or cremini mushrooms, thinly sliced

3 cloves garlic, finely chopped

1 tbsp (2 g) chopped fresh thyme

3 large eggs

1 cup (237 ml) milk

1 (16-oz [454-g]) loaf day-old gluten-free bread, cut into 1" (2.5-cm) cubes

1 cup (115 g) shredded sharp or mild cheddar cheese

½ cup (40 g) shredded Parmesan cheese

1 cup (156 g) frozen chopped spinach, thawed and moisture squeezed out

¼ cup (15 g) chopped fresh flat-leaf parsley, plus more for garnish

Zest of 1 lemon

1 tsp sea salt

1½ cups (355 ml) water

Place your healthy fat of choice in the Instant Pot and press sauté. Once the fat has melted, add the onion and mushrooms and cook, stirring occasionally, for 7 minutes, or until the onion and mushrooms are light golden brown and caramelized. Add the garlic and thyme and stir with a wooden spoon for 1 minute until fragrant, making sure to scrape up any browned bits at the bottom of the pot. Press keep warm/cancel. Transfer the onion mixture to a bowl and set aside.

Butter a 1½-quart (1.5-L) casserole dish (I use one that comes with a glass lid) that fits inside the Instant Pot. Set aside.

In a very large bowl, whisk together the eggs and milk until fully incorporated. Add the bread cubes, shredded cheeses, onion mixture, spinach, parsley, lemon zest and salt, then gently fold to combine. Pour the mixture into the prepared casserole dish and cover the dish with its glass lid. If your casserole dish doesn't come with a glass lid, you can cover the top of the dish with unbleached parchment paper, then top it with foil and secure it around the edges.

Pour the water into the Instant Pot and insert the steam trivet. Carefully set the covered casserole dish on top of the trivet. Secure the lid with the steam vent in the sealed position. Press manual and set on high pressure for 30 minutes.

Once the timer sounds, press keep warm/cancel. Allow the Instant Pot to release pressure naturally for 15 minutes. Using an oven mitt, do a quick release. If there is any steam left over, allow it to release until the silver dial drops, then carefully open the lid.

Carefully lift the trivet and the casserole dish out of the Instant Pot. Use oven mitts or towels because the Instant Pot and dish will be extremely hot. Carefully remove the hot lid. Optional, but highly recommended: Place the casserole dish on a baking sheet, then place in the oven under a preheated broiler for about 3 minutes to crisp the top of the strata. Allow to rest at room temperature for 10 minutes before serving.

DAIRY-FREE GLUTEN-FREE GRAIN-FREE

SOFT-BOILED EGGS
WITH TRUFFLE SALT & PROSCIUTTO

This is the breakfast I have almost every weekday morning. The soft yolk and truffle salt with a luscious slice of prosciutto will have you looking forward to breakfast. It's great for keto followers, too! **KB**

SERVES: 2

1 cup (237 ml) water
4 large eggs
1 tsp truffle salt
8 slices prosciutto

Pour the water into the Instant Pot and insert the steam trivet. Carefully place the eggs on the trivet.

Secure the lid with the steam vent in the sealed position. Press manual and immediately adjust the timer to 3 minutes. Check that the display light is beneath high pressure.

When the timer sounds, quick release the pressure and carefully remove the lid. Run the eggs under cold water until cool, then peel.

Sprinkle the eggs with truffle salt. Serve with the prosciutto slices.

DAIRY-FREE

EGGS IN A BOAT

Breakfast food is the best. The only thing that can bring breakfast food down a notch is the number of different pans you need for eggs, veggies and meat. Oh! And don't forget the toaster. Eggs in a Boat in the Instant Pot is your all-in-one breakfast dish with minimal cleanup! A crusty demi-baguette filled with eggs, greens and tomatoes is a perfect way to start the day. Eggs in a boat can be split between two people or eaten solo on those days when you wake up hangry. **SB**

SERVES: 4 to 6

½ cup (120 ml) water

3 to 4 demi-baguettes

½ cup (15 g) mixed fresh baby spinach and arugula

6 grape tomatoes, halved

6 to 8 large eggs

Salt

Freshly ground black pepper

Crushed red pepper flakes

Pour the water into the Instant Pot and insert the steam trivet.

Cut each demi-baguette to create a lid and well in the bread. Slice length-wise from end to end at a 45 degree angle about three-quarters of the way through the bread. Use your fingers to pull the "lid" off the baguette. Remove any stray pieces of bread from inside the well. You want to ensure there is enough room for the eggs.

To each demi-baguette, add a few leaves of spinach and arugula along with a few tomato halves. Crack 2 eggs into each bread boat. Top with salt, black pepper and a tiny pinch of red pepper flakes.

Arrange up to three bread boats inside the Instant Pot on top of the trivet.

Secure the lid with the steam vent in the sealed position. Press pressure cook until the display light is beneath high pressure. Use the plus and minus buttons to adjust the time until the display reads "4 minutes."

When the timer sounds, allow the pressure to naturally release for 3 minutes. After 3 minutes, quick release any remaining pressure.

Remove the boats with tongs and transfer to a plate. Allow the boats to cool for a minute or two so the bread will harden up a bit again, before slicing and serving.

GLUTEN-FREE GRAIN-FREE

JALAPEÑO CHEESY EGGS

I make these cheesy eggs often for our family. They're so quick and easy, plus they keep well and can be popped into the microwave for a quick weekday breakfast. **KB**

SERVES: 3

6 large eggs
½ cup (115 g) full-fat cottage cheese
½ cup (60 g) Mexican-blend shredded cheese
1 jalapeño pepper, minced
1 green onion, minced
1 cup (237 ml) water

In a high-powered blender, blend together all the ingredients except the water.

Pour the water into the Instant Pot and insert the steam trivet. Evenly divide the egg mixture among the wells of a six-bite egg mold. Carefully lower the mold onto the trivet.

Secure the lid with the steam vent in the sealed position. Press steam and immediately adjust the timer to 10 minutes. Check that the display light is beneath high pressure.

Once the timer sounds, allow the pressure to release naturally for 10 minutes, then quick release the pressure and carefully remove the lid. Carefully remove the eggs from the molds and serve immediately.

GF

GLUTEN-FREE

PARMESAN POLENTA
WITH EGGS

News flash! Polenta is not just for dinner. There is no better way to start the day than with a belly full of warm Parmesan polenta. Cooking polenta normally takes a lot of stirring and patience, but not when you make it in the Instant Pot. Top the polenta with a fried egg and mix the runny yolk into the polenta for added creaminess. **SB**

SERVES: 4

1 cup (175 g) uncooked polenta (not instant)

4 cups (946 ml) water

1 tsp salt, plus more if needed

¼ tsp freshly ground black pepper, plus more if needed

1 tbsp (15 ml) extra-virgin olive oil

4 large eggs

3 tbsp (43 g) unsalted butter

2 tbsp (30 ml) heavy whipping cream

2 oz (55 g) finely grated Parmesan cheese, plus more for topping

In the Instant Pot, mix together the polenta, water, salt and pepper until combined.

Secure the lid with the steam vent in the sealed position. Press pressure cook until the display light is beneath high pressure. Use the plus and minus buttons to adjust the time until the display reads "9 minutes."

While the polenta cooks, place a small to medium skillet over high heat. Heat the olive oil. Once the oil is shimmering, crack the eggs into the hot oil. Fry the eggs for about 4 minutes, or until the white part is firm.

Once the timer sounds, quick release the pressure from the Instant Pot.

Remove the lid and mix the butter, cream and cheese into the polenta. Taste the polenta and adjust the salt and pepper, if needed.

Transfer the polenta to four bowls and top each with a fried egg.

DAIRY-FREE GLUTEN-FREE
GRAIN-FREE VEGAN

CINNAMON-APPLE & BUTTERNUT SQUASH BREAKFAST SOUP

Butternut squash for breakfast? Yes! This cozy bowl of apples and butternut squash makes a unique and absolutely delicious breakfast! Packing in nutrients, fiber and healthy fats, this breakfast soup is sure to keep you full longer. Not too sweet and, as Goldilocks would say, "just right!" **AR**

SERVES: 4

3 cups (430 g) seeded, peeled and cut butternut squash (½" [1.3-cm] chunks)

1 apple, peeled, cored and cut into ½" (1.3-cm) chunks (I like Honeycrisp or Gala apples)

1 (13.5-oz [400-ml]) can full-fat coconut milk

2 tsp (5 g) ground cinnamon

1 tbsp (15 ml) pure maple syrup

Pinch of salt

½ cup (55 g) roasted and chopped pecans

In the Instant Pot, combine the butternut squash, apple pieces, coconut milk, cinnamon, maple syrup and salt.

Secure the lid with the steam vent in the sealed position. Select manual or pressure, and cook on high pressure for 6 minutes.

Use a quick release. Remove the lid once the steam has been completely released. Using an immersion blender or high-powered blender, blend until smooth.

Serve warm and top with pecans.

DAIRY-FREE

BACON & EGG FRIED RICE

Sometimes leftovers make the best breakfast. That is where I got the idea of a breakfast fried rice. You have a filling starch, a vegetable and protein. What else do you need first thing in the morning? The glory of this dish is you can make it for breakfast and then keep the pot on warm and have the rest for lunch or dinner! **SB**

SERVES: 4 to 6

1¼ cups (295 ml) water

1 cup (190 g) uncooked brown rice

Salt

1 tsp sesame oil

5 slices raw bacon, chopped

1 tsp soy sauce

3 large eggs, beaten

½ cup (65 g) frozen peas

Freshly ground black pepper

Sriracha sauce, for topping (optional)

4 green onions, sliced

In the Instant Pot, combine the water, rice and a pinch of salt.

Secure the lid with the steam vent in the sealed position. Press pressure cook until the display light is beneath high pressure. Use the plus and minus buttons to adjust the time until the display reads "15 minutes."

When the timer sounds, allow the pressure to naturally release. Once the float valve falls, remove the lid. Use a fork to fluff the rice, then transfer it to a large plate. Set aside.

Clean out the pot and then return it to the device. Set to sauté.

Once the display reads "hot," add the sesame oil along with the chopped bacon. Sauté for 5 to 7 minutes, stirring and turning regularly, until each piece is crispy.

Press sauté again until the display light is beneath less.

Stir in the soy sauce, then push the bacon to one side of the Instant Pot. Add the eggs to the opposite side of the pot. Gently push the eggs back and forth, using a rubber spatula, until they start to scramble slightly. Add the cooked rice and mix everything together quickly.

Press cancel and stir in the peas. Let the fried rice sit for a minute or two until the peas have thawed and warmed.

Season with salt and pepper to taste. Top with sriracha sauce (if using) and the green onions.

GLUTEN-FREE · **GRAIN-FREE**

CODDLED EGGS
WITH GARLICKY KALE

Garlic and kale for breakfast? Heck, yeah! Think of that extra pep in your step you will have from these two superfoods. I love to make a bunch of these little ramekins ahead of time. That way, if I am running late, I can just grab one of them and heat it up for a quick and nutritious breakfast. **SB**

SERVES: 4

1 tbsp (15 ml) extra-virgin olive oil

½ yellow onion, diced

2 cups (134 g) trimmed and chopped kale

Salt

Freshly ground black pepper

1 clove garlic, grated

1 cup (237 ml) water

Unsalted butter, for ramekins

4 large eggs

2 tsp (10 ml) heavy cream

Set the Instant Pot to sauté. Once the display reads "hot," add the olive oil. Let the oil heat for 1 minute, then add the onion. Sauté for 2 minutes. Mix in the kale along with a little salt and pepper. Sauté for 3 to 4 minutes, or until tender and slightly wilted. Add the garlic, stir to combine and sauté for an additional minute.

Press cancel. Remove the kale mixture and transfer to a small plate.

Clean the Instant Pot and return it to the device. Pour the water into the Instant Pot and insert the steam trivet.

Butter four small soufflé ramekins with unsalted butter. Place a little bit of the kale mixture in the bottom of each ramekin. Crack an egg into each ramekin, then top each egg with ½ teaspoon of the heavy cream, plus salt and pepper.

Place the ramekins on top of the trivet.

Secure the lid with the steam vent in the sealed position. Press steam. Use the plus and minus buttons to adjust the time until the display reads "3 minutes."

When the timer sounds, allow the pressure to naturally release for 2 minutes. Quick release any remaining pressure.

BLUEBERRY FRENCH TOAST

I love French toast, and this version is so simple with no flipping the toast in batches. It's almost like a bread pudding, but you get to enjoy it for brunch! A perfect weekend breakfast dish. **KB**

SERVES: 4

2 large eggs

1 cup (237 ml) whole milk

2 tbsp (30 g) light brown sugar

1 tsp pure vanilla extract

½ tsp ground cinnamon

1 small loaf French bread, cut into ½" (1.3-cm) cubes (about 7 slices)

Nonstick cooking spray, for pan

½ cup (75 g) blueberries, plus more for serving (optional)

1 cup (237 ml) water

Pure maple syrup, for serving

In a medium bowl, beat the eggs. Add the milk, brown sugar, vanilla and cinnamon, then whisk well until thoroughly combined. Add the bread cubes and press into the liquid until completely submerged. Cover and refrigerate for 30 minutes (or overnight if you want to make it ahead).

Spray a 7-inch (18.5-cm) round cake pan with nonstick cooking spray. Remove the bread mixture from the refrigerator and fold in the blueberries. Pour the mixture into the prepared pan.

Pour the water into the Instant Pot and insert the steam trivet. Cover the cake pan with foil and place on the trivet.

Secure the lid with the steam vent in the sealed position. Press manual and adjust the timer to 15 minutes. Check that the display light is beneath high pressure.

When the timer sounds, quick release the pressure and carefully remove the lid. Cut the French toast and serve with maple syrup and more fresh blueberries, if desired.

RASPBERRY PANCAKE BITES

This one is so simple that my girls will make it for themselves when they have friends over. It makes a great breakfast or snack. Add a few mini chocolate chips and it's almost a dessert! **KB**

SERVES: 2

1 cup (120 g) pancake mix, prepared as a batter according to the package directions

Small pinch of ground cinnamon

½ cup (65 g) raspberries

1½ cups (355 ml) water

Pure maple syrup, for serving

In a medium bowl, stir the cinnamon into the prepared pancake batter. Gently fold in the raspberries.

Pour the mixture into an egg bite mold until each well is about three-quarters full. Cover tightly with foil.

Pour the water into the Instant Pot and insert the steam trivet. Place the egg mold on top of the trivet.

Secure the lid with the steam vent in the sealed position. Press manual and adjust the timer to 5 minutes. Check that the display light is beneath high pressure.

Once the timer sounds, allow the pressure to release naturally for 2 minutes, then quick release the pressure and carefully remove the lid. Remove the pancake bites and serve with maple syrup, if desired.

GF GLUTEN-FREE   **V** VEGAN OPTION

BERRY CHIA PORRIDGE

This creamy bowl of goodness is reminiscent of oatmeal—without the grains! It's packed with antioxidants, nutrients, healthy fats and protein for a simple hearty breakfast. Top with additional berries, nuts or even shredded coconut for additional crunchy texture. A fantastic make-ahead breakfast you can also enjoy throughout the week! **AR**

SERVES: 2 to 3

6 oz (170 g) fresh raspberries, plus more for serving (optional)

½ cup (75 g) fresh blueberries, plus more for serving (optional)

1 (13.5-oz [400-ml]) can full-fat coconut milk

¼ cup (40 g) chia seeds

2 scoops collagen protein powder (optional)

2 tbsp (15 g) nuts, for serving (optional)

In the Instant Pot, combine the raspberries, blueberries, coconut milk and chia seeds. Give the mixture a quick stir.

Secure the lid with the steam vent in the sealed position. Select manual or pressure, and cook on high pressure for 1 minute.

Use a natural release for 8 minutes, then release any remaining steam. Stir in the collagen (if using).

Serve hot, at room temperature or chilled. Top with additional berries and nuts (if using).

GF
GLUTEN-FREE

PUMPKIN PIE OATMEAL

Who doesn't want pie for breakfast, especially when it comes together so quickly? This breakfast is simple, but always feels like a special treat. **KB**

SERVES: 4

2 cups (320 g) steel-cut oats

4½ cups (1.1 L) milk

1 (14.5-oz [411-g]) can pure pumpkin puree

¾ cup (170 g) light brown sugar

1 tsp ground cinnamon

½ tsp coarse salt

1 tsp pure vanilla extract

2 tbsp (28 g) unsalted butter, at room temperature

¼ cup (30 g) dried cranberries

¼ cup (28 g) chopped pecans

¼ cup (60 ml) pure maple syrup, for drizzling

In the Instant Pot, combine the oats, milk and pumpkin, then whisk until smooth. Add the brown sugar, cinnamon and salt and stir well.

Secure the lid with the steam vent in the sealed position. Press manual and immediately adjust the timer to 4 minutes. Check that the display light is beneath high pressure.

Once the timer sounds, allow the pressure to release naturally for 20 minutes. Open the lid of the Instant Pot and stir in the vanilla, butter, cranberries and pecans.

Serve immediately in bowls and drizzle the oatmeal with maple syrup.

GF GLUTEN-FREE **V** VEGAN OPTION

SINGLE-SERVING BERRY OATMEAL

This is what I make for my kids on many weekday mornings. It's so simple and fast, plus they can add whatever toppings they like. Try it with sliced peaches and a drizzle of cream in the summertime! **KB**

SERVES: 1

½ cup (80 g) steel-cut oats

1½ cups (355 ml) water, divided

½ cup (120 ml) almond, soy or dairy milk

2 tsp (10 g) light brown sugar

Pinch of salt

Fresh berries, for topping (optional)

In a large heatproof mug or small heatproof dish, mix together the oats, ½ cup (120 ml) of the water, milk, brown sugar and salt.

Pour the remaining cup (235 ml) of water into the Instant Pot and insert the steam trivet. Place the mug on the trivet. Press manual and adjust the timer to 10 minutes. Check that the display light is beneath high pressure.

When the timer sounds, quick release the pressure and carefully remove the lid. Using oven mitts, as it will be very hot, carefully remove the mug. Top with fresh berries, if desired.

STRAWBERRY CHEESECAKE OATMEAL

I never grew up an oatmeal kind of girl. But cheesecake? Yes. Cheesecake, I can get behind. If you tell me the way to have cheesecake for breakfast is with a healthy dose of oats, I will eat it and go back for seconds! In three minutes of cooking and with a little bit of stirring, you can get the creamiest oatmeal ever in the Instant Pot. Top it off with some fresh strawberries and crumbled graham crackers and you won't even realize you are eating breakfast. **SB**

SERVES: 4

1 cup (237 ml) plain unsweetened almond milk

1 cup (237 ml) water

1 cup (80 g) old-fashioned rolled oats

¼ tsp salt

1 cinnamon stick

1.5 oz (43 g) cream cheese, softened

½ tsp pure vanilla extract

1 cup (170 g) sliced strawberries

¼ cup (23 g) crumbled graham crackers

Honey, for drizzling

In the Instant Pot, combine the almond milk, water, oats, salt and cinnamon stick. Stir to distribute.

Secure the lid with the steam vent in the sealed position. Press pressure cook until the display light is beneath high pressure. Use the plus and minus buttons to adjust the time until the display reads "3 minutes."

When the timer sounds, allow the pressure to naturally release for 20 minutes. After 20 minutes, quick release any remaining pressure. Remove the lid. Stir the oats and remove the cinnamon stick.

Add the cream cheese and vanilla. Stir until the cream cheese is completely melted into the oats.

Place the cooked oats in four serving bowls and top with strawberries, graham crackers and a drizzle of honey.

MAPLE-PECAN STEEL-CUT OATS

For those cold weather mornings when you want a filling and cozy breakfast, these oats are the perfect solution! This recipe also has the perfect combination of high fiber, plant-based protein and a healthy fat with coconut milk, allowing you to be satisfied for hours. I love the way this recipe makes a large batch, allowing you to refrigerate and reheat throughout the week for busy weekday mornings. **AR**

SERVES: 4

2 cups (320 g) steel-cut oats

3 cups (710 ml) water

1 (13.5-oz [400-ml]) can full-fat coconut milk, divided

⅓ cup (80 ml) pure maple syrup, plus more to taste

½ tsp sea salt

½ cup (56 g) toasted pecan pieces

2 tsp (5 g) ground cinnamon (optional)

In the Instant Pot, combine the oats, water, 1 cup (237 ml) of the coconut milk, and the maple syrup and salt. Give the mixture a quick stir. Secure the lid with the steam vent in the sealed position.

Select manual or pressure, and cook on high pressure for 4 minutes.

Use a natural release for 15 minutes, then release any remaining steam before removing the lid.

After removing the lid, stir in the remaining coconut milk and additional maple syrup to taste.

Serve with the toasted pecans and sprinkle with the cinnamon (if using).

CINNAMON ROLL OATMEAL

Another dessert-for-breakfast recipe that will make the entire family happy. This is one I make often for my girls before they're off to school. **KB**

SERVES: 4

2 cups (180 g) old-fashioned rolled oats

4 cups (946 ml) milk

¼ cup (60 g) light brown sugar

1 tsp pure vanilla extract

½ tsp salt

1 tsp ground cinnamon

2 tbsp (28 g) unsalted butter, at room temperature

¼ cup (60 ml) pure maple syrup, for drizzling

In the Instant Pot, combine the oats, milk, brown sugar, vanilla, salt and cinnamon and stir well.

Secure the lid with the steam vent in the sealed position. Press manual and immediately adjust the timer to 4 minutes. Check that the display light is beneath high pressure.

Once the timer sounds, allow the pressure to release naturally for 20 minutes. Open the lid of the Instant Pot and stir in the butter.

Serve immediately in bowls and drizzle the oatmeal with maple syrup.

DAIRY-FREE   GRAIN-FREE

BACON JAM BREAKFAST SWEET POTATOES

Sweet potatoes coated in salty and sticky bacon jam. Yes. This recipe doesn't need a big explanation as to why it is amazing. It says it all in the title. Crisp that bacon, caramelize those onions and then toss in the sweet potatoes. Three minutes in the Instant Pot later, you have tender sweet potatoes coated in that jammy goodness. Even though this recipe cooks up fast, you will still have enough time to fry some eggs to serve on top. **SB**

SERVES: 4 to 6

1 tbsp (15 ml) extra-virgin olive oil

7 slices thick-cut bacon, diced

1 yellow onion, diced

1 tsp Worcestershire sauce

¼ cup (60 ml) bourbon or beef stock

3 sweet potatoes (about 19 oz [540 g] total), peeled and cut into large cubes

⅓ cup (80 ml) water

Salt

Freshly ground black pepper

¼ cup (38 g) loosely packed light brown sugar

¼ tsp cayenne pepper

Press sauté on the Instant Pot. Make sure the display light is beneath normal. Once the pot reads "hot," add the olive oil and bacon. Sauté for about 10 minutes, or until crispy, stirring regularly to prevent sticking.

Add the onion and sauté for an additional 5 to 7 minutes, or until the onion is starting to caramelize.

Deglaze the pot with the Worcestershire and bourbon. Use the edge of a wooden spoon to scrape up all the browned bacon bits from the bottom of the pot. Sauté for 2 more minutes.

Press cancel. Stir in the sweet potatoes along with the water, plus salt and black pepper to taste.

Secure the lid with the steam vent in the sealed position. Press pressure cook until the display light is beneath high pressure. Use the plus and minus buttons to adjust the time until the display reads "3 minutes." When the timer sounds, quick release the pressure.

Stir in the brown sugar and cayenne pepper. Let the potato mixture cool slightly before tasting and adjusting the salt and pepper, if needed.

GF GLUTEN-FREE   GRAIN-FREE

HAM & CARAMELIZED ONION HOME FRIES

Breakfast potatoes are a staple at any breakfast joint. They usually come in the form of hash browns or diced little baby potatoes with peppers and onions. Potatoes cook up in no time in the Instant Pot, so you definitely have time to play them up and add whatever you like. I wanted to take these vehicles for egg consumption to the next level by adding caramelized onion and salty ham. Now these potatoes have taken center stage, you don't even need an egg! **SB**

SERVES: 4 to 6

1 tbsp (15 ml) extra-virgin olive oil

2 tbsp (28 g) unsalted butter

2 yellow onions, diced

¾ cup (113 g) diced thick-cut ham

½ tsp chopped fresh rosemary

3 sprigs thyme

3 large russet potatoes, cut into 1" (2.5-cm) cubes

Salt

Freshly ground black pepper

¼ cup (60 ml) chicken stock

Press sauté and make sure the display light is beneath normal. Wait a minute or two for the pot to heat. Add the olive oil and butter. Once the butter melts, add the onions. Cook for about 9 minutes, or until the onions start to caramelize.

Add the ham, rosemary and thyme. Stir to combine. Sauté for another 3 minutes.

Press cancel. Stir in the potatoes, salt and pepper to taste and the stock. Using a wooden spoon, scrape up any bits from the bottom of the pan.

Secure the lid with the steam vent in the sealed position. Press pressure cook until the display light is beneath high pressure. Use the plus and minus buttons to adjust the time until the display reads "3 minutes." When the timer sounds, quick release the pressure.

Remove the lid, stir and add more salt or pepper if needed.

LUNCH

GF
GLUTEN-FREE

BROWN BUTTER PUMPKIN RISOTTO

If you haven't made risotto in the Instant Pot yet, why do you even have an Instant Pot? I'm kidding! But seriously, risotto is such a hands-on dish when it is cooked on a stovetop; you have to watch over it to get it just right. Making it in the Instant Pot is a hands-off way to get creamy risotto every time. No need to stand over the stove and add ladle after ladle of stock. Add the rice and stock to the pot. While it cooks, brown up some butter. Add the butter, pumpkin and cheese to the rice at the end, and you're done! Keep the risotto warm in the pot to maintain that creaminess. It really could not be easier! **SB**

SERVES: 4

4 tbsp (55 g) unsalted butter, divided

1 yellow onion, minced

2 cloves garlic, grated

2 cups (390 g) uncooked arborio rice

1 tbsp (15 ml) bourbon

4 cups (946 ml) vegetable or chicken stock

½ cup (123 g) pure pumpkin puree

½ cup (50 g) freshly finely grated Parmesan cheese, divided

Salt

Freshly ground black pepper

Press sauté on the Instant Pot. Wait 1 minute for the pot to heat. Add half of the butter. When the butter melts, add the onion and sauté until translucent, about 3 minutes.

Add the garlic and rice, stirring continuously to prevent browning. Once the rice is toasted, about 2 minutes, add the bourbon. Scrape any stuck bits off the bottom of the pot. Press cancel.

In a large measuring cup, heat the stock in a microwave for 1 minute. Add the warmed stock to the Instant Pot and stir to combine.

Secure the lid with the steam vent in the sealed position. Press pressure cook until the display light is beneath high pressure. Use the plus and minus buttons to adjust the time until the display reads "5 minutes."

While the risotto cooks, heat the remaining butter in a small pan over medium heat until the butter stops crackling and starts to brown. When the butter has dark golden bits floating in it, 3 to 5 minutes, remove from the heat.

When the timer sounds, quick release the pressure from the Instant Pot. Remove the lid.

Stir in the pumpkin puree and half of the grated Parmesan. Add salt and pepper to taste. Transfer the risotto to individual bowls. Top with the brown butter and the remaining Parmesan cheese.

LEMON-ARTICHOKE CHICKEN
WITH AVOCADO

DAIRY-FREE GLUTEN-FREE GRAIN-FREE

This is my spin on a warm salad. Minus lettuce. Simply marinated chicken served alongside big pieces of artichoke hearts and avocados is the perfectly balanced light lunch. I like to imagine bringing out a big dish of this at a book club meeting or a quick meal shared between friends. It is not only perfect flavor-wise, it is perfect because of the minimal amount of prep you have to do to make a stunner of a dish. Everything happens in the Instant Pot; just toss in the avocado at the end and get back to doing what you were doing. **SB**

SERVES: 4

2 tbsp (30 ml) extra-virgin olive oil

Juice of ½ lemon

1 tbsp (15 ml) white wine vinegar

Salt

Freshly ground black pepper

4 large boneless, skinless chicken breasts

¼ cup (60 ml) white wine

1 (14-oz [400-g]) can quartered artichoke hearts, drained

1 avocado, peeled, pitted and cubed

1 tsp chopped fresh parsley

Lemon wedges, for serving

In a gallon-size (4-L) resealable plastic bag, combine the olive oil, lemon juice, vinegar, salt, pepper and chicken. Seal the bag and shake to evenly coat the chicken. Marinate the chicken for at least 30 minutes and up to an hour in the refrigerator.

Press sauté on the Instant Pot and make sure the display light is beneath normal. Transfer the chicken and its marinade to the pot. Sauté for about 5 minutes on the first side. Flip the chicken, press cancel and then add the white wine. Stir the wine into the marinade.

Add the artichoke hearts to the pot.

Secure the lid with the steam vent in the sealed position. Press pressure cook and make sure the display light is beneath high pressure. Use the plus and minus buttons to adjust the time until the display reads "10 minutes."

When the timer sounds, quick release the pressure. Remove the lid and use tongs to transfer the chicken and artichoke hearts to a serving platter.

Add the avocado to the platter along with a few tablespoons (about 45 ml) of the cooking liquid left in the Instant Pot. Top with fresh parsley and add lemon wedges to the platter.

OPEN-FACED BEEF SANDWICHES
WITH SMOKY GOUDA SAUCE

This recipe works well with leftover pot roast. The creamy, cheesy sauce is to die for! **KB**

SERVES: 4

2 tsp (10 ml) olive oil

1 (2-lb [905-g]) chuck roast

Coarse salt

Freshly ground black pepper

1 medium onion, sliced

1 cup (237 ml) beef stock

¼ cup (30 g) all-purpose flour

2 cups (475 ml) whole milk

4 oz (115 g) shredded smoked Gouda cheese

1 loaf crusty bread, sliced and toasted

Press sauté to preheat the Instant Pot. When the word "hot" appears on the display, add the oil to the pot. Season your chuck roast well with salt and pepper, then add the roast to the Instant Pot and brown it well on all sides. Remove the roast and set aside.

Add the onion to the drippings in the pot and scrape up any browned bits on the bottom of the pot. Sauté the onion until it is soft and starting to caramelize, about 10 minutes.

Add the beef stock, taking care to scrape up any browned bits from the bottom of the pot. Place the roast directly into the liquid.

Secure the lid with the steam vent in the sealed position. Press manual and adjust the timer to 40 minutes. Check that the display light is beneath high pressure.

Meanwhile, in a small saucepan, whisk together the flour and milk to make a sauce. Cook over medium heat until it starts to thicken, about 3 to 4 minutes. Add the shredded cheese, 1 small handful at a time, gently stirring to incorporate before adding more. Season well with salt and pepper.

When the timer sounds, quick release the pressure and carefully remove the lid. Shred the meat with two forks and stir the meat into the liquid in the pot.

Divide the meat mixture among the toasted slices of bread. Drizzle with the cheese sauce and serve.

PHILLY CHEESESTEAK SLOPPY JOES

I love Philly cheesesteaks, but we can't get a good one around here. So, when I need my fix, I make these joes. We love to keep them on warm when we have a party and let everyone serve themselves, too! **KB**

SERVES: 4

2 tsp (10 ml) olive oil

1 medium onion, sliced

1 green bell pepper, seeded and sliced

8 oz (225 g) mushrooms, sliced

1 lb (455 g) ground beef

1 (10-oz [295-ml]) can French onion soup

¼ cup (60 ml) water

2 tsp (10 ml) Worcestershire sauce

6 buns, split, buttered and toasted

6 slices provolone cheese

Press sauté to preheat the Instant Pot. When the word "hot" appears on the display, add the olive oil, then the onion, bell pepper and mushrooms. Cook, stirring occasionally, until the onion is soft and the mushrooms have released their liquid and it has evaporated, 5 to 7 minutes. Add the beef and cook until almost no pink is left, about 5 minutes.

Add the French onion soup and water, taking care to scrape up any browned bits from the bottom.

Secure the lid with the steam vent in the sealed position. Press soup and immediately adjust the timer to 7 minutes. Check that the display light is beneath high pressure.

When the timer sounds, quick release the pressure and carefully remove the lid. Stir in Worcestershire sauce. Divide the meat mixture among the rolls and top each mixture with a slice of provolone (the heat from the meat will melt the cheese).

DAIRY-FREE   GLUTEN-FREE   GRAIN-FREE

CHIPOTLE EGG SALAD WRAPS

I love egg salad and this recipe takes it to the next level. It's creamy and a little spicy with a nice crunch from the peppers. Great for lunches and keto followers! **KB**

SERVES: 4

1 cup (237 ml) water

8 large eggs

½ cup (115 g) mayonnaise

1 chipotle pepper (from a can of chipotle peppers in adobo)

½ red bell pepper, seeded and diced

½ poblano pepper, diced

1 jalapeño pepper, minced

¼ cup (10 g) chopped fresh cilantro

¼ cup (25 g) chopped green onion

Salt

Freshly ground black pepper

4 large lettuce leaves

4 slices tomato, halved

Pour the water into the Instant Pot and insert the steam trivet. Carefully place the eggs on the trivet.

Secure the lid with the steam vent in the sealed position. Press manual and immediately adjust the timer to 5 minutes. Check that the display light is beneath high pressure.

Once the timer sounds, allow the pressure to release naturally for 10 minutes, then quick release the pressure and carefully remove the lid. Run the eggs under cold water until cool, then peel.

In a medium bowl, mix together the mayonnaise and chipotle pepper. Stir in the bell, poblano and jalapeño peppers, cilantro and green onion.

Chop the eggs and gently fold them into the mayonnaise mixture. Season with salt and pepper.

Divide the egg salad among the lettuce leaves, then top with the tomato slices

DAIRY-FREE   GLUTEN-FREE OPTION   GRAIN-FREE

ASIAN BEEF LETTUCE WRAPS

Spiced, tangy and Asian-flavored beef cooks perfectly under pressure in a simple sauce! Place inside lettuce wraps with additional toppings for a complete meal, or serve on top of a bowl of rice. **AR**

SERVES: 4

2 tbsp (30 ml) olive or avocado oil

2 lb (905 g) top sirloin steak or stew meat

½ cup (120 ml) soy sauce, gluten-free tamari or coconut aminos

¼ cup (60 ml) beef stock

2 tbsp (30 ml) rice vinegar

3 tbsp (45 g) coconut sugar

2 tbsp (30 ml) sriracha or chili garlic sauce

2 tsp (10 ml) sesame oil

1 tsp ground ginger

2 tbsp (16 g) arrowroot powder

2 tbsp (30 ml) water

1 head romaine lettuce

1 cup (130 g) matchstick-sliced carrot

⅓ cup (33 g) diced green onion

¼ cup (10 g) chopped fresh cilantro (optional)

Select sauté on the Instant Pot. Once hot, coat the bottom of the Instant Pot with the olive oil. Place the meat in the pot and brown on all sides. This should take 3 to 4 minutes. Select cancel.

In a medium bowl, whisk together the soy sauce, beef stock, vinegar, coconut sugar, sriracha, sesame oil and ginger. Pour the soy sauce mixture over the beef.

Secure the lid with the steam vent in the sealed position. Select manual or pressure, and cook on high pressure for 10 minutes.

Use a natural release for 15 minutes, then release any remaining steam.

After removing the lid, in a small bowl, stir together the arrowroot starch and water and pour into the pot. Select the sauté function and let the liquid come to a quick boil, then select cancel and let the sauce thicken.

Assemble the lettuce wraps by adding the beef, carrot, green onion and cilantro (if using).

GF GLUTEN-FREE   GRAIN-FREE

BUFFALO CHICKEN LETTUCE WRAPS

These easy wraps are perfect for a quick lunch. Sometimes I'll make a big salad out of the ingredients and skip the wrapping. I love that we can get our buffalo wing fix but it's much healthier. **KB**

SERVES: 4

½ cup (120 ml) chicken stock

2 lb (905 g) boneless, skinless chicken breast

½ cup (120 g) buffalo wing sauce

½ cup (50 g) chopped celery

¼ cup (30 g) crumbled blue cheese

2 green onions, chopped

8 large lettuce leaves

Ranch or blue cheese dressing, for drizzling

Pour the chicken stock into the Instant Pot, then add the chicken breast.

Secure the lid with the steam vent in the sealed position. Press manual and immediately adjust the timer to 6 minutes. Check that the display light is beneath high pressure.

In a medium bowl, mix together the wing sauce, celery, blue cheese and green onions. Remove the chicken from the pot, chop the chicken and mix it with the sauce mixture.

Divide the buffalo chicken among the lettuce leaves, then drizzle with dressing.

DAIRY-FREE

CARIBBEAN JERK PULLED PORK SANDWICHES

The flavor in this pulled pork is amazing and makes for a deliciously different sandwich! It's also great served with mashed potatoes or rice for a more hearty dinner. **KB**

SERVES: 8

2 tbsp (30 ml) olive oil

1 tsp ground cinnamon

2 tsp (4 g) allspice

1 tsp coarse salt

1 tsp freshly ground black pepper

¼ tsp freshly ground nutmeg

2 tsp (2 g) dried thyme

½ tsp cayenne pepper

1 (4-lb [1.8-kg]) pork shoulder

1 cup (237 ml) water or chicken broth

Crusty rolls

Sliced pineapple

In a small bowl, mix together the olive oil, cinnamon, allspice, salt, black pepper, nutmeg, thyme and cayenne. Rub the mixture all over the pork roast.

Press sauté to preheat the Instant Pot. When the word "hot" appears on the display, add the roast and brown it well on all sides, adding a little oil to the pot, if necessary.

Remove the roast and set aside. Add the water or broth to the pot, taking care to scrape up any browned bits from the bottom of the pot. Return the roast to the pot.

Secure the lid with the steam vent in the sealed position. Press manual and adjust the timer to 50 minutes. Check that the display light is beneath high pressure.

When the timer sounds, quick release the pressure and carefully remove the lid. Shred the meat with two forks and stir in with the liquid in the pot.

Divide the meat mixture among the rolls and top each with a slice of pineapple.

DAIRY-FREE

KOREAN BEEF SANDWICHES

If you're looking for a flavor twist from the usual sandwich, give this one a try. It's a deliciously different flavor and is great to make for a crowd. Just keep your Instant Pot setting on warm and set out the buns and toppings so everyone can make their own. **KB**

SERVES: 8

⅓ cup (80 ml) beef stock

½ cup (120 ml) soy sauce

⅓ cup (75 g) light brown sugar

4 cloves garlic, minced

2 tbsp (30 ml) sesame oil

2 tbsp (30 ml) rice vinegar

2 tbsp (12 g) grated fresh ginger

2 tbsp (30 ml) Korean chili sauce (gochujang)

3 lb (1.4 kg) chuck roast, cut into bite-sized pieces

8 rolls

Toppings: mayonnaise, sliced jalapeño pepper, cucumber, fresh cilantro

In a small bowl, whisk together the stock, soy sauce, brown sugar, garlic, sesame oil, vinegar, ginger and chili sauce. Pour the mixture into the Instant Pot and add the beef.

Secure the lid with the steam vent in the sealed position. Press manual and immediately adjust the timer to 40 minutes. Check that the display light is beneath high pressure.

When the timer sounds, quick release the pressure and carefully remove the lid. Divide the beef mixture among the rolls and add toppings as desired.

BBQ CHICKEN JALAPEÑO SLIDERS

This recipe was tested three times and then made another two times in a row. It was tested and cooked so many times not because I was having trouble with it, but because it was so good! My husband and I each ate six sliders for lunch one day and then for dinner the next! The trick to living off sliders for days in a row is to cook the meat in the Instant Pot ahead of time. Then, when the craving for these sticky sweet and spicy sliders hits, all you have to do is assemble and heat them in the oven. **SB**

SERVES: 4

2 large boneless, skinless chicken breasts

¼ cup (60 ml) water or chicken stock

1 tsp salt

½ tsp ground cumin

¼ tsp freshly ground black pepper

Juice of 1 lime

½ red onion, thinly sliced

1 clove garlic, grated

¼ cup (30 g) mild-medium sliced pickled jalapeño peppers

1 tbsp (15 ml) honey

12 brioche slider buns

6 oz (170 g) Gouda cheese, shredded

In the Instant Pot, combine the chicken, water or stock, salt, cumin, black pepper, lime juice, red onion, garlic, jalapeños and honey.

Secure the lid with the steam vent in the sealed position. Press pressure cook until the display light is beneath high pressure. Use the plus and minus buttons to adjust the time until the display reads "15 minutes."

Preheat the oven to 375°F (190°C). Line a half sheet pan with foil. Slice the slider buns in half horizontally, placing the bun bottoms on the prepared sheet pan.

When the timer sounds, quick release the pressure on the Instant Pot. Remove the lid. Use two forks to shred the chicken and mix together all the contents of the Instant Pot.

Use tongs to transfer equal amounts of the chicken mixture to each bun bottom. Top each little pile of chicken with a pinch of shredded cheese and then cover with the top bun.

Bake the sliders for 15 minutes, or until the cheese melts. Let cool slightly for 2 minutes before serving.

CRACK CHICKEN SANDWICHES

Tender chicken, a creamy ranch sauce and bacon? It's perfect on a toasted bun! It's rich, but the lettuce and tomato balance that out nicely. Wrap them in foil for a great picnic sandwich! **KB**

SERVES: 4

8 slices bacon

½ medium onion, chopped

½ cup (120 ml) chicken stock

2 lb (905 g) boneless, skinless chicken breast

1 (1-oz [28-g]) packet dried ranch seasoning mix

1 (8-oz [225-g]) package cream cheese

1 cup (115 g) shredded cheddar cheese

¼ cup (60 g) sour cream

4 buns, split, buttered and toasted

Lettuce, for topping

Sliced tomato, for topping

Press sauté to preheat the Instant Pot. When the word "hot" appears on the display, add the bacon. Cook until the bacon is browned and crispy, then remove it with a slotted spoon and place on paper towels to drain any excess fat. Add the onion to the drippings in the pot and cook until starting to soften, 3 to 4 minutes.

Add the chicken stock to the pot, taking care to scrape up any browned bits from the bottom of the pot. Then add the chicken, ranch seasoning and cream cheese.

Secure the lid with the steam vent in the sealed position. Press manual and immediately adjust the timer to 15 minutes. Check that the display light is beneath high pressure.

When the timer sounds, quick release the pressure and carefully remove the lid. Carefully shred the chicken. Add the cheddar cheese and sour cream, then stir to combine.

Divide the chicken mixture among the buns. Top each with 2 slices of bacon, lettuce and tomato.

POT ROAST SANDWICHES

You can also use this recipe with leftover pot roast. I always make extra just so I can make these sandwiches! The meat is also delicious scrambled with eggs and added to an English muffin for a tasty weekday breakfast. **KB**

SERVES: 6

2 tsp (10 ml) olive oil

1 (2-lb [905-g]) chuck roast

Coarse salt

Freshly ground black pepper

2 medium onions, sliced

2 cups (475 ml) beef stock

2 sprigs thyme

6 crusty rolls, split, buttered and toasted

6 slices Swiss cheese

Dijon mustard

Press sauté to preheat the Instant Pot. When the word "hot" appears on the display, add the oil to the pot.

Season the chuck roast well with salt and pepper, then add the roast to the Instant Pot and brown it well on all sides. Remove the roast and set aside.

Add the onions to the drippings in the pot and scrape up any browned bits on the bottom of the pot. Sauté the onions until they are soft and starting to caramelize, about 10 minutes.

Add the beef stock to the pot, taking care to scrape up any browned bits from the bottom of the pot. Place the roast and thyme sprigs directly into the liquid.

Secure the lid with the steam vent in the sealed position. Press manual and adjust the timer to 40 minutes. Check that the display light is beneath high pressure.

When the timer sounds, quick release the pressure and carefully remove the lid.

Divide the meat among the roll bottoms and top each with a slice of Swiss cheese (the heat from the meat will melt the cheese). Spread Dijon on the underside of the roll tops and place over the cheese.

BEEF & CHEDDAR CROISSANTS

I live outside of Chicago—the land of Polish sausages and beef sandwiches. Everybody has an opinion on who makes the best beef. I'll tell you who really makes the best beef. You do, now, with this recipe. I have never been much of a traditional beef sandwich lover but throw in some spicy cheese sauce and a croissant, and I am in! The Instant Pot allows you to get that slow-roasted medium-rare beef that is perfect for beef sandwiches; all you really have to do is let the beef hang out in the pot after pressure-cooking for 3 minutes. This recipe will make a convert of any beef sandwich doubter. **SB**

SERVES: 4 to 6

1 cup (237 ml) beef stock

1 (2½- to 3-lb [1.1- to 1.4-kg]) eye round roast

3 cloves garlic, cut in half

1 tbsp (15 ml) extra-virgin olive oil

1 tbsp (19 g) kosher salt

¾ tsp freshly ground black pepper, divided

1 tsp chopped fresh basil

1 tsp chopped fresh rosemary

1 tsp chopped fresh parsley

2 tbsp (28 g) unsalted butter

2 tbsp (15 g) all-purpose flour

1 cup (237 ml) milk

1 tsp prepared grated horseradish

½ tsp paprika

1 tsp salt

2 cups (225 g) shredded sharp cheddar cheese

10 croissants, cut in half

Pour the stock into the Instant Pot and insert the steam trivet.

Make six ½-inch (1.3-cm)-deep slits in the surface of the beef round, three on the top and three on the bottom. Insert ½ garlic clove into each slit.

Rub the olive oil all over the beef round. Season with the kosher salt, ½ teaspoon of the pepper, and the basil, rosemary and parsley and rub them all over the surface of the beef. Place the seasoned beef on the trivet.

Secure the lid with the steam vent in the sealed position. Press pressure cook until the display light is beneath high pressure. Use the plus and minus buttons to adjust the time until the display reads "3 minutes."

When the timer sounds, let the pressure naturally release for 2 hours. The pot will switch to keep warm. After 2 hours of the eye round sitting in the pot, it will be rare in the center. For a well-done beef, let the eye round stay in the pot for 3 hours.

While the beef cooks and then rests, make the cheese sauce: Heat the butter in a small saucepan over medium heat. Once the butter melts, whisk in the flour. Lower the heat to medium-low. Slowly add the milk, while whisking, to the pot. Stir in the horseradish, paprika, salt and remaining ¼ teaspoon of pepper. Cook for 2 to 3 minutes.

Once the milk starts to thicken, add the cheese. Lower the heat to low. Stir the cheese into the liquid. When the cheese melts, remove the pan from the heat. Cover with a lid and let sit until the beef is finished cooking.

Once the beef has reached your preferred doneness, remove it with tongs and transfer to a large cutting board. Let the beef rest for 7 to 10 minutes, then thinly slice.

Place the sliced beef inside the croissants, topped with a spoonful or two of cheese sauce.

DAIRY-FREE   GLUTEN-FREE   GRAIN-FREE

DIY TURKEY LUNCHMEAT

We have a batch of this on hand at all times. I love not having to stand in line at the deli counter, plus this is so much tastier! The smoked paprika flavor makes for a killer BLT with turkey. **KB**

SERVES: 6

1 tbsp (7 g) smoked paprika

1 tsp coarse salt

1 tsp freshly ground black pepper

3 lb (1.4 kg) turkey breast

1 cup (237 ml) water or chicken stock

In a small bowl, mix together the paprika, salt and pepper and rub the mixture all over the outside of the turkey breast.

Pour the water or chicken stock into the Instant Pot and insert the steam trivet. Place the turkey breast on the trivet.

Secure the lid with the steam vent in the sealed position. Press manual and immediately adjust the timer to 20 minutes. Check that the display light is beneath high pressure.

When the timer sounds, quick release the pressure and carefully remove the lid. Remove the turkey breast and place on a carving board. Once cooled enough to handle, thinly slice the turkey and place in an airtight container or resealable plastic bag and store in the refrigerator.

GF GLUTEN-FREE GRAIN-FREE

DILLY RANCH SALMON

I struggle with lunch sometimes. I want to eat more protein and less carbs, but don't really wanna fuss with creating a salad every day. I came up with the solution. At least once a week, I fire up the old Instant Pot and steam the most perfect piece of Dilly Ranch Salmon. Flaky and tender salmon coated in all the traditional ranch flavors with an extra punch of fresh dill. Nothing goes better with salmon than dill. Look at us, being all healthy with time to spare! **SB**

SERVES: 2 to 4

½ tsp salt

¼ tsp garlic powder

¼ tsp onion powder

¼ tsp dried chives

¼ tsp freshly ground black pepper

2 (12-oz [340-g]) salmon fillets

1 tbsp (15 ml) olive oil

1 tbsp (14 g) unsalted butter

Juice of ½ lemon

1 tbsp (15 ml) white wine

1½ tsp (2 g) chopped fresh dill

1½ tsp (2 g) chopped fresh parsley

In a small bowl, mix together the salt, garlic powder, onion powder, chives and pepper. Season each salmon fillet liberally with the mixture.

Press sauté on the Instant Pot. Make sure the display light is beneath normal. Once the display reads "hot," add the oil and butter.

Add the salmon fillets, skin side down. Sauté for 7 to 9 minutes, or until the skin is nice and crispy.

Press cancel and carefully remove the salmon with a fish spatula. Some parts of the skin might stick; work carefully so as to not break the fish. Transfer the fish to a large plate.

Deglaze the pot with the lemon juice and white wine. Scrape up any browned bits from the bottom of the pot.

Insert the steam trivet into the pot. Place the fillets on the trivet. Secure the lid with the steam vent in the sealed position. Press steam and then use the plus and minus buttons to adjust the time until the display reads "3 minutes."

When the timer sounds, quick release the pressure. Remove the lid and carefully transfer each fillet to a serving plate. Spoon some of the sauce from the pot over each fish, then top with fresh dill and parsley.

DAIRY-FREE GLUTEN-FREE GRAIN-FREE OPTION

MANGO-CHIPOTLE SHREDDED CHICKEN

Shredded chicken and the Instant Pot might be my two favorite things when it comes to lunch. I love the versatility of throwing this chicken in a salad, in a wrap, on top of cauliflower rice or in a tortilla. So easy and works perfectly for meal prep! The spicy-sweet combo in this recipe is really fun and one of my favorite ways to enjoy tacos. **AR**

SERVES: 6

2 tsp (5 g) smoked paprika

1 tsp ground cumin

½ tsp ground coriander

½ tsp chipotle chili powder

½ tsp sea salt

½ tsp garlic powder

2 lb (905 g) chicken breast

2 mangoes, peeled, pitted and diced

Juice of 1 lime

¼ cup (60 ml) coconut aminos

2 tbsp (30 ml) cider vinegar

⅓ cup (80 ml) water or chicken stock

1 clove garlic, crushed

¼ cup (10 g) fresh cilantro, chopped

1 tbsp (15 ml) chopped chipotle pepper in adobo sauce

Cooked rice, cauliflower rice or tortillas, for serving

Optional toppings: avocado, onion, mango, fresh cilantro, salsa, tomatoes

In a small bowl, mix together the paprika, cumin, coriander, chipotle chili powder, salt and garlic powder. Rub all sides of the chicken with the spice mixture.

Make the sauce: In a blender or food processor, combine the mangoes, lime juice, coconut aminos, vinegar, water or stock, garlic, cilantro and chipotle pepper in adobo sauce. Blend until smooth.

Place the chicken in the bottom of the Instant Pot. Pour the sauce over the chicken.

Secure the lid with the steam vent in the sealed position. Select manual or pressure, and cook on high pressure for 10 minutes,

Use a natural release for 15 minutes, then release any remaining steam. Remove the lid, then shred the chicken with a knife or fork.

Serve over rice or cauliflower rice, or with a tortilla. Add any additional toppings, such as avocado, onion, more mango, cilantro, salsa or tomatoes.

GLUTEN-FREE **GRAIN-FREE**

CHICKEN CAPRESE SALAD BOWLS

The balsamic glaze and tender chicken in this recipe is to die for. We eat this often during the summer months as it keeps our kitchen cool. And it's elegant enough for a dinner party! **KB**

SERVES: 4

1 cup (237 ml) water or chicken stock

2 lb (905 g) boneless, skinless chicken breast

Coarse salt

6 cups (330 g) spring mix lettuce

1 cup (150 g) cherry tomatoes, halved

15 mini mozzarella balls

1 avocado, peeled, pitted and chopped

¼ cup (60 ml) balsamic glaze

Pour the water or chicken stock into the pot, then add the chicken.

Secure the lid with the steam vent in the sealed position. Press manual and immediately adjust the timer to 7 minutes. Check that the display light is beneath high pressure.

When the timer sounds, quick release the pressure and carefully remove the lid. Remove the chicken and allow to cool completely, then slice. Season with a little coarse salt.

Place the spring mix in a large salad bowl. Top with the sliced chicken, cherry tomatoes, mozzarella balls and avocado. Drizzle with the balsamic glaze and serve immediately.

DAIRY-FREE GLUTEN-FREE

CAJUN CHICKEN BOWLS

There are just five ingredients in this simple dish, but you won't believe how much flavor it has. Toasting the rice really helps boost the flavor, so don't skip that quick step. **KB**

SERVES: 4

1¼ cups (244 g) uncooked long-grain white rice, rinsed

1¼ cups (295 ml) chicken stock

5 tsp (13 g) Cajun seasoning

2 lb (905 g) boneless, skinless chicken breast, cut into bite-size pieces

1 red bell pepper, seeded and chopped

Press sauté to preheat the Instant Pot. When the word "hot" appears on the display, add the rice. Toast the rice in the dry pot, stirring frequently, about 2 minutes.

Add the chicken stock, Cajun seasoning, chicken and bell pepper and stir.

Secure the lid with the steam vent in the sealed position. Press manual and immediately adjust the timer to 9 minutes. Check that the display light is beneath high pressure.

When the timer sounds, quick release the pressure and carefully remove the lid. Season to taste and serve.

DAIRY-FREE GLUTEN-FREE

COFFEE-RUBBED STEAK BURRITO BOWLS

I have been making and eating burrito bowls before they were even a thing. I love them. My only gripe with them is all the dishes! One pot for rice, one pan for meat, one for beans. For a while we didn't have a dishwasher, and lemme tell you, on burrito bowl night sometimes those dishes sat there for some time. Now, in the Instant Pot, you can steam perfect rice and have the tenderest beef all in one pot. Mix it and then add it to the pot. It could not be any easier! I will even come to your house and wash your one pot after this meal! **SB**

SERVES: 4

2 lb (905 g) boneless eye round, cut into ½" (1.3-cm) cubes

3 tbsp (15 g) ground coffee

1 tbsp (7 g) smoked paprika

1 tbsp (15 g) light brown sugar

1 tsp onion powder

1 tsp salt

½ tsp freshly ground black pepper

½ tsp crushed red pepper flakes

2 cups (380 g) uncooked brown rice

2½ cups (590 ml) water

¼ cup (60 ml) beef stock

Optional toppings: hot sauce, pico de gallo, avocado, sour cream, jalapeño peppers, shredded lettuce

In a large bowl, combine the beef, coffee, paprika, brown sugar, onion powder, salt, black pepper and red pepper flakes. Stir to evenly coat all the beef.

Place the brown rice and water in a 7-inch (18.5-cm) heatproof bowl.

Pour the beef stock into the Instant Pot, then place the coated beef into the stock in an even layer.

Place the trivet into the Instant Pot, slightly pressing it down into the beef. Place the bowl of the rice on top of the trivet.

Secure the lid with the steam vent in the sealed position. Press pressure cook until the display light is beneath high pressure. Use the plus and minus buttons to adjust the time until the display reads "15 minutes."

When the timer sounds, allow the pressure to naturally release.

Once the float valve falls, remove the lid. Carefully lift the bowl with rice out of the Instant Pot with oven mitt–covered hands. Fluff the rice with a fork. Transfer the rice to individual bowls.

Remove the trivet. Use a slotted spoon to remove the beef and place it on top of the rice. Add whichever additional toppings you desire.

DAIRY-FREE OPTION   GLUTEN-FREE

BEEF GYRO BOWLS

We have a local Greek place that we love and it has a bowl similar to this. It's my take on it and I think it's pretty close! Now we choose to just make it at home because it's so simple. **KB**

SERVES: 4

2 lb (905 g) flank steak, thinly sliced

1 medium onion, thinly sliced

3 cloves garlic, minced

1¼ cups (244 g) uncooked long-grain white rice, rinsed

1¼ cups (295 ml) chicken stock

Juice of ½ lemon

Suggested toppings: tzatziki sauce, lettuce, tomato, sliced onion, crumbled feta cheese

Press sauté to preheat the Instant Pot. When the word "hot" appears on the display, add the flank steak, onion and garlic. Cook for about 5 minutes, or until the meat is browned.

Add the rice, stock and lemon juice, taking care that the rice is completely submerged in the liquid.

Secure the lid with the steam vent in the sealed position. Press manual and immediately adjust the timer to 9 minutes. Check that the display light is beneath high pressure.

When the timer sounds, quick release the pressure and carefully remove the lid. Serve in bowls and add your desired toppings.

GF

GLUTEN-FREE
OPTION

SOUTHWEST SHRIMP & CORN SALAD

Tender shrimp steamed inside the Instant Pot in a spicy lime sauce. It's almost perfect as an appetizer alone. Almost. It tastes even better on top of a big salad served with corn, crunchy lettuce and cabbage. In fact, it tastes so good that somebody may have been so busy devouring the salad that they were two bites in before they noticed a rogue shrimp tail. Not that that happened to me or anything. **SB**

SERVES: 4

Juice and zest of 1 lime

1 tsp soy sauce or coconut aminos

1 tbsp (8 g) chili powder

2 cloves garlic, minced

1 jalapeño pepper, seeded and minced

½ tsp ground cumin

1 tsp smoked paprika

½ tsp salt, plus more to taste

¼ tsp freshly ground black pepper, plus more to taste

2 tbsp (30 ml) hot sauce, such as Valentina

1 lb (455 g) frozen and thawed deveined shrimp

2 ears corn, husked

1 head romaine lettuce, chopped

1 cup (70 g) shredded purple cabbage

½ cup (114 g) pico de gallo

DRESSING

2 tbsp (30 g) light sour cream

1 tbsp (15 ml) fresh lime juice

1 tsp sauce from the Instant Pot

Salt

Freshly ground black pepper

In the Instant Pot, mix together the lime juice and zest, soy sauce, chili powder, garlic, jalapeño, cumin, paprika, salt, black pepper and hot sauce. Add the shrimp and mix until evenly coated.

Insert the steam trivet into the Instant Pot on top of the shrimp. Place the ears of corn on the trivet. Secure the lid with the steam vent in the sealed position. Press steam. Use the plus and minus buttons to adjust the time until the display reads "2 minutes."

When the timer sounds, quick release the pressure. Use tongs to remove the ears of corn and transfer them to a cutting board. Stand an ear on one end. Use a knife to slice along each cob to remove the kernels from the cob.

To assemble the salad, place the lettuce and then cabbage on the bottom of a large bowl. Top with the pico de gallo, corn kernels and shrimp.

To prepare the dressing, in a separate bowl, whisk together the sour cream, lime juice, cooking liquid from the pot and salt and pepper to taste.

Dress the salad with the dressing. Add more salt and pepper to taste, if desired.

SALSA VERDE CHICKEN

DAIRY-FREE GLUTEN-FREE GRAIN-FREE

This chicken is a total game changer for any Mexican dish! A delicious roasted tomatillo sauce is tossed into your Instant Pot to make the yummiest shredded, tangy and flavorful chicken. Put inside a taco, in a salad or on a bed of rice for a versatile meal! **AR**

SERVES: 6

1½ lb (680 g) tomatillos, husks removed

1 large poblano pepper, seeded and sliced in half

2 jalapeño peppers, seeded and sliced in half

1 tbsp (15 ml) olive or avocado oil

⅔ cup (107 g) diced white onion

½ cup (20 g) fresh cilantro, chopped

2 cloves garlic, crushed

Juice of 1 lime

½ tsp sea salt, plus more to taste

2 lb (905 g) boneless chicken thighs

½ cup (120 ml) chicken stock

2 tsp (5 g) ground cumin

Salt

Begin by making the salsa verde: Preheat the oven to 425°F (220°C). Slice the tomatillos in half and place, cut side down, on a baking sheet. Place the peppers, cut side down, on the same sheet. Lightly brush with oil, then place in the oven. Roast for 12 to 15 minutes, or until the tops of the veggies are blistered. Remove from the oven.

In a blender, combine the roasted veggies, onion, cilantro, garlic, lime and salt. Pulse and blend until smooth (don't overblend).

Place the chicken in the Instant Pot. Pour the salsa verde on top. Add the chicken stock and cumin.

Secure the lid with the steam vent in the sealed position. Select manual or pressure, and cook on high pressure for 10 minutes.

Use a quick release and release all the steam before opening the lid. Shred the chicken with a fork and serve, adding salt to taste.

GF
GLUTEN-FREE GRAIN-FREE

HERB-LOADED WARM POTATO SALAD
WITH PEAS

There is a creamy potato salad recipe that is cherished in my family. You make it one way and don't mess with it. The Instant Pot not only steams potatoes perfectly, but it also keeps the salad the perfect warm temperature for ultimate creaminess. Serve the salad right out of the Instant Pot and save yourself a dish or two. **SB**

SERVES: 4

1½ lb (680 g) red and yellow baby potatoes, larger potatoes sliced in half

½ cup (120 ml) chicken or vegetable stock

Salt

Freshly ground black pepper

2 tbsp (20 g) minced red onion

2 tbsp (30 ml) white wine vinegar

¼ tsp sugar

¾ cup (96 g) frozen peas

1 tbsp (14 g) mayonnaise

1 tbsp (15 g) light sour cream

1 tbsp (4 g) chopped fresh parsley

1 tsp chopped fresh dill

¼ tsp dried oregano

¼ tsp crushed red pepper flakes

In the Instant Pot, combine the potatoes, stock and a pinch each of salt and pepper.

Secure the lid with the steam vent in the sealed position. Press steam. Use the plus and minus buttons to adjust the time until the display reads "2 minutes."

Meanwhile, in a small bowl, combine the red onion, vinegar and sugar. Let sit while the potatoes steam.

When the timer sounds, quick release the pressure. Remove the lid. Press keep warm/cancel.

Add the peas, mayonnaise, sour cream, herbs, salt and black pepper to taste and the red pepper flakes to the Instant Pot. Stir in the onion mixture until everything is combined. Let the salad warm for 1 minute. Adjust the salt and pepper to taste.

GF
GLUTEN-FREE

VEGETARIAN STUFFED POBLANO PEPPERS

Stuffed peppers are often times a giant meatball inside a pepper. If that's what you like, sorry, it isn't for me. I am in the market for something healthier that still has all that cheese! Balance, right? I wanted to make a stuffed pepper that had all the flavors of chiles rellenos, but not the calories. These stuffed peppers have lots of quinoa, vegetables, spice and cheese. The Instant Pot brings all the flavors together without turning the peppers to mush. This is a filling but not overwhelming dish that wipes the floor with the old stuffed peppers. **SB**

SERVES: 4 to 6

6 large poblano peppers

1 cup (185 g) cooked quinoa

½ cup (86 g) drained and rinsed black beans

½ cup (80 g) diced red onion

½ tsp ground cumin

½ tsp chili powder

Salt

Freshly ground black pepper

1 tbsp (15 ml) hot sauce

2 tbsp (30 g) tomato sauce

1 tbsp (3 g) chopped fresh cilantro, plus more for topping

1 cup (115 g) shredded pepper Jack cheese, divided

1 cup (237 ml) water

Slice vertically down one side of each poblano, from the stem to the tip, to remove a piece about 2 inches (5 cm) wide, leaving the stem attached. Dice the removed portion, leaving the rest of each pepper intact until ready to stuff.

In a large bowl, combine the diced poblano, quinoa, black beans, red onion, cumin, chili powder, salt and black pepper to taste, hot sauce, tomato sauce, cilantro and one-quarter of the pepper Jack cheese. Mix well.

Spoon the quinoa mixture into each reserved poblano pepper. Use the back of the spoon to press the filling into each pepper.

Once each pepper is filled, pour the water into the Instant Pot and insert the steam trivet. Arrange the peppers on top of the trivet. Top the peppers with the remaining cheese.

Secure the lid with the steam vent in the sealed position. Press pressure cook until the display light is beneath high pressure. Use the plus and minus buttons to adjust the time until the display reads "10 minutes."

When the timer sounds, quick release the pressure. Remove the lid and use tongs to carefully transfer the peppers individually to plates. Top the cooked peppers with fresh cilantro.

CHILI-GARLIC BOW TIES

Chili-Garlic Bow Ties are so, so good on their own as a quick hot or cold lunch. They are also a great base for an added protein of your choice, such as Chicken Saltimbocca with Dates (page 373). I also love to chill the noodles and use them for a big pasta salad filled with all the veggies. Noodles in the Instant Pot take half the time as they do on the stovetop. That even includes creating the perfect chili-garlic oil to infuse all through the noodles as they cook. You will find yourself making these over and over again. **SB**

SERVES: 4 to 6

2 tbsp (30 ml) extra-virgin olive oil

4 cloves garlic, minced

1 tsp crushed red pepper flakes

1 lb (455 g) farfalle pasta

3 cups (710 g) water

2 tsp (12 g) salt

1 tbsp (15 ml) fresh lemon juice

½ cup (50 g) grated Parmesan cheese

Press sauté on the Instant Pot and heat the oil. After 1 minute, add the garlic and red pepper flakes and stir continuously for 1 minute. Once the garlic starts to turn ever so slightly golden, press cancel.

Stir in the farfalle, water and salt.

Secure the lid with the steam vent in the sealed position. Press pressure cook until the display light is beneath high pressure. Use the plus and minus buttons to adjust the time until the display reads "5 minutes."

When the timer sounds, quick release the pressure. Remove the lid, add the lemon juice and stir well to combine.

Top the farfalle with the cheese and adjust the salt, if needed

DAIRY-FREE GLUTEN-FREE GRAIN-FREE

BLT CHICKEN SALAD

This easy recipe is great for your BLT lovers. The tender chicken and salty bacon is an irresistible combination, and makes a quick weekday lunch if you keep some in the fridge. It also makes a great sandwich! **KB**

SERVES: 4

½ lb (225 g) bacon

1 cup (237 ml) water or chicken stock

1½ lb (680 g) boneless, skinless chicken breast, cut into bite-size pieces

1 cup (150 g) cherry tomatoes, halved

½ cup (113 g) mayonnaise

Coarse salt

Freshly ground pepper

4 cups (220 g) spring mix lettuce

Press sauté to preheat the Instant Pot. When the word "hot" appears on the display, add the bacon. Cook until the bacon is browned and crispy, then remove it with a slotted spoon and place on paper towels to drain any excess fat. Discard the drippings but do not wipe clean.

Add the water or chicken stock to the pot, taking care to scrape up any browned bits from the bottom of the pot. Add the chicken.

Secure the lid with the steam vent in the sealed position. Press manual and immediately adjust the timer to 6 minutes. Check that the display light is beneath high pressure.

When the timer sounds, quick release the pressure and carefully remove the lid. Remove the chicken and allow to cool completely.

In a large bowl, mix together the chicken, tomatoes and mayonnaise. Crumble the bacon and gently fold into the chicken mixture. Season with salt and pepper.

Place 1 cup (55 g) of lettuce on each of the four plates. Evenly divide the chicken salad and place on top of the lettuce.

GF GLUTEN-FREE | GRAIN-FREE

GREEK CHICKEN SALAD

Meal prep . . . weekly meal prep is a thing these days. The only things I meal prep revolve around the Instant Pot. Greek chicken salad is at the top of my list. This chicken has so much flavor that when you add it to a salad, you don't really need much of a dressing. Little dressing means you can store it longer without all the salad wilting. This is my kind of meal prep. Ready-to-eat salad for days. Thanks, Instant Pot. **SB**

SERVES: 4

1 tbsp (15 g) sour cream

¼ cup (60 ml) extra-virgin olive oil, plus more for sautéing

1 clove garlic, grated

½ tsp fresh thyme leaves

¼ tsp crushed red pepper flakes

Salt

Freshly ground black pepper

½ tsp dried oregano

2 large boneless, skinless chicken breasts

Juice of ½ lemon

SALAD

2 jarred roasted red peppers, thinly sliced

½ red onion, thinly sliced

2 Persian cucumbers, thinly sliced

2 tbsp (13 g) pitted and sliced black olives

2 tbsp (13 g) pitted and sliced green olives

15 oz (425 g) mixed greens

Crumbled feta cheese, for topping

Juice of ½ lemon

1 tbsp (15 ml) olive oil

Salt

Freshly ground black pepper

In a gallon-size (4-L) resealable plastic bag, combine the sour cream, olive oil, garlic, thyme, red pepper flakes, salt and black pepper to taste and oregano. Seal the bag and shake until the entire marinade is combined.

Add the chicken breasts to the marinade. Store in the fridge for at least 15 minutes, or up to 3 hours at the most.

After the chicken has marinated, place about 1 teaspoon of olive oil in the Instant Pot. Press sauté. Use tongs to remove the chicken breasts from the marinade and add them to the pot. Sauté for about 3 minutes on each side. Use a silicone spatula to get under the chicken if it sticks a little. Remove the chicken from the pot and transfer to a plate.

Press cancel and add the lemon juice to the pot. Scrape up the browned bits of flavor from the bottom of the pot, using a wooden spoon or silicone spatula. Return the chicken to the pot.

Secure the lid with the steam vent in the sealed position. Press pressure cook until the display light is beneath high pressure. Use the plus and minus buttons to adjust the time until the display reads "10 minutes."

When the timer sounds, quick release the pressure. Remove the lid and let the chicken rest for 4 to 5 minutes before removing and slicing.

Assemble the salad: In a large serving bowl, toss the roasted red peppers, red onion, cucumbers, olives and mixed greens. Slice the chicken breasts. Top the salad with the chicken and then the feta cheese, lemon juice and olive oil. Season with a little bit of salt and black pepper.

DAIRY-FREE GLUTEN-FREE GRAIN-FREE

CILANTRO-LIME CHICKEN SALAD

This is the best salad to take to a potluck. Everyone always loves it! The poblano pepper, lime juice and cilantro give it an unexpected flavor twist. **KB**

SERVES: 4

½ cup (120 ml) chicken stock

2 lb (905 g) boneless, skinless chicken breast

½ cup (80 g) chopped red onion

2 cloves garlic, minced

1 cup (225 g) mayonnaise

1 poblano pepper, chopped

1 red bell pepper, seeded and chopped

Juice of 1 lime

½ cup (20 g) chopped fresh cilantro

Pour the chicken stock into the Instant Pot, then add the chicken breast.

Secure the lid with the steam vent in the sealed position. Press manual and immediately adjust the timer to 6 minutes. Check that the display light is beneath high pressure.

When the timer sounds, quick release the pressure and carefully remove the lid.

In a medium bowl, mix together the red onion, garlic, mayonnaise, poblano and bell peppers, lime juice and cilantro. Remove the chicken from the pot, chop the chicken and mix it with the sauce.

Refrigerate for at least 1 hour before serving.

DAIRY-FREE   GLUTEN-FREE

QUINOA-SPINACH SALAD
WITH SAUSAGE

This simple salad is refreshing because of the lemon and Dijon dressing. It comes together quickly and makes a great weeknight meal. **KB**

SERVES: 4

2 tsp (10 ml) olive oil

1 (7-oz [198-g]) package chicken sausage, any flavor

1 cup (173 g) uncooked quinoa

1 cup (237 ml) water

2 tbsp (30 ml) fresh lemon juice

¼ cup (60 ml) extra-virgin olive oil

1 tsp Dijon mustard

Coarse salt

Freshly ground pepper

3 to 4 cups (90 to 120 g) fresh spinach leaves

Press sauté to preheat the Instant Pot. When the word "hot" appears on the display, add the olive oil. When the oil is shimmering, add the sausage. Cook until the sausage is starting to brown, stirring occasionally, about 5 minutes.

Remove the sausage from the pot and set aside. Add the quinoa to the pot and cook, stirring frequently, for 2 to 3 minutes. Add the water and stir well to scrape up any browned bits from the bottom.

Secure the lid with the steam vent in the sealed position. Press manual and immediately adjust the timer to 1 minute. Check that the display light is beneath high pressure.

Meanwhile, in a small bowl, mix together the lemon juice, extra-virgin olive oil, Dijon, salt and pepper to make the dressing. Set aside.

Once the timer sounds, allow the pressure to release naturally for 15 minutes, then remove the lid of the pot (release any remaining pressure, if necessary). Stir the quinoa and allow to cool for a few minutes.

Stir the dressing into the quinoa and mix to coat thoroughly. Add the spinach and mix it in to wilt it slightly. Add the cooked sausage and mix well.

GF

GLUTEN-FREE

PESTO CHICKEN
WITH QUINOA

You cannot find a better method to cook quinoa than in the Instant Pot. It's fast, hands off and perfectly fork-fluffy! I love the addition of chicken bites in here, along with some pesto and fresh tomatoes. This complete meal is so easy, and it tastes delicious served warm or even at room temperature in a salad. Make it ahead on a weekend and enjoy it for lunches throughout the week! **AR**

SERVES: 5

1 cup (173 g) uncooked quinoa, rinsed

1½ cups (355 ml) chicken stock

½ tsp salt, plus more to taste

1 lb (455 g) chicken breast, cut into bite-size pieces

⅔ cup (173 g) homemade or store-bought pesto, divided (see note)

1 cup (150 g) sliced cherry tomatoes

⅓ cup (33 g) fresh Parmesan cheese, for garnish

Mixed greens, for serving

In the Instant Pot, combine the quinoa, chicken stock, salt, chicken breast and half of the pesto.

Secure the lid with the steam vent in the sealed position. Select manual or pressure, and cook on high pressure for 1 minute.

Use a natural release for 10 minutes, then release any remaining steam. Open the lid and fluff the quinoa with a fork.

Serve with sliced tomatoes, remaining pesto, Parmesan cheese and additional salt, if needed.

Alternatively, this recipe can be made ahead and stored in the fridge. Serve warm or at room temperature over a bed of greens.

NOTE: For a homemade pesto, blend together in a food processor or blender: 2 cups (80 g) of loosely packed fresh basil leaves, ⅓ cup (33 g) of grated Parmesan cheese, 2 minced garlic cloves, ½ cup (120 ml) of olive oil and ¼ teaspoon of sea salt.

DAIRY-FREE GLUTEN-FREE VEGAN OPTION

CRUSTLESS VEGGIE POTPIE

This comforting bowl of potpie filling is packed with vegetables, and the recipe I make when I need to pack in extra veggies for my family on a Meatless Monday! It comes together so much easier than a traditional potpie, and although you might be bummed without a crust, this lightened-up version can be served easily with some crusty bread or biscuits. **AR**

SERVES: 4

1 large head cauliflower, cut into florets

3 cups (710 ml) vegetable or chicken stock

1 cup (130 g) frozen peas

2 cups (260 g) sliced carrot

2 medium Yukon gold potatoes, peeled and diced

3 celery ribs, diced

1 medium yellow onion, diced

3 cloves garlic, minced

2 bay leaves

1½ tsp (9 g) sea salt, plus more to taste

½ tsp dried marjoram

2 tbsp (5 g) fresh thyme, for garnish (optional)

In the Instant Pot, combine the cauliflower florets and stock.

Secure the lid with the steam vent in the sealed position. Select manual or pressure, and cook on high pressure for 5 minutes.

Use a quick release and remove the lid. Using an immersion blender or blender, puree the cauliflower mixture to form the base of your potpie. (Place the mixture back in the pot if it was removed to blend.)

Add the frozen peas, carrot, potatoes, celery, onion, garlic and bay leaves to the cauliflower mixture. Sprinkle with the salt and marjoram and give the mixture a stir.

Secure the lid with the steam vent in the sealed position. Select manual or pressure, and cook on high pressure for 7 minutes. Use a quick release and remove the lid.

Serve hot and garnish with fresh thyme (if using), and additional salt to taste (if needed).

GRAIN-FREE

CRUSTLESS PEPPERONI, MUSHROOM & OLIVE PIZZA QUICHE

Pizza lovers, this crustless quiche is for you! It's packed with the flavors that so many of us love on our pizza—Italian herbs, tomatoes, pepperoni, mushrooms, olives and, of course, all of the cheesy goodness. Instead of picking up a slice, this egg-based version gets sliced and served on a plate with a fork. Take one bite of this quiche and you'll be in pizza heaven! **ESV**

SERVES: 6

Grass-fed butter, ghee or avocado oil, for casserole dish

3 oz (85 g) pepperoni, divided

5 large eggs

½ cup (120 ml) milk or heavy cream

1 tsp sea salt

1½ tsp (4.5 g) garlic granules

½ tsp onion powder

½ tsp dried oregano

½ tsp dried thyme

3 small tomatoes, seeded and chopped

¼ cup (15 g) chopped fresh flat-leaf parsley

1 cup (70 g) sliced mushrooms

½ cup (50 g) pitted and sliced black olives

1 cup (115 g) shredded mozzarella cheese

½ cup (40 g) shredded Parmesan cheese

1 cup (237 ml) water

Use your healthy fat of choice to grease a 1½-quart (1.5-L) casserole dish that fits inside the Instant Pot. Set it aside.

Chop 1 ounce (28 g) of the pepperoni, reserving the remaining pepperoni (left whole).

In a large mixing bowl, whisk together the eggs and milk until the eggs are fully incorporated. Add the salt, garlic granules, onion powder, oregano, thyme, tomatoes, parsley, mushrooms, olives, the chopped pepperoni and the cheeses, gently stirring to combine. Pour the mixture into the prepared casserole dish. In a uniform layer, place the remaining whole pieces of pepperoni on top of the filling. Cover the casserole dish with its glass lid. If your casserole dish doesn't have a glass lid, you can cover the top of the dish with unbleached parchment paper, then top it with foil and secure it around the edges.

Pour the water into the Instant Pot and insert the steam trivet. Carefully set the covered casserole dish on top of the trivet. Secure the lid on the Instant Pot with the steam vent in the sealed position. Press manual and set on high pressure for 25 minutes.

Once the timer sounds, press keep warm/cancel. Allow the Instant Pot to naturally pressure release for 10 minutes. Using an oven mitt, do a quick release. When the steam venting stops and the silver dial drops, carefully open the lid.

Carefully remove the casserole dish from the Instant Pot and remove the lid from the dish. If you prefer crispier pepperoni, place the casserole dish on a baking sheet and place in the oven under a preheated broiler for about 3 minutes, or just until the pepperoni becomes crispy around the edges.

Allow to rest for 15 minutes before serving.

DAIRY-FREE   GLUTEN-FREE

RED BEANS & RICE

I have never been to New Orleans. I have no idea how authentic red beans and rice tastes. My dad, however, has been to New Orleans. He was my head taste tester for the book and he told me that I came pretty close to getting it right. The recipe comes together in two steps. First, we make the rice. Second, we add our holy trinity: spices, sausage and pressure-cook. For a dish that normally cooks all day long, I don't think waiting 25 minutes for the Instant Pot to do its thing is that big a price to pay. **SB**

SERVES: 4 to 6

2 cups (380 g) uncooked brown rice

2½ cups (590 ml) water

1 tsp salt, plus a pinch and more to taste

1 tsp extra-virgin olive oil

12 oz (340 g) andouille sausage, sliced

2 yellow onions, diced

1 celery rib, diced

1 bell pepper, seeded and diced

5 cloves garlic, grated

1 tsp smoked paprika

¼ tsp freshly ground black pepper, plus more to taste

¼ to ½ tsp cayenne pepper

½ tsp dried basil

½ tsp dried oregano

2 (15.5-oz [439-g]) cans red kidney beans, drained and rinsed, divided

½ cup (120 ml) chicken stock

3 dried bay leaves

In the Instant Pot, combine the rice and water along with a pinch of salt.

Secure the lid with the steam vent in the sealed position. Press pressure cook until the display light is beneath high pressure. Use the plus and minus buttons to adjust the time until the display reads "1 minute."

When the timer sounds, allow the pressure to naturally release for 15 minutes.

After 15 minutes, quick release any remaining pressure. Remove the lid and use a fork to fluff the rice. Transfer the rice to a plate. Clean out the Instant Pot.

Place the olive oil in the pot. Press sauté. Once the oil is shimmering, add the sausage and sauté for 3 minutes.

Stir in the onions, celery and bell pepper. Sauté for 2 minutes.

Press cancel, then stir in the garlic, paprika, the remaining teaspoon of salt, black pepper, cayenne, basil and oregano.

Puree ½ cup (128 g) of the kidney beans in a food processor until smooth. Add to the pot along with the remaining beans, stock and bay leaves.

Secure the lid with the steam vent in the sealed position. Press pressure cook until the display light is beneath high pressure. Use the plus and minus buttons to adjust the time until the display reads "5 minutes."

When the timer sounds, quick release the pressure. Remove the lid and stir the sausage and beans. Add more salt and black pepper, if needed. Serve the beans and sausage over the brown rice.

DAIRY-FREE

FRESH SWEET & SPICY TOMATO JAM
WITH TOAST

Everybody that knows me knows I could live off tomatoes alone. Tomato season is my favorite time of year. I hoard fresh tomatoes and try to make sauces or jams for the rest of the year. This tomato jam is my favorite addition to toast with a little butter and even a fried egg on top. I also love to hand this jam out as a gift or serve it with a big cheeseboard and crackers. The Instant Pot takes all the mixing and guesswork out of making jam. Keep that tomato season alive longer with some tomato jam. **SB**

SERVES: 4 to 6

1 lb (455 g) tomatoes, cut into eighths

½ cup (100 g) sugar

¼ cup (60 ml) white wine vinegar

¼ to ½ tsp crushed red pepper flakes

¼ tsp salt

1 tbsp (15 ml) water

Toast or crackers, for serving

In the Instant Pot, combine all the ingredients except for toast.

Secure the lid with the steam vent in the sealed position. Press pressure cook until the display light is beneath high pressure. Use the plus and minus buttons to adjust the time until the display reads "10 minutes."

When the timer sounds, quick release the pressure.

Remove the lid and use a potato masher to mash the tomatoes into small pieces. As the jam cools, it will thicken. When the jam is completely cool, transfer to a pint-size (473 ml) Mason jar with a lid. Store in the refrigerator for up to 3 weeks.

Spread the jam on toast or crackers.

GF
GLUTEN-FREE

BUFFALO JACKFRUIT TOSTADAS

I like to say I could coat anything in buffalo sauce and my husband would eat it. Case in point: jackfruit. Have you ever tried it? It has the same consistency as pulled pork and doesn't taste fruity at all. It can now be found in most freezer sections at the grocery store. I prefer buying smoked jackfruit for this recipe. The glory of the Instant Pot is that I can toss in the frozen jackfruit along with some sauce and veggies, and voilà!—lunch on the double. Not only would this buffalo jackfruit be great on tostadas, it works well on nachos and tacos, too. Even the pickiest meat eaters can be fooled into loving this recipe. **SB**

SERVES: 4 to 6

20 oz (586 g) frozen smoked jackfruit

1 carrot, thinly sliced

1 celery rib, thinly sliced

½ red onion, thinly sliced

¼ cup (60 ml) vegetable stock

¼ cup (60 ml) buffalo sauce

½ tsp salt

¼ tsp freshly ground black pepper

¼ tsp ground cumin

¼ tsp garlic powder

¼ tsp onion powder

8 to 10 corn tostadas

Shredded Mexican cheese or blue cheese crumbles, for topping

In the Instant Pot, combine all the ingredients, except the tostadas and cheese.

Secure the lid with the steam vent in the sealed position. Press pressure cook until the display light is beneath high pressure. Use the plus and minus buttons to adjust the time until the display reads "5 minutes."

When the timer sounds, quick release the pressure.

Remove the lid and stir well with a fork, shredding any big pieces of jackfruit, if necessary.

Transfer the buffalo jackfruit to the tostadas and top with your preferred cheese.

SOUPS AND STEWS

DAIRY-FREE   GLUTEN-FREE OPTION   GRAIN-FREE

BEEF & CHORIZO PUMPKIN CHILI

Calling all meat lovers! This beanless chili is one that I am sure will have a permanent place in your dinner rotation. I love the hint of sweetness and thickness of the pumpkin, and the two different types of meat that make every bite so delicious! Your taste buds will also love the hints of smoky chipotle and dark beer. Because of the robust flavor, this is one of those meals that tastes better the second day. My favorite way to prepare this recipe is to make it the night before, or on the morning I want to serve it and let it sit all day on warm. **AR**

SERVES: 6 to 8

1 tbsp (15 ml) avocado oil

1 medium yellow onion, diced

1 jalapeño pepper, seeded and diced

1 poblano pepper, diced

1 red bell pepper, seeded and diced

3 cloves garlic, minced

1 lb (455 g) ground beef

1 lb (455 g) chorizo sausage

1 (28-oz [800-g]) can whole tomatoes

1 (15-oz [425-g]) can pure pumpkin puree

1 chipotle pepper in adobo sauce, diced

1 tbsp (15 ml) adobo sauce

2 tbsp (32 g) tomato paste

3 tbsp (23 g) chili powder

1 tbsp (7 g) paprika

1 tbsp (7 g) ground cumin

1 tsp salt, plus more to taste

¾ cup (175 ml) dark beer (see note)

1 tbsp (15 ml) cider vinegar

Optional toppings: fresh cilantro, jalapeño peppers, cheddar cheese, onion, avocado

Select sauté on the Instant Pot. Once hot, coat the bottom of your pot with the oil. Cook the onion and jalapeño, poblano and red bell peppers for about 3 minutes, then add the garlic and cook for another 30 seconds, or until fragrant.

Add the ground beef and chorizo and continue to cook for another 5 to 6 minutes. Most of the meat will be browned, but doesn't need to be cooked all the way. Select cancel.

Add the tomatoes, pumpkin, chipotle pepper, adobo sauce, tomato paste, chili powder, paprika, cumin and salt. Stir, coating the meat and vegetable mixture with the spices. Pour in the beer and vinegar. Give a quick stir.

Secure the lid with the steam vent in the sealed position. Select manual or pressure, and cook on high pressure for 12 minutes.

Use a quick release, ensuring all the steam is released before opening the lid. Give a quick stir and adjust with any additional seasonings and salt.

Serve hot with such toppings as fresh cilantro, jalapeños, cheddar cheese, onion or avocado.

NOTE: The beer adds a unique and delicious flavor to this chili. For a gluten-free variation, find a good gluten-free beer.

MEATBALL SOUP

I love to keep meatballs on hand just to make this easy soup. It makes for a hearty meal and is a real family pleaser! A good loaf of crusty bread and a salad round this meal out nicely. **KB**

SERVES: 6

2 tsp (10 ml) olive oil

1 medium onion, chopped

2 carrots, chopped

1 celery rib, chopped

3 cloves garlic, minced

½ tsp dried basil

½ tsp dried oregano

4 cups (946 g) beef stock

1 (14.5-oz [411-g]) can fire-roasted diced tomatoes

½ cup (50 g) dried mini penne pasta

1 lb (455 g) Italian meatballs

¼ cup (25 g) grated Parmesan cheese

Press sauté to preheat the Instant Pot. When the word "hot" appears on the display, add the oil. Add the onion, carrots and celery and cook until the onion is soft, about 5 minutes, stirring frequently. Add the garlic, basil and oregano and cook for 1 more minute, stirring frequently.

Add the beef stock to the pot, taking care to scrape any browned bits from the bottom. Add the tomatoes, pasta and meatballs to the pot, taking care that the pasta is completely submerged.

Secure the lid with the steam vent in the sealed position. Press manual and immediately adjust the timer to 6 minutes. Check that the display light is beneath high pressure.

When the timer sounds, quick release the pressure and carefully remove the lid. Stir in the Parmesan and serve.

GF

GLUTEN-FREE

BACON-PARMESAN POTATO-LEEK SOUP

Enjoy the sweet flavor of leeks with creamy potatoes in this filling soup. Aged Parmesan and smoky bacon enhance this delightful soup and make a nice, complex profile for the palate. **ESV**

SERVES: 4 to 6

2 tbsp (28 g) grass-fed butter

1 medium leek, sliced finely and washed well

4 cloves garlic, chopped finely

3 large celery ribs, sliced about ¼" (6-mm) thick

4 large russet potatoes, peeled and diced

6 oz (170 g) precooked crispy bacon or turkey bacon, crumbled

4 cups (946 ml) chicken or vegetable stock

1 tsp sea salt

1 tsp dried thyme

1 tsp dried dill

1 cup (237 ml) milk

2 tbsp (15 g) gluten-free all-purpose flour

½ cup (120 ml) heavy cream

¼ cup (20 g) shredded Parmesan cheese, plus more for garnish (optional)

¼ cup (15 g) freshly chopped flat-leaf parsley, plus more for garnish (optional)

Place the butter in the Instant Pot and press sauté. Once the butter has melted, add the leek and sauté for 5 minutes, stirring occasionally. Add the garlic and sauté for 1 minute, stirring occasionally. Press keep warm/cancel.

Add the celery, potatoes, bacon, stock, salt, thyme and dill, then give the mixture a quick stir.

Secure the lid with the steam vent in the sealed position. Press manual and set on high pressure for 9 minutes.

While the soup is cooking, pour the milk into a large measuring cup or medium bowl, then sprinkle the flour on the top and whisk until the flour is mostly incorporated. Set aside.

Once the timer sounds, press keep warm/cancel. Using an oven mitt, do a quick release. When the steam venting stops and the silver dial drops, carefully open the lid.

Press sauté and add the milk mixture, cream, Parmesan and parsley. Allow the soup to come to a simmer, then quickly stir until the milk, cream and Parmesan are fully mixed in. Simmer for about 5 minutes, or until the soup slightly thickens. Press keep warm/cancel. Taste for seasoning and adjust salt to taste. Allow to rest for 10 minutes.

Serve immediately, garnished with shredded Parmesan and chopped fresh parsley (if using).

GF GLUTEN-FREE   GRAIN-FREE

CHICKEN POTPIE SOUP

I love chicken potpie but don't like all the effort on a busy weeknight. This soup has all the same flavors and satisfies that craving in a snap! **KB**

SERVES: 4 to 6

2 tsp (10 ml) olive oil

1 lb (455 g) boneless, skinless chicken breast, cut into small bite-size pieces

1 medium onion, chopped

2 cloves garlic, minced

Pinch of dried thyme

4 cups (946 ml) chicken stock

2 cups (300 g) diced red baby potatoes

1 (12-oz [340-g]) package frozen vegetables, such as peas and carrots

1 cup (237 ml) heavy cream

2 tbsp (16 g) cornstarch

Coarse salt

Freshly ground black pepper

2 tbsp (8 g) chopped fresh parsley

Press sauté to preheat the Instant Pot. When the word "hot" appears on the display, add the olive oil, then the chicken. Cook until starting to brown, 3 to 4 minutes. Remove the chicken and set aside.

Add the onion to the pot. Cook, stirring occasionally, until the onion is soft, about 5 minutes. Add the garlic and thyme and cook for 1 more minute Press cancel to turn off the Instant Pot.

Add the chicken stock, taking care to scrape up any browned bits from the bottom of the pot. Add back the chicken along with the potatoes and vegetables.

Secure the lid with the steam vent in the sealed position. Press manual and immediately adjust the timer to 15 minutes. Check that the display light is beneath high pressure.

Once the timer sounds, allow the pressure to release naturally for 5 minutes, then quick release the pressure and carefully remove the lid. In a small bowl, mix together the cream and cornstarch and add to the pot, stirring well until thickened. Season well with salt and pepper, then stir in the chopped parsley.

DAIRY-FREE · GLUTEN-FREE · GRAIN-FREE · VEGAN

LEMON-LENTIL-SPINACH SOUP

If there is one thing I always have on hand in my kitchen, it is lemons. Lemons add so much to any dish. Lentil soup is normally a hearty, not-so-pretty soup that makes me wanna take a nap with a full belly. Add a burst of lemon and some fresh spinach and bang!—you won't be wanting to take a nap. Also, sorry to tell you, you won't have time for a nap with a twelve-minute cook time in the Instant Pot. **SB**

SERVES: 4 to 6

1 tsp extra-virgin olive oil

1 yellow onion, diced

1 tsp salt

1 tsp ground cumin

¼ tsp ground turmeric

¼ tsp freshly ground black pepper

¼ tsp ground coriander

32 oz (946 ml) vegetable stock

2 lb (905 g) dried red lentils

Juice of 1½ lemons

3 cups (90 g) baby spinach

Croutons, for topping (optional)

Press sauté on the Instant Pot. Heat the oil in the pot. After 1 minute, add the onion. Sauté for 2 minutes, or until translucent.

Press cancel and add the salt, cumin, turmeric, pepper, coriander, stock and lentils. Stir to combine.

Secure the lid with the steam vent in the sealed position. Press pressure cook until the display light is beneath high pressure. Use the plus and minus buttons to adjust the time until the display reads "12 minutes."

When the timer sounds, quick release the pressure. Remove the lid. Add the lemon juice. Use an immersion blender to puree the soup until smooth.

Mix in the fresh spinach and top with croutons, if using. Once the spinach slightly wilts, adjust the salt and pepper to taste.

SLOW COOKER METHOD: In the Instant Pot, combine all the ingredients, except the lemon juice and spinach, and stir. Press slow cook until the display light is beneath less. Use the plus and minus buttons to adjust the time until the display reads "8 hours." After 8 hours, remove the lid, mix in the lemon juice and use an immersion blender to puree. Stir in the spinach.

GF GLUTEN-FREE GRAIN-FREE

CHEESEBURGER SOUP

When you can't get your cheeseburger fix, make this soup! It's a fun twist on an American favorite. It's creamy and rich, and the pickles add a nice flavor contrast. **KB**

SERVES: 4

2 tsp (10 ml) olive oil

1 lb (455 g) ground beef

½ medium onion, chopped

2½ cups (590 ml) chicken stock

8 oz (225 g) baby red potatoes, chopped into small pieces

1 (14.5-oz [411-g]) can fire-roasted diced tomatoes

1½ cups (355 ml) half-and-half or heavy cream

2 cups (225 g) shredded mild cheddar cheese

4 oz (113 g) cream cheese, softened, cut into small cubes

Coarse salt

Freshly ground pepper

Chopped dill pickles, for topping (optional)

Press sauté to preheat the Instant Pot. When the word "hot" appears on the display, add the olive oil, then the ground beef and onion. Cook, stirring occasionally, until the onion is soft and the meat has no more pink, about 5 minutes. Press cancel to turn off the Instant Pot.

Add the chicken stock, taking care to scrape up any browned bits from the bottom of the pot. Add the potatoes and fire-roasted tomatoes.

Secure the lid with the steam vent in the sealed position. Press soup and immediately adjust the timer to 20 minutes. Check that the display light is beneath high pressure.

When the timer sounds, quick release the pressure and carefully remove the lid. Stir in the cream, cheddar cheese and cream cheese until the cheeses are completely melted into the soup. Season well with salt and pepper. Top each bowl with some chopped dill pickles, if desired.

DAIRY-FREE GLUTEN-FREE GRAIN-FREE

SAUSAGE, KALE & SWEET POTATO SOUP

This soup has all the warming comfort and indulgent taste that our body craves in the colder months, but done so in a lighter and healthier way! It is packed with protein and veggies and the elegant addition of white wine. Sweet potatoes are fiber and nutrient rich, but also very filling, and complete this meal in a bowl. **AR**

SERVES: 4

2 tbsp (30 ml) avocado oil or extra-virgin olive oil

1 lb (455 g) ground turkey or pork sausage

1 medium white onion, chopped

3 cloves garlic, minced

2 large sweet potatoes, skinned and chopped

10 oz (280 g) sliced mushrooms

4 cups (950 ml) chicken stock

1 cup (237 ml) dry white wine

2 tbsp (30 ml) cider vinegar

1 tbsp (5 g) dried basil

1 tsp sea salt, plus more to taste

½ tsp freshly ground black pepper

3 cups (201 g) roughly chopped kale

2 tbsp (5 g) chopped fresh thyme (optional)

Select sauté on the Instant Pot. Once hot, add the oil to coat the pot and toss in the ground sausage. Cook until almost cooked through, about 5 minutes. Add the onion and garlic. Cook for another 2 to 3 minutes.

Toss in the sweet potatoes, mushrooms, chicken stock, wine, vinegar, basil, salt and pepper.

Secure the lid with the steam vent in the sealed position. Select manual or pressure, and cook on high pressure for 8 minutes.

Use a quick release. Select cancel.

Open the lid and add the kale. Let it cook on keep warm with the lid open for another 3 to 4 minutes, or until the kale is softened but not wilted. Add more salt, if needed. Garnish with the fresh thyme (if using) and serve.

GF GLUTEN-FREE   GRAIN-FREE

CREAMY VEGETARIAN SALSA VERDE CHILI

For a long time in my life, I was a vegetarian. It has been ten-plus years since I reintroduced meat into my diet. Still to this day, though, I try to make and eat meat-free dishes at least once a week. Ya know, minimizing that whole carbon footprint thing? Chili is a really versatile dish that has so many flavors, you won't even miss the meat. **SB**

SERVES: 4 to 6

1 tbsp (15 ml) extra-virgin olive oil

1 yellow onion, diced

1 green bell pepper, seeded and diced

1 jalapeño pepper, seeded and diced

1 clove garlic, grated

1 tsp ground cumin

1 tsp ground coriander

¼ tsp cayenne pepper

4 cups (946 ml) vegetable stock

2 (15.5-oz [429-g]) cans cannellini beans, drained and rinsed

1 cup (260 g) salsa verde

Salt

Freshly ground black pepper

4 oz (115 g) cream cheese, softened

Press sauté on the Instant Pot and allow the pot to heat up for 2 minutes. Add the oil, onion, bell pepper and jalapeño to the pot. Sauté for 3 minutes. Stir in the garlic.

Press cancel. Add the cumin, coriander, cayenne, stock, beans, salsa verde and salt and black pepper to taste. Stir to combine.

Secure the lid with the steam vent in the sealed position. Press pressure cook until the display light is beneath high pressure. Use the plus and minus buttons to adjust the time until the display reads "5 minutes."

When the timer sounds, quick release the pressure. Remove the lid and mix in the cream cheese. Once the cream cheese melts, adjust the salt and pepper to taste.

CORN & POTATO SOUP

This is the easiest recipe and has amazing flavor! The best part—besides how good it tastes—is that you don't have to peel the potatoes or drain anything after cooking! Stir in some shredded cheese, if you like, too. **KB**

SERVES: 4 to 6

½ lb (225 g) bacon, cut crosswise into 1" (2.5-cm) pieces

½ medium onion, chopped

3 tbsp (23 g) all-purpose flour

1 (32-oz [950-ml]) container low-sodium chicken stock

3 lb (1.4 kg) red potatoes, quartered

1½ lb (680 g) frozen corn kernels

2 cups (475 ml) whole milk

1 tbsp (18 g) coarse salt, plus more to taste

Freshly ground black pepper

Press sauté to preheat the Instant Pot. When the word "hot" appears on the display, add the bacon. Cook until the bacon is browned and crispy, then remove it with a slotted spoon and place on paper towels to drain any excess fat.

Add the onion to the drippings in the pot and cook until the onion is soft, about 5 minutes, stirring frequently. Add the flour and cook for 1 more minute, stirring constantly. Press cancel to turn off the Instant Pot.

Add the chicken stock, taking care to scrape any browned bits from the bottom of the pot. Add the potatoes and corn.

Secure the lid with the steam vent in the sealed position. Press manual and immediately adjust the timer to 20 minutes. Check that the display light is beneath high pressure.

When the timer sounds, quick release the pressure and carefully remove the lid. Using a potato masher or something similar, crush the potatoes to thicken the soup, leaving some chunks but allowing some to "melt" into the soup, then stir in the milk. Season generously with salt and pepper.

RED LENTIL CURRY SOUP

This soup is one of my favorite meals to eat, ever! I love the delicious spices, the creamy coconut milk and the way it fills me up in the best way possible. This recipe is such a breeze to make that I often prepare it to keep on hand for lunches or an easy dinner. Pair with a salad or some naan for an easy Meatless Monday dinner! **AR**

SERVES: 4 to 5

1 tbsp (15 ml) avocado oil or extra-virgin olive oil

1 medium yellow onion, diced

2 cloves garlic, minced

1 tbsp (6 g) chopped fresh ginger

1 red bell pepper, seeded and diced

2 cups (400 g) split red lentils

6 cups (1.4 L) vegetable or chicken stock

1 (14.5-oz [411-g]) can diced tomatoes

2 tbsp (30 g) red curry paste

2 tsp (4 g) garam masala

1 tsp curry powder

1 tsp sea salt, plus more to taste

1 (13.5-oz [400-ml]) can full-fat coconut milk

Juice of 1 lime

¼ cup (10 g) chopped fresh cilantro, for garnish (optional)

Select sauté on the Instant Pot. Once the pot is hot, coat the pan with the oil. Add the onion, garlic, ginger and bell pepper. Sauté for about 3 minutes, then select cancel.

Add the lentils, stock, tomatoes, curry paste, garam masala, curry powder and salt. Give the mixture a quick stir.

Secure the lid with the steam vent in the sealed position. Select manual or pressure, and cook on high pressure for 5 minutes.

Use a quick release and remove the lid. Pour in the coconut milk and lime juice and stir.

Enjoy hot, topping with fresh cilantro and additional salt to taste.

DAIRY-FREE OPTION · GLUTEN-FREE · GRAIN-FREE · VEGAN OPTION

SPINACH & TOMATO CURRY SOUP

This warming yellow curry soup is full of wholesome veggies and packs both the savory and sweet spices of mild curry plus herby aromatics from the sweet licorice-like Thai basil and vibrant, lemony cilantro. **ESV**

SERVES: 4 to 6

2 tbsp (28 g) grass-fed butter, ghee or avocado oil

1 yellow onion, peeled and diced

5 cloves garlic, finely minced

3 large celery ribs, thinly sliced

2 organic russet potatoes, peeled and diced

3 small tomatoes, seeded and diced

1½ tbsp (10 g) yellow curry powder

1½ tsp (4 g) ground cumin

1 tsp sea salt, plus more to taste

1 tsp dried thyme

½ tsp ground coriander

4 cups (946 ml) chicken or vegetable stock

2 large bunches fresh spinach (about 1½ lb [680 g] total), leaves only, cleaned well

¼ cup (10 g) roughly chopped fresh cilantro, plus more for garnish

¼ cup (10 g) fresh Thai basil or basil leaves

1½ cups (355 ml) coconut milk

⅓ cup (80 ml) fresh lime juice

Lime wedges, for garnish (optional)

Place your healthy fat of choice in the Instant Pot and press sauté. Once the fat has melted, add the onion and sauté for 7 minutes, stirring occasionally, then add the garlic and continue to sauté for 1 minute, stirring occasionally. Add the celery, potatoes, tomatoes, curry, cumin, salt, thyme, coriander and stock, then give it a stir. Press keep warm/cancel.

Secure the lid with the steam vent in the sealed position. Press manual and set on high pressure for 7 minutes.

Once the timer sounds, press keep warm/cancel. Using an oven mitt, do a quick release. When the steam venting stops and the silver dial drops, carefully open the lid.

Press sauté and add the spinach, cilantro, basil, coconut milk and lime juice. Allow the soup to come to a simmer, stirring, until the spinach has fully wilted. Press keep warm/cancel. Taste for seasoning and adjust the salt to taste.

Serve immediately. Garnish with chopped fresh cilantro and lime wedges (if using).

NOTES: If possible, use organic spinach since spinach is on the EWG's "Shopper's Guide to Pesticides in Produce" Dirty Dozen list.

Use a curry powder that uses a blend of such ingredients as coriander, turmeric, mustard, cumin, fenugreek, paprika, cayenne, cardamom, nutmeg, cinnamon and cloves, preferably an organic brand.

PUMPKIN-BUTTERNUT SQUASH BISQUE

A comforting bowl of fabulously delicious fall flavors! A blend of pumpkin, butternut squash and even some apple for a slightly sweet taste, this bisque makes a perfect main course or starter for any fall feast. Perfect for the holidays, too! **AR**

SERVES: 4 to 5

1 (3- to 4-lb [1.4- to 1.8-kg]) butternut squash

1 (2- to 3-lb [1- to 1.4-kg]) pie pumpkin

2 tbsp (30 ml) avocado oil or extra-virgin olive oil

1 medium white onion, diced

2 cloves garlic, minced

1 large apple (see note)

3 to 4 cups (710 to 946 ml) vegetable or chicken stock

2 tbsp (30 ml) cider vinegar

2 tsp (3 g) dried basil

2 tsp (2 g) dried sage

1 tsp salt, plus more to taste

½ cup (120 ml) coconut milk, coconut cream, or light or heavy dairy cream

½ cup (70 g) pumpkin seeds, for garnish

2 tbsp (3 g) fresh rosemary or thyme

Peel the skin off your butternut squash. Cut in half vertically and remove the seeds, then cut into 1-inch (2.5-cm) chunks. Cut the pumpkin in half and remove the seeds, then continue cutting to carve out the inside flesh of the pumpkin. Cut the pumpkin into 1-inch (2.5 cm) chunks.

Select sauté on the Instant Pot and, once hot, coat the bottom with the oil. Add the onion and cook for 2 to 3 minutes, then add the garlic and cook for another 1 to 2 minutes.

Add the squash, pumpkin and apple. Top with 3 cups (710 ml) of the stock and the vinegar, basil, sage and salt.

Secure the lid with the steam vent in the sealed position. Select manual or pressure, and cook on high pressure for 14 minutes.

Use a natural release for 15 minutes, then release the remaining steam before opening the lid.

Add the coconut milk, and blend your soup with an immersion blender or in batches in a regular blender (to prevent overheating). If the soup is too thick, add an additional ½ to 1 cup (120 to 237 ml) of stock.

Garnish with pumpkin seeds and fresh herbs.

NOTE: I use a Honeycrisp apple, but a Braeburn or Pink Lady would also work in this recipe.

GF GLUTEN-FREE GRAIN-FREE

LOBSTER BISQUE

Smooth and creamy, this mouthwatering lobster bisque is certainly elegant. It warms you to the core with its rich, yet simple, delectable flavors. It cooks quickly in the Instant Pot, too! **ESV**

SERVES: 4 to 6

2 tbsp (28 g) grass-fed butter

1 large onion, diced

5 fresh cloves garlic, chopped

½ cup (120 ml) dry white wine

2 large russet potatoes, peeled and roughly chopped

2 large celery ribs, thinly sliced

1 large carrot, peeled and thinly sliced

1 tsp sea salt

½ tsp smoked paprika

2 tsp (2 g) finely chopped fresh thyme leaves, plus more for garnish (optional)

2 tsp (3 g) finely chopped fresh dill, plus more for garnish (optional)

1 tsp finely chopped fresh chives, plus more for garnish (optional)

1 bay leaf

Zest of 1 lemon

2 tbsp (8 g) chopped fresh flat-leaf parsley

3 cups (710 ml) lobster, fish, chicken or veggie stock

1 lb (455 g) cooked lobster meat, plus more to garnish (optional)

¾ cup (175 ml) heavy cream

Place the butter in the Instant Pot and press sauté. Once the butter has melted, add the onion and sauté for 5 minutes, stirring occasionally. Then, add the garlic and sauté for 2 minutes, stirring occasionally. Add the white wine, then give the mixture a stir. Press keep warm/cancel.

Add the potatoes, celery, carrot, salt, paprika, thyme, dill, chives, bay leaf, lemon zest, parsley, stock and lobster, then give the mixture a quick stir.

Secure the lid with the steam vent in the sealed position. Press manual and set on high pressure for 10 minutes.

Once the timer sounds, press keep warm/cancel. Allow the Instant Pot to release pressure naturally for 5 minutes. Using an oven mitt, do a quick release. If there is any steam left over, allow it to release until the silver dial drops, then carefully open the lid. With tongs or a spoon, remove and discard the bay leaf.

Carefully pour the soup into a high-powered blender, leaving at least 3 inches (7.5 cm) of headspace to the top of the blender, then blend on low speed just until fully incorporated, about 10 seconds. You may need to do this in batches. Alternatively, leave the soup in the Instant Pot and use an immersion blender instead.

Taste for seasoning and adjust the salt to taste. Add the soup back to the Instant Pot and press sauté (reheating helps get the bubbles from blending out of the soup), bring to a boil and give it a few stirs. Then, press keep warm/cancel. Add the cream, then stir until it's mixed in.

Serve immediately. Garnish with fresh thyme, dill or chives, or a few pieces of lobster meat.

NOTES: For a lower-carb version, 2 cups (200 g) of fresh or frozen cauliflower florets can be substituted for the potatoes.

Look for lobster tails instead of whole lobster; they are usually easy to find and tend to be much more affordable. Most natural food stores will have them in the frozen section.

BBQ CHICKEN SOUP

This soup is my daughter's absolute favorite dinner ever! She requests it all the time, and luckily for me, it couldn't be easier to make. Only a few ingredients, and usually ones that I keep on hand at all times. I also love how it packs in flavor with plenty of protein and fiber. It also makes the perfect lunch throughout the week! **AR**

SERVES: 4

2 tbsp (30 ml) avocado oil or extra-virgin olive oil

½ large red onion

1 cup (130 g) frozen corn

1 lb (455 g) chicken breast

4 cups (946 ml) chicken stock

⅔ cup (165 g) barbecue sauce

Fresh cilantro, for garnish (optional)

Select sauté on the Instant Pot. Once the pot is hot, coat with the oil, then toss in the red onion. Cook for 2 minutes, then add the frozen corn. Continue to cook for another 2 to 3 minutes, then select cancel.

Add the chicken breast, stock and barbecue sauce.

Secure the lid with the steam vent in the sealed position. Select manual or pressure, and cook on high pressure for 7 minutes.

Use a quick release. Serve hot with fresh cilantro, for garnish.

NOTE: Use your own personal favorite barbecue sauce in this recipe, or a homemade version.

DAIRY-FREE GLUTEN-FREE

GRAIN-FREE VEGAN

CREAMY ROASTED RED PEPPER SOUP

My normal go-to version of this soup is totally me being lazy. I dump a jar of roasted red peppers in a blender with some milk and call it soup. I think we can do better. Even on our laziest days, we can put just a tad more effort into our food, right? We take a few minutes to sauté before we pressure-cook in the Instant Pot. You can always find a few minutes here and there in a day. After that, we can get back to being lazy while the Instant Pot takes care of the rest. **SB**

SERVES: 4 to 6

1 tbsp (15 ml) extra-virgin olive oil

1 yellow onion, diced

2 cloves garlic, grated

1 tbsp (15 ml) sherry vinegar

2 (16-oz [455-g]) jars roasted red peppers, drained

1 (14.5-oz [411-g]) can fire-roasted diced tomatoes

2 cups (475 ml) water or vegetable stock

1 tsp fresh lemon juice

Salt

Freshly ground black pepper

1 cup (237 ml) coconut milk

Croutons, for topping (optional)

Press sauté on the Instant Pot. Place the oil in the pot. Once the oil is hot, after about 2 minutes, add the onion. Sauté for 2 minutes, or until translucent.

Press cancel and then add the garlic and vinegar. Stir to combine. Add the roasted red peppers, tomatoes, water and lemon juice along with salt and pepper to taste.

Secure the lid with the steam vent in the sealed position. Press pressure cook until the display light is beneath high pressure. Use the plus and minus buttons to adjust the time until the display reads "7 minutes."

When the timer sounds, quick release the pressure. Remove the lid. Stir in the coconut milk. Use an immersion blender to puree the soup until smooth. Add more salt and pepper to taste and top with croutons, if using.

NOTE: If you do not have an immersion blender, wait until the soup is slightly cooled and then puree in batches in a blender until smooth.

CREAMY & SMOOTH VEGETABLE SOUP

GF GLUTEN-FREE   GRAIN-FREE

This vegetable soup is a great way to get some beans and veggies in! It's delicious, with a wonderfully creamy texture. It's just as good without the cream, so try it both ways and see which one you like best! **KB**

SERVES: 6

2 tsp (10 ml) olive oil

½ onion, chopped

1 lb (455 g) carrots, chopped

3 celery ribs, chopped

2 cloves garlic, minced

Large pinch of dried thyme

Large pinch of dried oregano

2½ cups (590 ml) chicken stock

8 oz (225 g) baby red potatoes, quartered

1 (15-oz [425-g]) can white beans, drained and rinsed

¼ cup (60 ml) heavy cream

Coarse salt

Freshly ground black pepper

Press sauté to preheat the Instant Pot. When the word "hot" appears on the display, add the oil. Add the onion, carrots and celery and cook until the onion is soft, about 5 minutes, stirring frequently. Add the garlic, thyme and oregano and cook for 1 more minute, stirring frequently.

Add the chicken stock, taking care to scrape any browned bits from the bottom. Add the potatoes and beans.

Secure the lid with the steam vent in the sealed position. Press manual and immediately adjust the timer to 20 minutes. Check that the display light is beneath high pressure.

When the timer sounds, quick release the pressure and carefully remove the lid. Using an immersion blender, puree the soup until very smooth. Stir in the cream and season well with salt and pepper.

DAIRY-FREE GLUTEN-FREE GRAIN-FREE

VEGETABLE BEEF STEW

Every home cook needs a go-to beef stew recipe, and this one is, hands down, the best I've ever tasted. This classic cold-weather dish is cooked perfectly in the Instant Pot! We love to have it on a snow day, or even Christmas Eve. It also tastes delicious paired with a glass of red wine! **AR**

SERVES: 6

2 tbsp (30 ml) avocado oil or extra-virgin olive oil

2 lb (905 g) top sirloin steak, fat trimmed, cut into 1" (2.5-cm) pieces

1 yellow onion, diced

2 cloves garlic, minced

3 tbsp (24 g) tapioca starch

1 cup (130 g) frozen peas

1 (14.5-oz [411-g]) can diced tomatoes, with juices

4 carrots, peeled and diced

1 large russet potato, peeled and diced

1 cup (100 g) diced celery

3 cups (710 ml) beef stock

½ cup (120 ml) red wine (e.g., a cabernet sauvignon or zinfandel)

2 tbsp (30 ml) red wine vinegar

1 tbsp (15 g) dark brown sugar

1 tsp dried thyme

1 tsp dried rosemary

2 bay leaves

2 tsp (12 g) salt, plus more to taste

Fresh rosemary or thyme, for garnish

Select sauté on the Instant Pot. Once hot, coat the bottom of the pan with the oil. Sauté the beef until it is starting to brown, about 3 minutes. Toss in the onion and garlic and cook another 3 minutes. Select cancel. Coat the beef mixture with tapioca starch and stir.

Add the frozen peas, tomatoes, carrots, potato, celery, stock, wine, vinegar, brown sugar, thyme, rosemary, bay leaves and salt.

Secure the lid with the steam vent in the sealed position. Select the meat/stew function, and cook on high pressure for 35 minutes.

Use a natural release for 15 minutes, and then release any remaining steam. Remove the lid and take out the bay leaves.

Serve hot, garnished with fresh rosemary or thyme and additional salt to taste.

NOTE: This stew tastes better after sitting all day, or serve the following day after it is made.

DAIRY-FREE GLUTEN-FREE GRAIN-FREE

SWEET POTATO SOUP
WITH COCONUT MILK

The flavor of coconut milk combined with the sweet potatoes make this easy soup a wonderful weeknight meal. I like to top mine with candied bacon for an indulgent treat, but it's perfect on its own with a loaf of crusty bread, too. **KB**

SERVES: 8

2 tsp (10 ml) olive oil

1 small onion, chopped

2 carrots, peeled and chopped

2 cloves garlic, minced

4 cups (946 ml) chicken stock

5 large sweet potatoes, peeled and cut into small chunks

1 (13.5-oz [400 ml]) can coconut milk

Coarse salt

Freshly ground black pepper

Press sauté to preheat the Instant Pot. When the word "hot" appears on the display, add the oil. Add the onion and carrots and cook until the onion is soft, about 5 minutes, stirring frequently. Add the garlic and cook for 1 more minute, stirring frequently.

Add the chicken stock, taking care to scrape any browned bits from the bottom. Add the sweet potatoes.

Secure the lid with the steam vent in the sealed position. Press manual and immediately adjust the timer to 20 minutes. Check that the display light is beneath high pressure.

When the timer sounds, quick release the pressure and carefully remove the lid. Using an immersion blender, puree the soup until very smooth. Add the coconut milk, then taste and season well with salt and pepper.

GF GLUTEN-FREE   GRAIN-FREE

CREAMY PUMPKIN WHITE CHICKEN CHILI

This is the recipe that is on consistent repeat in my house during the fall months! A perfect meal to make for guests, co-workers and even a chili cook-off. Our family tradition is to enjoy this the night of Halloween, but we eat it many other times during cooler months. **AR**

SERVES: 6

2 tbsp (30 ml) avocado oil or extra-virgin olive oil

1 medium yellow onion, diced

2 jalapeño peppers, seeded and chopped

2 poblano peppers, diced

2 lb (905 g) chicken breast

1 tbsp (8 g) chili powder

2 tsp (5 g) paprika

2 tsp (5 g) ground cumin

½ tsp cayenne pepper

1 tsp sea salt

1 (14.5-oz [411-g]) can diced tomatoes

1 (15-oz [425-g]) can pure pumpkin puree

2 (4-oz [115-g]) cans diced green chiles

1 cup (237 ml) chicken stock

8 oz (225 g) cream cheese, softened

Chopped fresh cilantro, for garnish

Select sauté on the Instant Pot. Once hot, coat the bottom of the pot with the oil and add the onion. Cook for 2 to 3 minutes, then add the jalapeño and poblano peppers. Continue to sauté for another 2 to 3 minutes. Select cancel.

Add the chicken, chili powder, paprika, cumin, cayenne, salt, diced tomatoes, pumpkin, diced green chiles and chicken stock and stir.

Secure the lid with the steam vent in the sealed position. Select manual or pressure, and cook on high pressure for 8 minutes.

Use a quick release. Remove the lid once the steam is released, and transfer the chicken to a cutting board. Using a fork or knife, shred the chicken and place it back in the Instant Pot.

Stir in the cream cheese and allow it to melt into the chili. Serve hot with fresh cilantro and any other chili toppings.

DAIRY-FREE OPTION · GLUTEN-FREE · GRAIN-FREE

SEAFOOD STEW

This deeply flavored seafood stew is chock-full of sustainable seafood and lots of tantalizing textures. It's also overflowing with veggies and fresh herbs that give it lots of bold flavor, plus a touch of capers for a nice little salty bite. **ESV**

SERVES: 4 to 6

2 tbsp (28 g) grass-fed butter, ghee or avocado oil

1 large onion, diced

1 small fennel bulb, thinly sliced

4 fresh cloves garlic, chopped

½ cup (120 ml) dry white wine

3 large celery ribs with leaves, sliced about ¼" (6 mm) thick

2 carrots, peeled and thickly sliced

1 tsp sea salt

1 fresh or dried bay leaf

Zest of 1 lemon

¼ cup (15 g) chopped fresh flat-leaf parsley, plus more for garnish (optional)

1 tbsp (3 g) thinly chopped fresh basil, plus more for garnish (optional)

1 tbsp (4 g) chopped fresh dill, plus more for garnish (optional)

2 tsp (2 g) fresh thyme leaves

1 tsp chopped fresh rosemary

3 tbsp (26 g) drained capers

2 lb (905 g) assorted fresh sustainable seafood; e.g., Dungeness crab or canned lump crabmeat, lobster tail, clams (cleaned), mussels (cleaned), jumbo shrimp (peeled and deveined) or scallops

1 lb (455 g) sustainable white fish (e.g., halibut, cod or sea bass), cut into 3" (7.5-cm) pieces

4 cups (946 ml) fish, lobster, crab, chicken or vegetable stock

Extra-virgin olive oil, for garnish

Place your healthy fat of choice in the Instant Pot and press sauté. Once the fat has melted, add the onion and fennel and sauté, stirring occasionally, for 7 minutes, or until caramelized. Then, add the garlic and sauté for 1 minute, stirring occasionally. Add the white wine, then give the mixture a stir. Press keep warm/cancel.

Add the celery, carrots, salt, bay leaf, lemon zest, parsley, basil, dill, thyme, rosemary, capers, seafood, fish and stock, then give the mixture a quick stir.

Secure the lid with the steam vent in the sealed position. Press manual and set for 6 minutes.

Once the timer sounds, press keep warm/cancel. Using an oven mitt, do a quick release. When the steam venting stops and the silver dial drops, carefully open the lid.

Taste for seasoning and adjust the salt to taste.

Serve immediately. Garnish with fresh parsley, basil or dill and drizzle with extra-virgin olive oil

NOTES: Use the Monterey Bay Aquarium's Seafood Watch website or app to make sure you choose low-mercury, sustainable fish.

GF
GLUTEN-FREE GRAIN-FREE

LOADED CAULIFLOWER SOUP

This low-carb soup is bound to be a new favorite comfort food! Cauliflower creates a creamy and filling, delicious soup that is perfect for a cold night. You can easily load up with your favorite toppings: cheddar, chives, bacon and even sour cream! **AR**

SERVES: 4 to 5

2 tbsp (28 g) unsalted butter

1 cup (225 g) diced leeks

2 celery ribs, diced

3 cloves garlic, crushed

1 large head cauliflower, cut into florets

3 cups (710 ml) vegetable or chicken stock

1 tsp sea salt, plus more to taste

3 tbsp (45 g) cream cheese

½ cup (120 ml) half-and-half or milk

4 strips cooked bacon, crumbled

¾ cup (86 g) shredded sharp cheddar cheese

Diced green onion, for garnish (optional)

Sour cream, for garnish (optional)

Select sauté on the Instant Pot. Once hot, melt the butter. Toss in the leeks. Sauté for 2 to 3 minutes, or until fragrant, then add the celery and garlic. Cook for another 2 minutes. Select cancel.

Add the cauliflower, then pour the stock on top. Stir in the salt.

Secure the lid with the steam vent in the sealed position. Select manual or pressure, and cook on high pressure for 6 minutes.

Use a quick release, and remove the lid once the steam is completely released.

Add the cream cheese and half-and-half. Using a blender or immersion blender, blend until smooth.

Pour into individual bowls and top with the bacon, cheddar and optional green onion and sour cream.

GF
GLUTEN-FREE

HEARTY CLAM CORN CHOWDER

Clam chowder plus corn chowder—they're a match made in heaven. Known for being thick, rich and full of different textures—both crunchy and soft—this simple bowl of deliciousness is wonderful enjoyed as-is or with a gluten-free biscuit or crusty piece of buttered gluten-free bread. **ESV**

SERVES: 4 to 6

2 tbsp (28 g) grass-fed butter

1 large yellow onion, finely diced

4 fresh cloves garlic, finely chopped

2 tbsp (15 g) gluten-free all-purpose flour

2 large celery ribs, sliced about ¼" (6 mm) thick

1 large carrot, peeled and diced

1 large russet potato, peeled and diced

10 oz (280 g) fresh or frozen corn kernels

¼ cup (15 g) chopped fresh flat-leaf parsley

1 cup (237 ml) clam juice

1 cup (237 ml) fish, chicken or vegetable stock

1 tsp sea salt

1 tsp dried thyme

1 tsp dried dill

1 tsp dried basil

½ tsp freshly ground black pepper

½ tsp dried oregano

Zest of 1 lemon

13 oz (370 g) canned clams, drained

1 cup (237 ml) milk

¾ cup (175 ml) heavy cream

Place the butter in the Instant Pot and press sauté. Once the butter has melted, add the onion and sauté for 4 minutes, stirring occasionally. Add the garlic and sauté for 1 minute, stirring occasionally. Add the flour and stir for 1 more minute. Press keep warm/cancel.

Add the celery, carrot, potato, corn, parsley, clam juice, stock, salt, thyme, dill, basil, pepper, oregano, lemon zest and clams, then give the mixture a quick stir.

Secure the lid with the steam vent in the sealed position. Press manual and set on high pressure for 9 minutes.

Once the timer sounds, press keep warm/cancel. Using an oven mitt, do a quick release. When the steam venting stops and the silver dial drops, carefully open the lid.

Press sauté, add the milk and cream, then stir until they are fully mixed in. Allow to come to a simmer and cook for about 5 minutes, or until the chowder slightly thickens. Press keep warm/cancel. Taste for seasoning and adjust the salt to taste. Allow to rest for 10 minutes.

Serve immediately.

NOTE: Look for sustainable canned clams; usually you can find them in larger natural food stores or online. Otherwise, look for BPA-free lined cans or clams and/or clam juice that comes in glass jars.

CURRIED CAULIFLOWER SOUP

DAIRY-FREE GLUTEN-FREE GRAIN-FREE

This soup has such great taste for such a short ingredient list! The curry flavor is actually quite mild, so there's plenty of cauliflower flavor shining through. It's one of our family's favorites. **KB**

SERVES: 4

2 tsp (10 ml) olive oil

1 medium onion, chopped

3 cloves garlic, minced

1 tbsp (15 g) red curry paste

3 cups (710 ml) chicken stock

1 large head cauliflower, broken into florets, core discarded

1 (13.5-oz [400-m]) can coconut milk

1 tsp coarse salt

Press sauté to preheat the Instant Pot. When the word "hot" appears on the display, add the olive oil, then the onion. Cook, stirring occasionally, until the onion is soft, about 5 minutes. Add the garlic and red curry paste. Cook for about another minute, stirring frequently. Press cancel to turn off the Instant Pot.

Add the chicken stock, taking care to scrape up any browned bits from the bottom of the pot. Add the cauliflower florets.

Secure the lid with the steam vent in the sealed position. Press soup and immediately adjust the timer to 20 minutes. Check that the display light is beneath high pressure.

Once the timer sounds, allow the pressure to release naturally for 10 minutes, then quick release the pressure and carefully remove the lid. Stir in the coconut milk and salt. Using an immersion blender, puree the soup until smooth. Serve immediately.

DAIRY-FREE OPTION · GLUTEN-FREE · GRAIN-FREE

BEEF MINESTRONE SOUP

I love a classic minestrone soup because of its many veggies, but it becomes even better when you pack in some protein! This variation includes ground beef (substitute ground turkey, if you wish) and cannellini beans. A very filling soup that makes a fantastic dinner during colder months! **AR**

SERVES: 6

2 tbsp (30 ml) avocado oil or extra-virgin olive oil

1 yellow onion, diced

2 cloves garlic, minced

1 lb (455 g) ground beef

1 medium zucchini, diced

3 carrots, sliced and diced

3 celery ribs, diced

1 (14.5-oz [411-g]) can diced tomatoes

3 tbsp (48 g) tomato paste

1 (15-oz [425-g]) can cannellini beans, drained and rinsed

1 tbsp (6 g) Italian seasoning

5 cups (1.2 L) chicken stock

2 tbsp (30 ml) red wine vinegar

1 tsp salt, plus more to taste

¼ cup (10 g) chopped fresh basil

⅓ cup (30 g) shredded Parmesan cheese, for garnish (optional)

Select sauté on the Instant Pot. Once hot, add the oil to the pot, then the onion and garlic. Cook for 2 to 3 minutes, then add the ground beef. Continue to cook for another 5 to 6 minutes, or until the ground beef is mostly cooked. Select cancel.

Add the zucchini, carrots, celery, diced tomatoes, tomato paste, beans, Italian seasoning, stock, vinegar and salt.

Secure the lid with the steam vent in the sealed position. Select manual or pressure, and cook on high pressure for 6 minutes.

Use a quick release. Remove the lid once the steam is completely released.

Serve hot and garnish with fresh basil and Parmesan cheese (if using).

DAIRY-FREE GLUTEN-FREE GRAIN-FREE

MOROCCAN CARROT SOUP

I always love adding a new soup to the regimen. We all have our standard soups we always make when weather turns chilly. Adding a new one really livens things up. Moroccan carrot soup is dairy-free and packed with warm spices. Twelve minutes in the Instant Pot and this bright soup comes together. No boiling, no sautéing, just a little bit of pureeing. **SB**

SERVES: 4 to 6

1 yellow onion, diced

2 cloves garlic, minced

½ tsp ground cinnamon

½ tsp ground cumin

¼ to ½ tsp cayenne pepper (depending on how spicy you like things)

Salt

Freshly ground black pepper

1 tsp grated fresh ginger

Juice of ½ lemon

1 lb (455 g) carrots, peeled and roughly chopped

2 cups (475 ml) vegetable stock

1 cup (237 ml) water

1 tsp honey

¾ cup (175 ml) canned coconut milk

Chopped green onion, for topping (optional)

Pomegranate seeds, for topping (optional)

In the Instant Pot, combine the onion, garlic, cinnamon, cumin, cayenne, salt and black pepper to taste, ginger, lemon juice, carrots, stock and water. Stir to combine.

Secure the lid with the steam vent in the sealed position. Press pressure cook until the display light is beneath high pressure. Use the plus and minus buttons to adjust the time until the display reads "12 minutes."

When the timer sounds, quick release the pressure. Remove the lid. Stir in the honey and coconut milk.

Puree the soup until smooth and creamy, using an immersion blender. Adjust the salt, black pepper and cayenne to taste.

Serve with green onion and pomegranate seeds on top, if desired.

SLOW COOKER METHOD: In the Instant Pot, combine all the ingredients, except the honey and coconut milk. Secure the lid with the steam vent open. Press slow cook until the display light is beneath less. Use the plus and minus buttons to adjust the time until the display reads "6 hours." When the timer sounds, remove the lid. Stir in the honey and coconut milk. Use an immersion blender to puree until smooth.

DAIRY-FREE OPTION GLUTEN-FREE GRAIN-FREE

TUSCAN SOUP

Of all of my Instant Pot soup recipes, this is probably the one I make the most! The sausage, potato, kale and lightly creamy combo is so comforting and filling on a cold night. The crushed red pepper added at the end gives this soup a nice little kick! **AR**

SERVES: 4

2 tbsp (30 ml) olive or avocado oil

1 medium yellow onion, chopped

3 cloves garlic, minced

1 lb (455 g) Italian sausage (can be turkey or chicken)

5 cups (1.2 L) chicken stock

3 large russet potatoes, peel on, cut into 1" (2.5-cm) chunks

2 tsp (3 g) dried basil

1 tsp dried fennel

1 tsp sea salt, plus more to taste

2 cups (134 g) chopped large-leaf curly kale

½ cup (120 ml) full-fat coconut milk or heavy cream (see note)

1 to 2 tsp (1 to 2 g) crushed red pepper flakes (optional)

Freshly ground black pepper

Select sauté on the Instant Pot. Once hot, coat the bottom of the pot with the oil. Add the onion and sauté for 2 to 3 minutes, then toss in the garlic and sausage. Brown the sausage until cooked, about 5 minutes. Select cancel.

Pour the chicken stock over the sausage, then add the potatoes, basil, fennel and salt. Secure the lid with the steam vent in the sealed position. Select manual or pressure, and cook on high pressure for 12 minutes.

Use a quick release. Remove the lid and select the sauté function. Add the kale. Stir for a few minutes until the kale begins to wilt. Add the coconut milk.

Season with red pepper flakes (if using), and additional salt and pepper to taste.

NOTE: I normally make this soup dairy-free, using coconut milk. The coconut taste is nonexistent but gives off just the right amount of creaminess.

DAIRY-FREE
OPTION

GF
GLUTEN-FREE

MEXICAN CHICKEN NOODLE SOUP

Chicken soup is known for being a cure-all, plus it's simply just one of those comforting soups that makes you feel cozy and nourished. This Mexican-inspired version is filled with tender chicken, veggies, pasta, delicious spices and a touch of zesty lime. **ESV**

SERVES: 6 to 8

2 tbsp (28 g) grass-fed butter, ghee or avocado oil

1 large yellow onion, thickly sliced

5 cloves garlic, finely minced

½ cup (90 g) crushed tomatoes or diced fresh tomatoes

½ small green cabbage, thickly sliced

1 large celery rib, thickly sliced

2½ lb (1.1 kg) organic skinless, boneless chicken breast or thighs

6 cups (1.4 L) chicken stock

1½ cups (355 ml) filtered water

1 tbsp (8 g) chili powder

1½ tsp (9 g) sea salt

1½ tsp (4 g) ground cumin

½ tsp ground coriander

½ tsp dried oregano

½ tsp dried thyme

⅓ cup (80 ml) fresh lime juice

2 cups (210 g) gluten-free dried pasta; e.g., fusilli, macaroni, penne, egg noodles or broken-up tagliatelle

Fresh cilantro, for garnish

Lime wedges, for garnish

Place your healthy fat of choice in the Instant Pot and press sauté. Once the fat has melted, add the onion and sauté for 7 minutes, stirring occasionally, then add the garlic and continue to sauté for 1 minute, stirring occasionally. Add the tomatoes, cabbage, celery, chicken, stock, water, chili powder, salt, cumin, coriander, oregano, thyme and lime juice, then give the mixture a stir. Press keep warm/cancel.

Secure the lid with the steam vent in the sealed position. Press manual and set on high pressure for 12 minutes.

Once the timer sounds, press keep warm/cancel. Using an oven mitt, do a quick release. When the steam venting stops and the silver dial drops, carefully open the lid.

Transfer the chicken to a large plate and shred the meat, using the tines of two forks. Set aside.

Press sauté. As soon as the soup comes to a boil, add the pasta. Cook your pasta al dente according to the package directions—usually this is anywhere from 4 to 8 minutes. Press keep warm/cancel.

Return the shredded chicken to the Instant Pot and give it a stir.

Serve immediately, garnished with chopped fresh cilantro and lime wedges.

DAIRY-FREE

BEEF PHO

Did you know that traditional pho (pronounced fuh) broth takes hours to simmer and draw out all those flavors? In the Instant Pot, however, it takes about 30 minutes. That's right! You get that from-scratch beef pho broth in a fraction of the time. Cooking the broth under pressure extracts all the flavor from the dried mushrooms and spices. The next best things about pho, aside from the broth, are the noodles and toppings. While the soup cooks, you still have enough time to get all your favorite pho toppings arranged. **SB**

SERVES: 4

1 lb (455 g) boneless beef eye round

1 tbsp (18 g) salt, plus more to season the beef

Freshly ground black pepper

1 tbsp (15 ml) canola oil

2 small yellow onions, cut in half, skin on

2 cloves garlic, smashed

1 cinnamon stick

2 whole cloves

1 bay leaf

4 peppercorns

2 star anise

1 oz (28 g) dried shiitake mushrooms

5 cups (1.2 L) water

3 cups (710 ml) beef stock

9.5 oz (270 g) ramen or udon noodles

Toppings: shredded red cabbage, thinly sliced red onion, hot sauce, fresh cilantro, lime wedges, sliced jalapeño and sesame seeds

Season all sides of the beef with salt and pepper.

Place the oil in the Instant Pot. Press sauté. Once the oil is shimmering, add the beef. Sear each side of the beef for about 5 minutes.

Add the onions, garlic, cinnamon stick, cloves, bay leaf, peppercorns, star anise and dried mushrooms to the pot as well. Continue to sear the beef for 5 more minutes while stirring the vegetables and herbs around.

Press cancel and then remove the beef, transferring it to a nearby plate. Tent with foil and let rest.

Pour the water and stock into the pot and add the salt. Stir to combine.

Secure the lid with the steam vent in the sealed position. Press pressure cook until the display light is beneath high pressure. Use the plus and minus buttons to adjust the time until the display reads "20 minutes."

When the timer sounds, quick release the pressure. Remove the lid. Use a fine-mesh strainer with a handle to remove the onions, garlic, mushrooms and spices from the broth.

Discard the onions, garlic and spices, reserving the mushrooms. Add the mushrooms back to the pot.

Press sauté and wait a minute or two until the stock starts to bubble. Add the noodles and cook for 5 minutes, or until tender.

Ladle the broth into bowls. Use tongs to transfer the noodles to the bowls. Top with red cabbage, sliced red onion, hot sauce, fresh cilantro, lime wedges, sliced jalapeño and sesame seeds.

SPICY BEEF & BROCCOLI ZOODLE SOUP

DAIRY-FREE GLUTEN-FREE GRAIN-FREE

This Asian-style soup is reminiscent of a giant bowl of ramen noodles, without the carbs! I love the hot and sour flavor, combined with zucchini noodles and veggies for that perfect texture. So yummy on a cold day! **AR**

SERVES: 4 to 5

2 tbsp (30 ml) avocado oil

3 tbsp (18 g) minced fresh ginger

2 cloves garlic, minced

1½ lb (680 g) top sirloin steak tips, about 1" (2.5-cm) pieces

3 level cups (270 g) fresh broccoli florets

8 oz (225 g) sliced cremini mushrooms

6 cups (1.4 L) beef stock

¼ cup (60 ml) rice vinegar

¼ cup (60 ml) coconut aminos or soy sauce

¼ cup (60 ml) buffalo hot sauce or sriracha (see note)

1 large zucchini, spiralized into noodles

⅓ cup (33 g) chopped fresh green onion

Select sauté on the Instant Pot. Once hot, add the oil, ginger, garlic and steak tips. Cook for a few minutes, until the beef is lightly browned on each side and the garlic and ginger are fragrant. Select cancel.

Add the broccoli, mushrooms, beef stock, vinegar, coconut aminos and hot sauce and stir. At this point, you can remove and set aside the broccoli and add with the zoodles after the soup has cooked, if you want the broccoli to be crisper.

Secure the lid with the steam vent in the sealed position. Select manual or pressure, and cook on high pressure for 8 minutes.

Use a quick release to let the steam out, then open the lid and add more hot sauce if you desire a spicier broth. Add the spiralized zucchini, top with fresh green onion and serve hot.

NOTE: The ¼ cup (60 ml) of hot sauce is for a mild version. You can add up to ½ cup (120 ml) for a spicier version. Adjust to your taste!

GLUTEN-FREE **GRAIN-FREE**

CREAMY SPINACH SOUP

We call this "Popeye and Olive's Soup" in my home because you get a hefty dose of spinach in this pureed soup—we all know the animated character got his strength from eating spinach. But have no fear; this soup is so much better than any can of "Popeye spinach"—it's highly seasoned with layers of flavor from celery, herbs, garlic, sour cream, cheddar cheese and a touch of allspice. **ESV**

SERVES: 4 to 6

2 tbsp (28 g) grass-fed butter, ghee or avocado oil

1 yellow onion, peeled and diced

5 fresh cloves garlic, finely minced

2 large celery ribs, thickly sliced

1 lb (455 g) frozen organic spinach, thawed and moisture squeezed out

2 organic russet potatoes, peeled and cubed

1 tsp sea salt

1 tsp dried thyme

1 tsp dried dill

¼ tsp ground allspice

4 cups (946 ml) chicken or vegetable stock

8 oz (225 g) sour cream, plus more for garnish (if using)

1 cup (115 g) shredded cheddar cheese

Extra-virgin olive oil, for garnish (optional)

Place your healthy fat of choice in the Instant Pot and press sauté. Once the fat has melted, add the onion and sauté for 7 minutes, stirring occasionally, then add the garlic and continue to sauté for 1 minute, stirring occasionally. Add the celery, spinach, potatoes, salt, thyme, dill, allspice and stock, then give the mixture a stir. Press keep warm/cancel.

Secure the lid with the steam vent in the sealed position. Press manual and set on high pressure for 9 minutes.

Once the timer sounds, press keep warm/cancel. Using an oven mitt, do a quick release. When the steam venting stops and the silver dial drops, carefully open the lid.

In batches, ladle the soup into a blender, taking care to fill the blender only about halfway (hot liquids will expand in the blender, so please use caution). Blend on a low setting just until pureed and combined. Return the pureed soup to the Instant Pot and press sauté (reheating helps get the bubbles out of the soup), bring to a boil and give it a few stirs. Add the sour cream and cheese and stir until fully combined. Press keep warm/cancel.

Serve immediately. Garnish with a dollop of sour cream or a drizzle of quality extra-virgin olive oil (if using).

DAIRY-FREE   GRAIN-FREE

EGG DROP SOUP

While we were growing up, my siblings and I thrived off getting to pick the weekend takeout. We got to choose between pizza or Chinese. Once we learned to drive, we could venture out to get our own food, but somehow we still picked between the two places our dad would go to get food. Chinese food was always my pick. I love the complex flavors and comfort that kind of food gives me. I have learned now about how long some of those broths, sauces and bases can take to make. That's why I wanted to take a classic soup recipe from my takeout days and hurry it up a bit in the Instant Pot. Now, nobody has to make the takeout run! **SB**

SERVES: 4 to 6

4 cups (946 ml) water

1 carrot, cut in half widthwise

2 celery ribs, cut in half widthwise

1 yellow onion, cut in half

1 clove garlic, peeled and smashed

1 tsp soy sauce

½ tsp salt, plus a pinch

½ tsp black peppercorns

1 star anise

1 (1" [2.5-cm]) piece fresh ginger

4 large eggs

4 tsp (11 g) cornstarch

Freshly ground black pepper

4 green onions, sliced

In the Instant Pot, combine the water, carrot, celery, onion, garlic, soy sauce, ½ teaspoon of salt, and the peppercorns, star anise and ginger.

Secure the lid with the steam vent in the sealed position. Press pressure cook until the display light is beneath high pressure. Use the plus and minus buttons to adjust the time until the display reads "10 minutes."

When the timer sounds, quick release the pressure.

Remove the lid. Insert a mesh strainer into a large bowl or stockpot. Pour the stock through the strainer into the bowl. Discard the vegetables and spices. Return the stock to the pot. Press sauté. After 3 to 4 minutes, the stock should start to bubble up a bit.

In small bowl, whisk together the eggs, cornstarch and a pinch each of salt and pepper.

Slowly pour the eggs into the stock while whisking the whole time. The eggs should start to form fine ribbons as they cook.

Press cancel and adjust the salt and pepper to taste. Top with the green onions.

DAIRY-FREE GLUTEN-FREE GRAIN-FREE

SPLIT PEA SOUP
WITH HAM

This is my mom's recipe that I adapted for the Instant Pot. We had it often while growing up and it's a soup I love making for my family now. It's simple, inexpensive and hearty! **KB**

SERVES: 4 to 6

2 tsp (10 ml) olive oil

1 medium onion, chopped

2 celery ribs, chopped

3 carrots, chopped

6 cups (1.4 L) chicken stock

1 ham bone

1 lb (455 g) dried split peas

1 bay leaf

Coarse salt

Freshly ground black pepper

Press sauté to preheat the Instant Pot. When the word "hot" appears on the display, add the olive oil, then the onion, celery and carrots. Cook, stirring occasionally, until the onion is soft, about 5 minutes. Press cancel to turn off the Instant Pot.

Add the chicken stock, taking care to scrape up any browned bits from the bottom of the pot. Add the ham bone, split peas and bay leaf.

Secure the lid with the steam vent in the sealed position. Press soup and immediately adjust the timer to 20 minutes. Check that the display light is beneath high pressure.

Once the timer sounds, allow the pressure to release naturally for 10 minutes, then quick release the pressure and carefully remove the lid. Remove the ham bone, and any meat that fell from the ham bone, from the pot. Remove and discard the bay leaf. Using an immersion blender, puree the soup until smooth. Remove the meat from the ham bone and add it and any other meat that was removed back to the pot. Season well with salt and pepper, then serve.

DAIRY-FREE OPTION   GLUTEN-FREE   GRAIN-FREE OPTION

STUFFED PEPPER SOUP

All the flavors of yummy stuffed peppers in soup form! So simple to make, and perfectly cozy for a chilly evening. This family-friendly dinner is sure to become a weeknight staple in colder months! **AR**

SERVES: 4 to 5

2 tbsp (30 ml) avocado oil or extra-virgin olive oil

1 yellow onion, diced

3 cloves garlic, minced

1 lb (455 g) ground beef

2 green bell peppers, seeded and diced

1 red bell pepper, seeded and diced

2 (14.5-oz [411-g]) cans fire-roasted diced tomatoes

1 (15-oz [425-g]) can tomato sauce

2 cups (475 ml) beef stock

2 tbsp (30 ml) red wine vinegar

2 tsp (4 g) Italian seasoning

2 tsp (12 g) sea salt

2 cups (340 g) cooked rice or (220 g) cauliflower rice

¼ cup (20 g) shredded Parmesan cheese, for garnish (optional)

Fresh basil, for garnish

Select sauté on the Instant Pot. Coat the bottom of the pot with oil, then add the onion and garlic. Sauté for 3 to 4 minutes, then add the ground beef. Continue to cook until the beef is no longer pink, about 3 to 4 minutes. Select cancel.

Top the beef mixture with the bell peppers, diced tomatoes, tomato sauce, beef stock, red wine vinegar, Italian seasoning and salt.

Secure the lid with the steam vent in the sealed position. Select manual or pressure, and cook on high pressure for 6 minutes.

Use a quick release and remove the lid. Stir in the rice or cauliflower rice. Serve hot and garnish with Parmesan cheese (if using) and fresh basil.

ZUPPA TOSCANA

I make this recipe all the time because it has so much flavor from just a few ingredients. Plus, it's hearty and makes enough for leftovers! **KB**

SERVES: 6

1 lb (455 g) hot Italian sausage, casings removed

1 small onion, chopped

4 to 5 cloves garlic, minced

3 cups (450 g) diced red potatoes

4 to 5 cups (946 ml to 1.2 L) low-sodium chicken stock

3 cups (201 g) chopped kale

1 cup (237 ml) heavy cream

Coarse salt

Freshly ground black pepper

Press sauté to preheat the Instant Pot. When the word "hot" appears on the display, add the sausage. Cook until the sausage is browned, about 5 minutes. Add the onion and cook until the onion is soft, about 5 minutes, stirring frequently. Add the garlic and cook for 1 more minute, stirring frequently.

Add the potatoes and chicken stock, taking care to scrape any browned bits from the bottom.

Secure the lid with the steam vent in the sealed position. Press manual and immediately adjust the timer to 12 minutes. Check that the display light is beneath high pressure.

When the timer sounds, quick release the pressure and carefully remove the lid. Add the kale and cream, stirring until the kale is wilted. Season generously with salt and pepper.

GF
GLUTEN-FREE

CREAMY SPINACH LASAGNA SOUP

Enjoy a classic pasta recipe—soup-style, with all the flavor of your favorite lasagna. This comforting soup is packed with meaty protein, veggies, herbs and gluten-free pasta and has a creamy base with Italian mascarpone cheese. Top your bowl with a good sprinkling of shredded cheeses and a drizzle of quality extra-virgin olive oil. **ESV**

SERVES: 6 to 8

3 tbsp (43 g) grass-fed butter, ghee or avocado oil

1 lb (455 g) grass-fed ground beef

1 medium yellow onion, peeled and diced

8 oz (225 g) cleaned white button or cremini mushrooms, thinly sliced

5 cloves garlic, finely minced

1 cup (180 g) crushed tomatoes or diced fresh tomatoes

1 tsp sea salt

1 tsp dried thyme

½ tsp dried oregano

½ tsp finely chopped fresh rosemary leaves

6 cups (1.4 L) chicken or vegetable stock

2 cups (210 g) gluten-free dried pasta; e.g., broken-up lasagna or tagliatelle

2 large bunches fresh spinach, leaves only, cleaned well

¼ cup (6 g) fresh basil leaves

½ cup (120 ml) heavy cream

¼ cup (60 g) mascarpone or cream cheese

¼ cup (30 g) shredded mozzarella cheese, for garnish

¼ cup (20 g) shredded Parmesan or Asiago cheese, for garnish

Quality extra-virgin olive oil, for garnish (optional)

Place your healthy fat of choice in the Instant Pot and press sauté. Once the fat has melted, add the ground beef and sauté for 7 minutes, stirring often, allowing the meat to brown, then transfer the cooked beef to a plate and set aside. Add the onion and mushrooms to the pot and sauté for 5 minutes, stirring occasionally, then add the garlic and continue to sauté for 1 minute, stirring occasionally. Add the cooked meat, tomatoes, salt, thyme, oregano, rosemary and stock, then give the mixture a stir. Press keep warm/cancel.

Secure the lid with the steam vent in the sealed position. Press manual and set on high pressure for 5 minutes.

Once the timer sounds, press keep warm/cancel. Using an oven mitt, do a quick release. When the steam venting stops and the silver dial drops, carefully open the lid.

Press sauté. As soon as the soup comes to a boil, add the pasta. Cook your pasta al dente according to the package directions—usually this is anywhere from 4 to 8 minutes. Then, add the spinach and basil, stirring until the spinach has fully wilted. Press keep warm/cancel. Add the cream and mascarpone cheese, stirring until incorporated. Taste for seasoning and adjust the salt to taste.

Serve immediately. Garnish with the shredded cheeses and a drizzle of quality extra-virgin olive oil (if using).

NOTE: If possible, use organic spinach since spinach is on the EWG's "Shopper's Guide to Pesticides in Produce" Dirty Dozen list.

DAIRY-FREE OPTION · GLUTEN-FREE · GRAIN-FREE

BUFFALO CHICKEN CHOWDER

For all of my hot wing–loving friends, this recipe is for you! All the flavor of your favorite wing sauce, in the form of soup. Veggie and protein packed with plenty of tang and spice, and a creamy finish to balance it out. Loved by healthy eaters and those who crave chicken wings! **AR**

SERVES: 4

2 tbsp (30 ml) olive or avocado oil

1 white or yellow onion, chopped

1⅓ lb (600 g) chicken breast

1 cup (120 g) diced celery

1 cup (130 g) diced carrot

1½ cups (225 g) diced Yukon gold potato

5 cups (1.2 L) chicken stock

¾ cup (175 ml) buffalo hot sauce

⅔ cup (160 ml) full-fat canned coconut milk or half-and-half

¼ cup (10 g) fresh cilantro, for garnish (optional)

Select sauté on the Instant Pot. Coat the bottom of the pot with the oil once hot, add the onion and sauté for 2 to 3 minutes. Select cancel.

Place the chicken in the Instant Pot first. Then add the celery, carrot, potato, chicken stock and buffalo sauce on top of the chicken.

Secure the lid with the steam vent in the sealed position. Select manual, and cook on high pressure for 12 minutes.

Use a quick release, placing a kitchen towel over the valve to prevent a mess. Once the steam is completely released, remove the lid.

Add the coconut milk. Top with the fresh cilantro (if using) and serve.

DAIRY-FREE GLUTEN-FREE

COLOMBIAN CHICKEN SOUP

A classic chicken soup with a flavor twist from just a few ingredients. The fresh lime juice gives a nice freshness and cilantro brings all the flavors together. **KB**

SERVES: 4 to 6

2 tsp (10 ml) olive oil

1 medium onion, chopped

1 celery rib, chopped

3 cloves garlic, minced

½ tsp dried oregano

4 cups (946 ml) chicken stock

2 lb (905 g) boneless, skinless chicken breast, cut into bite-size pieces

1 lb (455 g) baby red potatoes, cut into bite-size pieces

1½ cups (195 g) frozen corn kernels

1 tbsp (15 ml) fresh lime juice

¼ cup (10 g) chopped fresh cilantro

Coarse salt

Freshly ground black pepper

1 avocado, peeled, pitted and chopped

Press sauté to preheat the Instant Pot. When the word "hot" appears on the display, add the onion and celery to the pot. Cook, stirring occasionally, until the onion is soft, about 5 minutes. Add the garlic and oregano and cook for 1 more minute. Press cancel to turn off the Instant Pot.

Add the chicken stock, taking care to scrape up any browned bits from the bottom of the pot. Add the chicken, potatoes and corn.

Secure the lid with the steam vent in the sealed position. Press manual and immediately adjust the timer to 20 minutes. Check that the display light is beneath high pressure.

When the timer sounds, quick release the pressure and carefully remove the lid. Stir in the lime juice and cilantro. Season well with salt and pepper. Serve in bowls, topped with avocado.

GF GLUTEN-FREE   GRAIN-FREE

TUSCAN BEAN SOUP

This soup is hearty and flavorful, and the contrasting colors make it pretty to look at, too! It's perfect with a loaf of crusty bread. **KB**

SERVES: 4 to 6

2 tsp (10 ml) olive oil

1 medium onion, chopped

2 celery ribs, chopped

2 carrots, chopped

3 cloves garlic, minced

½ tsp Italian seasoning

4 cups (946 ml) chicken stock

2 (14.5-oz [411-g]) cans fire-roasted diced tomatoes

2 (15-oz [425-g]) cans white beans

1 bay leaf

12 oz (340 g) fresh spinach leaves

Coarse salt

Freshly ground black pepper

½ cup (50 g) grated Parmesan cheese

Press sauté to preheat the Instant Pot. When the word "hot" appears on the display, add the olive oil, then the onion, celery and carrots to the pot. Cook, stirring occasionally, until the onion is soft, about 5 minutes. Add the garlic and Italian seasoning and cook for 1 minute more. Press cancel to turn off the Instant Pot.

Add the chicken stock to the pot, taking care to scrape up any browned bits from the bottom of the pot. Add the fire-roasted tomatoes, beans and bay leaf.

Secure the lid with the steam vent in the sealed position. Press soup and immediately adjust the timer to 20 minutes. Check that the display light is beneath high pressure.

When the timer sounds, quick release the pressure and carefully remove the lid. Remove the bay leaf. Add the spinach leaves and stir until wilted. Season well with salt and pepper. Top each bowl with some grated Parmesan.

DAIRY-FREE GLUTEN-FREE GRAIN-FREE

FIVE-INGREDIENT BLACK BEAN SOUP

Yep! Five ingredients! Well, not counting salt, pepper and optional garnishes, but that's just a given. This homemade, thick and rich black bean soup that tastes as if it took all day, takes five minutes in the Instant Pot. The trick to getting all the flavors is using a little store-bought salsa. Don't believe me? I cannot wait to prove you wrong! **SB**

SERVES: 4 to 6

2 cups (475 ml) chicken or vegetable stock

¾ cup (195 g) jarred salsa

1 (30-oz [850-g]) can black beans, drained and rinsed

1 jalapeño, seeded and diced

½ yellow onion, diced

Salt

Freshly ground black pepper

Fresh cilantro, lime, sour cream and avocado, for garnish (optional)

In the Instant Pot, combine all the ingredients except for the garnishes, including salt and pepper to taste. Secure the lid with the steam vent in the sealed position. Press pressure cook until the display light is beneath high pressure. Use the plus and minus buttons to adjust the time until the display reads "5 minutes."

When the timer sounds, quick release the pressure. Remove the lid and use an immersion blender to puree about half of the soup. You still want to see a few beans in the soup.

Adjust the salt and pepper to taste and top with cilantro, lime, sour cream and avocado (if using).

GARLICKY SPINACH, MUSHROOM & CHICKPEA SOUP

This brothy soup is packed with bold flavors from garlic, cumin and coriander, which go perfectly with the sweet spinach and hearty chickpeas. It's so delicious served with fresh homemade biscuits or toasted gluten-free bread to sop up the beautiful spiced broth. **ESV**

SERVES: 6 to 8

2 tbsp (28 g) grass-fed butter, ghee or avocado oil

1 yellow onion, peeled and diced

8 oz (225 g) cleaned white button or cremini mushrooms, thinly sliced

7 cloves garlic, finely minced

2 large celery ribs, thinly sliced

1 organic russet potato, peeled and diced

1 tbsp (7 g) ground cumin

1 tsp ground coriander

1 tsp sea salt

½ tsp dried thyme

½ tsp ground allspice

6 cups (1.4 L) chicken or vegetable stock

2 large bunches fresh spinach (about 1½ lb [680 g] total), leaves only, cleaned well

2 cups (480 g) canned or cooked chickpeas

Sour cream, for garnish (optional)

Quality extra-virgin olive oil, for garnish (optional)

Place your healthy fat of choice in the Instant Pot and press sauté. Once the fat has melted, add the onion and mushrooms and sauté for / minutes, stirring occasionally, then add the garlic and continue to sauté for 1 minute, stirring occasionally. Add the celery, potato, cumin, coriander, salt, thyme, allspice and stock, then give the mixture a stir. Press keep warm/cancel.

Secure the lid with the steam vent in the sealed position. Press manual and set on high pressure for 7 minutes.

Once the timer sounds, press keep warm/cancel. Using an oven mitt, do a quick release. When the steam venting stops and the silver dial drops, carefully open the lid.

Press sauté and add the spinach and chickpeas. Allow the soup to come to a simmer, stirring until the spinach has fully wilted. Press keep warm/cancel. Taste for seasoning and adjust the salt to taste.

Serve immediately. Garnish with a dollop of sour cream or a drizzle of quality extra-virgin olive oil (if using).

NOTE: If possible, use organic spinach and potatoes since spinach and potatoes are on the EWG's "Shopper's Guide to Pesticides in Produce" Dirty Dozen list.

GF GLUTEN-FREE GRAIN-FREE

CREAMY TOMATO-BASIL SOUP

What could be better than a comforting bowl of creamy tomato-basil soup? Nothing, except when it's made in the Instant Pot, of course! This classic soup is ridiculously easy in the Instant Pot, and one that you will be sure to make over and over. Serve along with a simple salad or the classic grilled cheese sandwich for an easy weeknight meal on a cold evening. **AR**

SERVES: 4

2 tbsp (30 ml) avocado oil or extra-virgin olive oil

1 yellow onion, diced

4 cloves garlic, minced

2 large carrots, peeled and diced

2 tbsp (16 g) arrowroot starch

3 cups (710 ml) vegetable or chicken stock

1 (28-oz [800-g]) can San Marzano whole tomatoes, with juice

2 tsp (4 g) Italian seasoning

1 tsp sea salt, plus more to taste

1 cup (237 ml) half-and-half or heavy cream

½ cup (20 g) fresh basil leaves, chopped, divided

⅓ cup (33 g) freshly grated Parmesan cheese (optional)

Select sauté on the Instant Pot, set to "medium," if possible. Once the pot is hot, coat the bottom of the pot with the oil. Add the onion, garlic and carrots. Cook until the vegetables are softened, about 5 minutes. Select cancel. Sprinkle the mixture with the arrowroot starch.

Add the stock, tomatoes, Italian seasoning and salt. Give the mixture a stir

Secure the lid with the steam vent in the sealed position. Select manual, and cook on high pressure for 6 minutes.

Use a quick release, allowing the steam to completely release before opening the lid. Stir in the half-and-half and ¼ cup (10 g) of the basil. Blend the soup, using an immersion blender or high-powered blender, until smooth.

Serve hot, adding more salt to taste, garnishing with the remaining basil and topping with the Parmesan cheese (if using).

DAIRY-FREE GLUTEN-FREE GRAIN-FREE

THAI CHICKEN CURRY SOUP
WITH ZUCCHINI "RAMEN"

This bowl of goodness is sure to be comforting on a chilly night! Packed with veggies and a delicious coconut-curry-lime flavor, it's bound to become a new weeknight staple. Zucchini noodles add that extra special touch! **AR**

SERVES: 6

2 tbsp (30 ml) avocado oil or coconut oil

½ large white onion, diced

1 tbsp (6 g) chopped fresh ginger

3 cloves garlic, minced

3 cups (710 ml) chicken stock

1 (14.5-oz [411-g]) can fire-roasted diced tomatoes

2 tbsp (30 g) Thai red curry paste

1 tsp sea salt, plus more to taste

1 yellow bell pepper, seeded and diced

3 carrots, peeled and diced

1½ lb (680 g) chicken breast

1 (13.5-oz [400-ml]) can full-fat coconut milk

Juice of 1 lime

2 large zucchini, spiralized into noodles

¼ cup (10 g) chopped fresh cilantro (optional)

Select sauté on the Instant Pot, set to "medium," if possible. Coat the bottom of the pot with the oil, and once hot, add the onion. Cook for 2 to 3 minutes, then toss in the ginger and garlic. Once the vegetables are gently browned, about another 3 minutes, select cancel.

Add the chicken stock, fire-roasted tomatoes, Thai curry paste, salt, bell pepper, carrots and chicken.

Secure the lid with the steam vent in the sealed position. Select manual or pressure, and cook on high pressure for 8 minutes.

Use a quick release and remove the lid. Remove the chicken breast and shred with a fork and knife, then place the chicken back in the pot. Stir in the coconut milk, lime juice and spiralized zucchini. Let sit for about 10 minutes before serving.

Pour into individual bowls and add additional salt to taste. Garnish with fresh cilantro (if using).

PASTAS

BROWN BUTTER-
CAULIFLOWER GNOCCHI

Cauliflower is still going through this big trendsetting moment when you can find cauliflower in everything. From cauliflower pizza crust to cauliflower rice, it is everywhere. I like the good old standard cauliflower. A quick steam in the Instant Pot with a little brown butter and gnocchi is all it needs to really shine. No fancy food trends here, just a good old practical dinner. **SB**

SERVES: 4

5 tbsp (70 g) unsalted butter

1 lb (455 g) gnocchi

3 cups (300 g) fresh cauliflower florets

1 tbsp (15 ml) extra-virgin olive oil

Juice of ½ lemon

¼ cup (60 ml) vegetable stock

¼ cup (60 ml) water

½ tsp dried oregano

½ tsp dried thyme

Salt

Freshly ground black pepper

Press sauté on the Instant Pot. After 2 minutes, the pot will be hot. Add the butter and cook until it stops popping and starts to turn golden, about 4 minutes.

Add the gnocchi and then sauté for another 2 minutes so the gnocchi absorbs that toasty butter.

Press cancel and add all the remaining ingredients, including salt and pepper to taste.

Secure the lid with the steam vent in the sealed position. Press pressure cook until the display light is beneath high pressure. Use the plus and minus buttons to adjust the time until the display reads "3 minutes."

When the timer sounds, quick release the pressure. Remove the lid and give the ingredients a good stir. Adjust the salt and pepper to taste.

GF
GLUTEN-FREE

SUN-DRIED TOMATO-PESTO CHICKEN PENNE ALFREDO

Pesto and Alfredo lovers, you're going to swoon for this chicken pasta dish. It's got all the sweet and salty flavors—sun-dried pesto combined with lemony creamy Alfredo. This delicious meal is sure to please! **ESV**

SERVES: 4 to 6

SUN-DRIED TOMATO PESTO

7 olive oil–packed sun-dried tomatoes

¾ cup (30 g) fresh basil leaves, stems removed

2 tsp (3 g) chopped fresh flat-leaf parsley

1 clove garlic, smashed

Zest of 1 lemon

1 tbsp (15 ml) fresh lemon juice

1 tbsp (15 ml) extra-virgin olive oil

1.5 oz (43 g) Parmesan cheese, cut into chunks

¼ tsp sea salt

PASTA

2 tbsp (28 g) grass-fed butter, ghee or avocado oil

1 lb (455 g) boneless, skinless chicken breast, cut into 1" (2.5-cm) cubes

2 cups (475 ml) filtered water

¼ cup (60 ml) chicken or vegetable stock

¾ tsp sea salt

2 cups (210 g) gluten-free dried penne

¾ cup (175 ml) heavy cream

4 oz (115 g) mascarpone cheese or cream cheese

1¼ cups (100 g) shredded Parmesan cheese, plus more for garnish

Zest of 1 lemon

¼ cup (15 g) roughly chopped fresh flat-leaf parsley or basil, for garnish (optional)

Prepare the pesto: In a food processor, combine all the pesto ingredients. Pulse until fully blended and smooth, about 30 seconds. Set aside.

Prepare the pasta: Place your healthy fat of choice in the Instant Pot and press sauté. Once the fat has melted, add the chicken and sauté, stirring occasionally, for 5 to 7 minutes, or until the pink color is gone.

Add the water, stock, salt and pasta to the Instant Pot, making sure the pasta is submerged in the liquid.

Secure the lid with the steam vent in the sealed position. Press manual and set on high pressure for 5 minutes.

Once the timer sounds, press keep warm/cancel. Allow the Instant Pot to naturally pressure release for 5 minutes. Using an oven mitt, do a quick release. When the steam venting stops and the silver dial drops, carefully open the lid.

Press sauté, immediately give the pasta a stir to help it not stick together, then add the cream, mascarpone and Parmesan. Allow to come to a simmer, then quickly stir until the Parmesan is fully mixed in. Add the pesto, give the mixture another stir and simmer for about 3 minutes, or until the sauce slightly thickens. Press the keep warm/cancel button. Add the lemon zest and gently stir to combine, then allow the pasta to rest for 10 minutes.

Serve immediately garnished with shredded Parmesan and chopped fresh parsley or basil (if using).

PASTA PUTTANESCA

Pasta is my love language. We have a date night, pasta. Just had a baby, you get some pasta! Lost a loved one, you get some pasta! There is something so comforting about the humble noodle that almost all people can appreciate. Lucky for us, we can dish out love a lot quicker than most, thanks to the convenience of the one-pot wonder, the Instant Pot. **SB**

SERVES: 4

1 lb (455 g) thin spaghetti

3½ cups (840 ml) water

1 pint (300 g) grape tomatoes, cut in half

2 tbsp (17 g) capers

½ cup (50 g) pitted black olives, cut in half

¾ cup (75 g) pitted Castelvetrano olives, cut in half

2 tbsp (8 g) chopped fresh parsley

1 tbsp (3 g) chopped fresh basil

1 tsp salt, plus more to taste

½ tsp freshly ground black pepper, plus more to taste

2 tbsp (30 ml) extra-virgin olive oil

Crack the spaghetti noodles in half to ensure they fit inside the pot. In the Instant Pot, combine the noodles along with all the remaining ingredients. Give them a toss and stir, using tongs.

Secure the lid with the steam vent in the sealed position. Press pressure cook until the display light is beneath high pressure. Use the plus and minus buttons to adjust the time until the display reads "5 minutes."

When the timer sounds, quick release the pressure. Remove the lid and use the tongs to toss and mix the pasta together.

Add more salt and pepper to taste, if needed.

GF
GLUTEN-FREE

CREAMY MUSHROOM-BEEF STROGANOFF

Full of mushrooms, tender chunks of beef and lots of herbs, this creamy pasta dish is true bliss. The original version may not have had mushrooms, but this classic quickly became popular with earthy mushrooms and other additions. **ESV**

SERVES: 4 to 6

2 tbsp (28 g) grass-fed butter, ghee or avocado oil

1 medium yellow onion, peeled and diced

8 oz (225 g) cleaned white button or cremini mushrooms, thinly sliced

5 cloves garlic, finely minced

2 tbsp (15 g) gluten-free all-purpose flour

1 lb (455 g) grass-fed stew meat, cut into 1" (2.5-cm) cubes

¼ cup (60 ml) quality dry white wine

1 tsp sea salt

1 tsp dried thyme

1 tsp dried dill

½ tsp dried oregano

½ tsp freshly ground black pepper

2 tbsp (30 ml) coconut aminos

1 tsp Dijon mustard

1 tsp cider vinegar

1 tsp Asian fish sauce

2½ cups (590 ml) filtered water, divided

2 cups (210 g) gluten-free dried pasta; e.g., tagliatelle or fettuccine

¼ cup (15 g) finely chopped fresh flat-leaf parsley, plus more for garnish

4 oz (115 g) cream cheese

¼ cup (58 g) sour cream

¼ cup (20 g) shredded Parmesan cheese, for garnish

Place your healthy fat of choice in the Instant Pot and press sauté. Once the fat has melted, add the onion and mushrooms and sauté for 7 minutes, stirring occasionally, then add the garlic and flour and continue to sauté for 2 minutes, stirring occasionally. Transfer the onion mixture to a plate and set aside.

Add the stew meat to the pot and cook, stirring occasionally, until the meat is browned on all sides, about 5 minutes. Add the white wine, giving the mixture a quick stir and scraping up any browned bits with a wooden spoon. Press keep warm/cancel. Add the salt, thyme, dill, oregano, pepper, coconut aminos, Dijon, vinegar, fish sauce and 1 cup (237 ml) of the filtered water.

Secure the lid with the steam vent in the sealed position. Press manual and set on high pressure for 10 minutes.

Once the timer sounds, press keep warm/cancel. Using an oven mitt, do a quick release. When the steam venting stops and the silver dial drops, carefully open the lid.

Add the pasta and remaining 1½ cups (355 ml) of filtered water to the Instant Pot, making sure the pasta is submerged in the liquid.

Secure the lid with the steam vent in the sealed position. Press manual and set on high pressure for 4 minutes.

Once the timer sounds, press keep warm/cancel. Allow the Instant Pot to naturally pressure release for 5 minutes. Using an oven mitt, do a quick release. When the steam venting stops and the silver dial drops, carefully open the lid.

Press sauté, then add the parsley, cream cheese and sour cream, stirring until incorporated. Press keep warm/cancel. Let the pasta rest for 10 minutes to thicken.

Serve immediately, garnished with shredded Parmesan and chopped fresh flat-leaf parsley.

GF
GLUTEN-FREE

CAULIFLOWER MAC & CHEESE

I grew up eating lots of mac and cheese, the boxed kind—I'm an '80s child and that stuff was quite popular back then. Ever since, I have been an avid mac and cheese fan, but my palate changed quite a bit. Now I prefer homemade versions, such as this divine recipe. It comes together great in the Instant Pot and is always family- and kid-approved. **ESV**

SERVES: 4 to 6

1 cup (237 ml) water

2½ cups (250 g) cauliflower florets, cut into bite-size pieces

2 cups (210 g) gluten-free dried macaroni pasta

2 cups (475 ml) filtered water

¼ cup (60 ml) chicken or vegetable stock

2 tbsp (28 g) grass-fed butter

½ tsp sea salt

¼ cup (60 ml) heavy cream

1¾ cups (201 g) shredded cheddar cheese

¼ cup (20 g) shredded Parmesan cheese

¼ cup (15 g) finely chopped fresh flat-leaf parsley, for garnish (optional)

Pour the cup (237 ml) of water into the Instant Pot and insert a steamer basket. Layer the cauliflower florets in the steamer basket.

Secure the lid with the steam vent in the sealed position. Press manual and set on high pressure for 2 minutes.

Once the timer sounds, press keep warm/cancel. Using an oven mitt, do a quick release. When the steam venting stops and the silver dial drops, carefully open the lid. Immediately remove the steamer basket and cauliflower, using caution because both are very hot. Set aside. Discard the water in the Instant Pot.

Add the pasta, 2 cups (475 ml) of filtered water, stock, butter and salt to the Instant Pot, making sure the pasta is submerged in the liquid. Secure the lid with the steam vent in the sealed position. Press manual and set on high pressure for 4 minutes.

Once the timer sounds, press keep warm/cancel. Allow the Instant Pot to naturally pressure release for 5 minutes. Using an oven mitt, do a quick release. When the steam venting stops and the silver dial drops, carefully open the lid.

Press sauté. Immediately give the pasta a stir to help it not stick together, then add the cream, cheddar and Parmesan. Allow to come to a simmer, then quickly stir until the cheeses are fully mixed in. Simmer for about 3 minutes, or until the sauce slightly thickens. Press keep warm/cancel. Add the cooked cauliflower, give it a gentle stir to combine, then allow the pasta to rest for 10 minutes.

Serve immediately garnished with chopped fresh flat-leaf parsley (if using).

NOTE: Gluten-free dried fusilli, penne or shell pasta can be substituted for the macaroni pasta.

MACARONI & BEER CHEESE

This recipe combines my two loves, craft beer and cheese. The glory of making mac and cheese in the Instant Pot is not only that you use one pot, it is that the sauce sort of takes care of itself. No need for starting with a roux to thicken the sauce. Add your noodles, beer and seasonings, then, when the timer sounds, mix in your cheese. Ta-da! For a big part of making this book, this recipe was front runner for my favorite. Give it a try and you will find out why. **SB**

SERVES: 4 to 6

1 lb (455 g) dried macaroni noodles

¾ cup (175 ml) water

1 cup (237 ml) your favorite pale ale

2 cups (475 ml) low-sodium chicken stock

1 tsp salt, plus more to taste

¼ tsp onion powder

¼ tsp garlic powder

¼ tsp cayenne pepper

½ tsp prepared grated horseradish

½ tsp smoked paprika

8 oz (225 g) sharp cheddar cheese, grated

In the Instant Pot, combine the macaroni, water, ale, chicken stock, salt, onion powder, garlic powder, cayenne, horseradish and smoked paprika. Stir well.

Secure the lid with the steam vent in the sealed position. Press pressure cook until the display light is beneath high pressure. Use the plus and minus buttons to adjust the time until the display reads "5 minutes."

When the timer sounds, quick release the pressure. Remove the lid and stir in the grated cheese until it is melted, creamy and combined. Adjust the salt, if needed.

SAUSAGE PASTA
IN CHIPOTLE-TOMATO SAUCE

The chipotle peppers in this sauce add a wonderful flavor twist from your usual red sauce. It's a meld of Italian and Mexican flavors that your family will love. Don't miss this one! **KB**

SERVES: 4

2 tsp (10 ml) extra-virgin olive oil

½ onion, chopped

2 cloves garlic, minced

1 tsp ground cumin

3 cups (710 ml) low-sodium chicken stock

1 lb (455 g) dried spaghetti, broken in half

1 (12-oz [340-g]) package Italian chicken sausage

1 (28-oz [800-g]) can crushed tomatoes

2 chipotle peppers, chopped

¼ cup (25 g) grated Parmesan cheese

Press sauté to preheat the Instant Pot. When the word "hot" appears on the display, add the olive oil. When the oil is shimmering, add the onion and cook until the onion is soft, about 5 minutes, stirring frequently. Add the garlic and cumin and cook for 1 more minute. Press cancel to turn off the Instant Pot.

Add the chicken stock and stir to scrape up all the browned bits from the bottom of the pot. Add the pasta and sausage, then pour the tomatoes over the sausage (do not stir). Top with the chipotle peppers, making sure the pasta is submerged in the liquid.

Secure the lid with the steam vent in the sealed position. Press manual and immediately adjust the timer to 6 minutes. Check that the display light is beneath high pressure.

When the timer sounds, quick release the pressure and carefully remove the lid. Top with the Parmesan and serve.

GF
GLUTEN-FREE

LASAGNA-STYLE CREAMY ITALIAN PASTA

Lasagna is total comfort food and can easily be made in the Instant Pot! This spinach and mushroom vegetarian version is packed with all of the lasagna basics, with a lot of cheesy goodness. **ESV**

SERVES: 3 to 4

3 tbsp (43 g) grass-fed butter, ghee or avocado oil

1 medium yellow onion, peeled and diced

8 oz (225 g) cleaned white button or cremini mushrooms, thinly sliced

5 cloves garlic, finely minced

1 cup (180 g) crushed tomatoes

1 tsp sea salt

1 tsp dried thyme

¾ tsp dried oregano

2 cups (210 g) gluten-free dried pasta; e.g., broken-up lasagna or tagliatelle

2¼ cups (533 ml) filtered water

1 large bunch fresh spinach (about 12 oz [340 g]), leaves only, cleaned well

¼ cup (10 g) fresh basil leaves

¼ cup (60 ml) heavy cream

4 oz (113 g) mascarpone cheese or cream cheese

¼ cup (25 g) shredded Parmesan cheese

¼ cup (29 g) shredded Romano or provolone cheese

¼ cup (28 g) shredded mozzarella cheese

¼ cup (15 g) roughly chopped fresh flat-leaf parsley or basil, for garnish (optional)

Place your healthy fat of choice in the Instant Pot and press sauté. Once the fat has melted, add the onion and mushrooms and sauté for 7 minutes, stirring occasionally, then add the garlic and continue to sauté for 1 minute, stirring occasionally. Add the crushed tomatoes, salt, thyme and oregano, then give the mixture a stir. Press keep warm/cancel.

Add the pasta and filtered water, making sure the pasta is submerged in the liquid.

Secure the lid with the steam vent in the sealed position. Press manual and set on high pressure for 4 minutes.

Once the timer sounds, press keep warm/cancel. Allow the Instant Pot to naturally pressure release for 5 minutes. Using an oven mitt, do a quick release. When the steam venting stops and the silver dial drops, carefully open the lid.

Press sauté, then add the spinach and basil, stirring until the spinach has fully wilted. Add the cream, mascarpone, Parmesan, Romano and mozzarella, stirring until incorporated. Press keep warm/cancel. Let the pasta rest for 10 minutes to thicken.

Serve immediately, garnished with the chopped fresh flat-leaf parsley or basil (if using).

NOTE: If possible, use organic spinach since spinach is on the EWG's "Shopper's Guide to Pesticides in Produce" Dirty Dozen list.

LIME-BUTTER CRAB LINGUINE

Lime, butter, crabs and noodles—need I say more? This is a bright and luscious recipe that is so easy to throw together. The glorious thing about cooking the crab with the noodles in the Instant Pot is that all that salty seafood flavor gets infused into the noodles. This dish is simple because all that flavor from the crab and lime is all you really need. **SB**

SERVES: 4

1 lb (455 g) linguine noodles, cracked in half

2¾ cups (651 ml) water

Juice and zest of 2 limes

1 tsp salt

¼ tsp freshly ground black pepper

1 (4-oz [115-g]) can mild diced green chiles

2 (6-oz [170-g]) cans lump crabmeat, drained

3 tbsp (42 g) unsalted butter

In the Instant Pot, combine the pasta, water, lime juice and zest, salt, black pepper, green chiles and crabmeat. Toss with tongs to mix.

Secure the lid with the steam vent in the sealed position. Press pressure cook until the display light is beneath high pressure. Use the plus and minus buttons to adjust the time until the display reads "6 minutes."

When the timer sounds, quick release the pressure. Remove the lid and stir in the butter. Toss to combine. Add more salt and pepper to taste.

LEMON ALFREDO PASTA

Hands down, fettuccine Alfredo has always been one of my favorite pastas. I've always viewed it as a "gourmet" pasta since it's so rich and decadent. It's not one of those light pasta dishes that you can eat often, which is part of why it's extra special. I have always made my version with lots of healthy fats and lemon zest—the lemon adds a wonderful flavor and helps cut through the richness. **ESV**

SERVES: 4 to 6

1½ cups (355 ml) chicken or vegetable stock

1 cup (237 ml) milk

¾ cup (175 ml) heavy cream

2 tbsp (28 g) grass-fed butter

¾ tsp sea salt

1½ lb (680 g) gluten-free dried fettuccine pasta, broken in half

4 oz (115 g) mascarpone cheese or cream cheese

1¼ cups (100 g) shredded Parmesan cheese, plus more for garnish

Zest of 2 lemons

¼ cup (15 g) finely chopped fresh flat-leaf parsley, for garnish (optional)

Combine the stock, milk, cream, butter, salt and pasta in the Instant Pot, making sure the pasta is submerged in the liquid.

Secure the lid with the steam vent in the sealed position. Press manual and set on high pressure for 5 minutes.

Once the timer sounds, press keep warm/cancel. Allow the Instant Pot to naturally pressure release for 5 minutes. Using an oven mitt, do a quick release. When the steam venting stops and the silver dial drops, carefully open the lid.

Press sauté, immediately give the pasta a stir to help it not stick together, then add the mascarpone and Parmesan. Allow to come to a simmer and quickly stir until the Parmesan is fully mixed in. Simmer for about 5 minutes, or until the sauce slightly thickens. Press keep warm/cancel. Add the lemon zest, gently stir to combine, then allow the fettuccine to rest for 10 minutes.

Serve immediately, garnished with shredded Parmesan and chopped fresh flat-leaf parsley (if using).

CHICKEN FLORENTINE

This is one of those rich recipes that tastes so amazing and everyone always loves. The pop of flavor from the cherry tomatoes and the earthy spinach is heavenly. **KB**

SERVES: 4

2 tsp (10 ml) olive oil

½ medium onion, chopped

2 cloves garlic, minced

½ tsp dried basil

½ tsp dried oregano

½ cup (120 ml) white wine

2 lb (905 g) boneless, skinless chicken breast, cut into bite-size pieces

1 pint (300 g) cherry tomatoes

½ lb (225 g) dried penne pasta

1½ cups (355 ml) chicken stock

1 cup (120 g) shredded mozzarella cheese

3 cups (90 g) fresh spinach leaves

Coarse salt

Freshly grated pepper

½ cup (50 g) grated Parmesan cheese

¼ cup (10 g) chopped fresh basil

Press sauté to preheat the Instant Pot. When the word "hot" appears on the display, add the oil and onion to the pot. Cook, stirring occasionally, until the onion is soft, about 5 minutes. Add the garlic, basil and oregano and cook for 1 more minute. Pour in the wine and deglaze the pot. Boil for 3 to 4 minutes, or until the wine is reduced by half.

Add the chicken, tomatoes, pasta and stock, taking care to ensure that the pasta is fully submerged in the liquid.

Secure the lid with the steam vent in the sealed position. Press manual and immediately adjust the timer to 6 minutes. Check that the display light is beneath high pressure.

When the timer sounds, quick release the pressure and carefully remove the lid. Add the mozzarella and spinach to the pot, then gently stir. Season to taste with salt and pepper. Top each plate with grated Parmesan and fresh basil.

CHICKEN PESTO PASTA

This is one of my go-to meals for busy weeknights. I like to keep a jar of pesto on hand since it makes the dish so flavorful with minimal effort—just dump it all into your Instant Pot. Everyone loves it and it's so easy! **KB**

SERVES: 4

1½ lb (680 g) boneless, skinless chicken breast, cut into bite-size pieces

4 cups (946 ml) chicken stock

1 lb (455 g) dried penne pasta

1 (6-oz [170-g]) jar basil pesto

1 red bell pepper, seeded and chopped

In the Instant Pot, combine all the ingredients, making sure that the pasta is completely submerged in the liquid.

Secure the lid with the steam vent in the sealed position. Press manual and immediately adjust the timer to 4 minutes. Check that the display light is beneath high pressure.

When the timer sounds, quick release the pressure and carefully remove the lid. Gently stir the pasta and serve immediately.

GF
GLUTEN-FREE

CREAMY SUN-DRIED TOMATO-PESTO PASTA

My husband and I are huge sun-dried tomato fans and I can't get enough homemade pesto during the summer months when basil is in abundance. We love making sun-dried tomato pesto and adding it to pasta. It's such a treat! This herby, sweet and salty pesto goes so well in this creamy pasta dish. **ESV**

SERVES: 4 to 6

SUN-DRIED TOMATO PESTO

9 olive oil–packed sun-dried tomatoes

1½ cups (60 g) fresh basil leaves

1 tbsp (4 g) chopped fresh flat-leaf parsley

2 cloves garlic, smashed

Zest of 1 lemon

2 tbsp (30 ml) fresh lemon juice

2 tbsp (30 ml) extra-virgin olive oil

3 oz (85 g) Parmesan cheese, cut into chunks

¼ tsp sea salt

PASTA

2 cups (210 g) gluten-free dried fusilli or penne pasta

2 cups (475 ml) filtered water

¼ cup (60 ml) chicken or vegetable stock

2 tbsp (28 g) grass-fed butter

½ tsp sea salt

¼ cup (60 ml) heavy cream

4 oz (115 g) cream cheese

½ cup (50 g) shredded Parmesan cheese

½ cup (57 g) shredded Romano or provolone cheese

¼ cup (15 g) roughly chopped fresh flat-leaf parsley or basil, for garnish (optional)

Prepare the pesto: In a food processor, combine all the pesto ingredients. Pulse until fully blended and smooth, about 30 seconds. Set aside.

Prepare the pasta: combine the pasta, filtered water, stock, butter and salt in the Instant Pot, making sure the pasta is submerged in the liquid.

Secure the lid with the steam vent in the sealed position. Press manual and set on high pressure for 4 minutes.

Once the timer sounds, press keep warm/cancel. Allow the Instant Pot to naturally pressure release for 5 minutes. Using an oven mitt, do a quick release. When the steam venting stops and the silver dial drops, carefully open the lid.

Press sauté, immediately give the pasta a stir to help it not stick together, then add the pesto, cream, cream cheese and shredded cheeses. Allow to come to a simmer, then quickly stir until the cheeses are fully mixed in. Simmer for about 3 minutes, or until the sauce slightly thickens. Press keep warm/cancel. Allow the pasta to rest for 10 minutes.

Serve immediately, garnished with fresh flat-leaf parsley or basil (if using).

CAJUN SPAGHETTI

Do I have a spice-packed pasta for you guys or what? This pasta is loaded with cayenne pepper, garlic and chili powder. I took the traditional jambalaya and turned it upside down. Well, not really. I made it into a quick flavorful protein-loaded pasta. **SB**

SERVES: 4

1 tbsp (15 ml) extra-virgin olive oil

1 yellow onion, diced

1 bell pepper (any color), seeded and diced

1 celery rib, diced

1 lb (455 g) andouille chicken sausage

2 tbsp (20 g) minced garlic

2 tbsp (30 ml) Worcestershire sauce

1 tbsp (8 g) chili powder

½ tsp onion powder

½ tsp smoked paprika

¼ to ½ tsp cayenne pepper

1 tsp salt

¼ tsp freshly ground black pepper

1 lb (455 g) peeled and deveined shrimp

2 cups (490 g) tomato sauce

1 (14.5-oz [411-g]) can fire-roasted diced tomatoes

1 cup (237 ml) water

1 lb (455 g) dried spaghetti noodles, cracked in half

Chopped fresh parsley, for garnish

Grated or shaved Parmesan cheese, for garnish

Press sauté on the Instant Pot. Heat the olive oil. After 1 minute, add the onion, bell pepper and celery. Sauté for 3 minutes.

Mix in the sausage and garlic and sauté for 3 more minutes. Press cancel. Deglaze the pot with the Worcestershire.

Add the chili powder, onion powder, paprika, cayenne, salt and black pepper. Stir to combine.

Add the shrimp, tomato sauce, fire-roasted tomatoes and water. Stir, scraping up any browned bits from the bottom of the pot. Add the noodles, pressing them down into the sauce.

Secure the lid with the steam vent in the sealed position. Press pressure cook until the display light is beneath high pressure. Use the plus and minus buttons to adjust the time until the display reads "5 minutes."

When the timer sounds, quick release the pressure. Remove the lid and use tongs to toss the pasta and shrimp together.

Top with chopped fresh parsley and grated or shaved Parmesan cheese.

GF
GLUTEN-FREE

LINGUINE ALLE VONGOLE

This popular Italian dish that is commonly known as spaghetti with clam sauce is so easy to make and the result is so rewarding. No need to go out to a restaurant when you can make this simple pasta dish at home with the help of the Instant Pot. **ESV**

SERVES: 4 to 6

3½ cups (827 ml) filtered water, divided

1 lb (455 g) small clams in their shells, cleaned and scrubbed

2 tbsp (28 g) grass-fed butter, ghee or avocado oil

1 medium shallot, peeled and thinly sliced

5 cloves garlic, finely minced

¼ cup (60 ml) quality dry white wine

1 tsp sea salt

1 tsp dried thyme

½ tsp freshly ground black pepper

Zest of 1 lemon

Juice of 1 small lemon

1 lb (455 g) gluten-free dried pasta; e.g., spaghetti or linguine

¼ cup (15 g) finely chopped fresh flat-leaf parsley, plus more for garnish

¼ cup (20 g) shredded Parmesan cheese, plus more for garnish

Pour the 1 cup (237 ml) of the filtered water into the Instant Pot and insert a steamer basket or trivet. Place the clams in the basket or on the trivet.

Secure the lid with the steam vent in the sealed position. Press manual and set on high pressure for 4 minutes.

Once the timer sounds, press keep warm/cancel. Using an oven mitt, do a quick release. When the steam venting stops and the silver dial drops, carefully open the lid.

Using tongs, discard any clams that did not open, as they will not be safe to eat. Carefully transfer the rest of the clams to a bowl and set aside; discard the cooking water.

Place your healthy fat of choice in the Instant Pot and press sauté. Once the fat has melted, add the shallot and sauté for 5 minutes, stirring occasionally, then add the garlic, continuing to sauté for 1 minute, stirring occasionally. Add the white wine, giving the mixture a quick stir. Press keep warm/cancel.

Add the salt, thyme, pepper, lemon zest and juice, the remaining 2½ cups (590 ml) of filtered water and the pasta, making sure the pasta is submerged in the liquid.

Secure the lid with the steam vent in the sealed position. Press manual and set on high pressure for 4 minutes.

Once the timer sounds, press keep warm/cancel. Allow the Instant Pot to naturally pressure release for 5 minutes. Using an oven mitt, do a quick release. When the steam venting stops and the silver dial drops, carefully open the lid.

Press sauté, then give the pasta a stir with tongs. Add the parsley and Parmesan, stirring until incorporated, then add the cooked clams and gently fold them into the pasta with the tongs. Press keep warm/cancel. Let the pasta rest for 10 minutes to thicken.

Serve immediately, garnished with shredded Parmesan and chopped fresh flat-leaf parsley.

PIZZA SUPREME ORZO

The original concept for this dish was, "How could I make a supreme pizza into a dish for ladies who lunch?" I love all the supreme pizza toppings; pepperoni, mushrooms, peppers, onion and sausage. But nothing about a big old messy slice of pizza is fancy. However, orzo—yeah, orzo—just sounds fancy. It's almost like a warm pizza pasta salad. Sauté the veggies and meat in the Instant Pot, toss in the pasta and then, four minutes later, all those pizza flavors. Pass me a fork. **SB**

SERVES: 4 to 6

1 tbsp (15 ml) extra-virgin olive oil

½ lb (225 g) ground mild Italian sausage

3 oz (85 g) pepperoni slices, chopped

1 green bell pepper, seeded and diced

¾ cup (70 g) stemmed and sliced shiitake mushrooms

⅓ cup (55 g) diced red onion

½ tsp salt

¼ tsp freshly ground black pepper

¼ tsp crushed red pepper flakes

½ tsp dried oregano

1 (14.5-oz [411-g]) can fire-roasted diced tomatoes

1 cup (170 g) dried orzo

2⅓ cups (553 ml) water

Press sauté on the Instant Pot. Once hot, add the oil. Sauté the sausage, breaking it into small pieces, for about 4 minutes.

Mix in the pepperoni, bell pepper, mushrooms and red onion. Sauté for 5 minutes.

Season with the salt, black pepper, red pepper flakes and oregano. Stir to combine. Press cancel.

Add the fire-roasted tomatoes, orzo and water. Stir to combine, scraping up any bits from the bottom of the pot.

Secure the lid with the steam vent in the sealed position. Press pressure cook until the display light is beneath high pressure. Use the plus and minus buttons to adjust the time until the display reads "4 minutes."

When the timer sounds, quick release the pressure. Remove the lid and stir the pasta. Let cool slightly and then adjust the salt and pepper to taste.

MAINS

BUTTERED-HERB RUMP ROAST

Rump roast tends to be a less expensive cut of beef than a chuck roast or brisket and has a lot less fatty parts—so you just get a bunch of good-quality meat. This chunky shredded meat melts into a simple, delectable, buttery-herb sauce with hints of celery. It's so good you'll want to add it to your monthly meal planning! **ESV**

SERVES: 6 to 8

8 tbsp (112 g) grass-fed butter, divided

2 to 3 lb (905 g to 1.4 kg) grass-fed beef rump roast

1 large yellow onion, thickly sliced

3 large celery ribs, thinly sliced

5 cloves garlic, chopped

1 tsp chopped fresh thyme leaves

1 tsp chopped fresh rosemary leaves

¾ cup (175 ml) filtered water, or beef or chicken stock

¼ cup (60 ml) coconut aminos

¼ cup (15 g) finely chopped fresh parsley

1 tsp sea salt

Place 2 tablespoons (28 g) of the butter in the Instant Pot and press sauté. Once the butter has melted, add the roast and brown for about 3½ minutes per side. Remove the roast and transfer to a plate. Set aside. Add the remaining 6 tablespoons (84 g) of butter and the onion, celery, garlic, thyme and rosemary to the pot and sauté, stirring occasionally, for 5 minutes, or until fragrant. Add the filtered water or stock and coconut aminos, giving the mixture a quick stir and scraping up any browned bits with a wooden spoon. Add the parsley and salt, then give the mixture another stir. Press keep warm/cancel.

Place the browned roast in the Instant Pot. Secure the lid with the steam vent in the sealed position. Press manual and set on high pressure for 40 minutes.

Once the timer sounds, press keep warm/cancel. Allow the Instant Pot to release pressure naturally for 15 minutes. Using an oven mitt, do a quick release. If there is any steam left over, allow it to release until the silver dial drops, then carefully open the lid.

Carefully remove the roast, place on a large plate or cutting board and cut into shredded chunks. Add the shredded beef back to the Instant Pot. Secure the lid with the steam vent in the sealed position. Press manual and set on high pressure for 5 minutes.

Once the timer sounds, press keep warm/cancel. Using an oven mitt, do a quick release. When the steam venting stops and the silver dial drops, carefully open the lid.

To reduce the sauce, press sauté and allow the sauce and shredded beef to simmer for 5 to 10 minutes to thicken. Once the sauce has reduced, allow the shredded beef to rest in the Instant Pot for about 15 minutes before serving.

Serve immediately or refrigerate for later use.

DAIRY-FREE **GLUTEN-FREE** **GRAIN-FREE OPTION**

CHIPOTLE-LIME SALMON

Salmon cooks to perfection in the Instant Pot with a flaky texture that melts in your mouth! This particular dish is dressed up with an amazing chipotle-lime vinaigrette that is sure to please. Serve over a bed of rice or cauliflower rice for a complete dinner. **AR**

SERVES: 3 to 4

1 cup (237 ml) water

¾ tsp sea salt, divided

½ tsp chipotle chili powder

1 tsp ground cumin

3 to 4 (5-oz [140-g]) salmon fillets with skin, about 1" (2.5 cm) thick

Juice of 2 limes

1 tbsp (15 ml) white vinegar

½ cup (120 ml) avocado oil or olive oil

1 chipotle pepper in adobo sauce

1 tbsp (15 ml) adobo sauce

¼ cup (10 g) chopped fresh cilantro

Cooked rice or cauliflower rice, for serving

Pour the water into the Instant Pot and insert the steam trivet.

In a small bowl, combine ¼ teaspoon of the salt and the chipotle chili powder and cumin. Season the salmon with the spice mixture, rubbing it onto the fillets. Place the salmon, skin side down, on the steam trivet.

Secure the lid with the steam vent in the sealed position. Select steam or manual and use the plus and minus buttons to adjust the time until the display reads "4 minutes." If the salmon is thicker than 1 inch (2.5 cm), add an additional 1 minute per ½ inch (1.3 cm).

Meanwhile, make the chipotle-lime vinaigrette: In a blender or food processor, combine the lime juice, vinegar, oil, chipotle pepper, adobo sauce, cilantro and remaining ½ teaspoon of salt and blend until smooth. Set aside.

When the salmon is finished cooking, use a quick release. Serve the salmon over a bed of rice or cauliflower rice and pour the vinaigrette on top.

MISSISSIPPI POT ROAST

This is my go-to roast for weekends when I don't have much time to prep. The pepperoncini peppers and onion add incredible flavor! Perfect served over mashed potatoes or cauliflower. **KB**

SERVES: 8

2 tsp (10 ml) olive oil

1 (5-lb [2.3-kg]) chuck roast

1 large onion, sliced

1 (10.5-oz [310-ml]) can French onion soup

¼ cup (60 ml) water

1 (1-oz [28-g]) packet dried ranch seasoning mix

1 (1-oz [28-g]) packet dried beef gravy mix

½ (16-oz [455-g]) jar pepperoncini peppers (half of both peppers and juice)

¼ cup (60 ml) heavy cream

Press sauté to preheat the Instant Pot. When the word "hot" appears on the display, add the olive oil. When the oil is shimmering, add the chuck roast and brown on all sides, about 10 minutes. Remove the roast and set aside.

Add the sliced onion. Cook until the onion is starting to soften, about 5 minutes. Press cancel to turn off the Instant Pot.

Add the French onion soup and water to the pot, stirring well to scrape up any browned bits from the bottom. Return the roast to the pot. Add the ranch and gravy mixes, then the pepperoncinis and their juice.

Secure the lid with the steam vent in the sealed position. Press manual and immediately adjust the timer to 80 minutes. Check that the display light is beneath high pressure.

When the timer sounds, quick release the pressure and carefully remove the lid. Remove the roast and place on a serving platter.

Using a gravy or fat separator, or just a spoon skimming from the top, remove the fat from the liquid in the pot. Stir in the cream. Pour the gravy over the roast, serving the extra on the side.

GF GLUTEN-FREE **GRAIN-FREE**

MUSHROOM BOURGUIGNON

A long time ago, I made Julia Child's beef bourguignon. It was so delicious but definitely time consuming, with many, many steps and many, many pots and pans. I am older and wiser and strapped for time these days. I also have something Julia didn't have: an Instant Pot. I made a version that rivals the traditional beef bourguignon – with mushrooms. They pack as much, if not more, flavor than beef, in my opinion. **SB**

SERVES: 4 to 6

2 tbsp (30 ml) extra-virgin olive oil

2 tbsp (28 g) unsalted butter

1 lb (455 g) whole white mushrooms, cut in half

1 yellow onion, diced

2 carrots, peeled and sliced

1 celery rib, diced

Salt

Freshly ground black pepper

½ tsp dried thyme

1 clove garlic, grated

1 tbsp (15 ml) balsamic vinegar

1 cup (237 ml) dry red wine

1 cup (237 ml) water

¾ cup (175 ml) beef or vegetable stock, divided

1 oz (28 g) dried shiitake mushrooms

1 tbsp (8 g) cornstarch

2 tbsp (32 g) tomato paste

Press sauté on the Instant Pot and wait for the display to say "hot." Once the pot is hot, add the oil and butter.

When the butter melts, add the white mushrooms. Cook for 15 minutes, or until the mushrooms are golden.

Add the onion, carrots, celery, salt and pepper to taste, thyme and garlic. Sauté for 3 minutes.

Press cancel, then mix in the vinegar, red wine, water, ½ cup (115 ml) of the stock and the dried mushrooms.

Secure the lid with the steam vent in the sealed position. Press pressure cook until the display light is beneath high pressure. Use the plus and minus buttons to adjust the time until the display reads "9 minutes."

When the timer sounds, quick release the pressure. Remove the lid.

In a small bowl, whisk together the cornstarch and remaining ¼ cup (60 ml) of stock.

Stir the cornstarch slurry into the pot along with the tomato paste. Adjust the salt and pepper to taste.

DAIRY-FREE GLUTEN-FREE GRAIN-FREE OPTION

BEEF BURGUNDY

This classic French dish is an elegant meal that is perfect for a special occasion, holiday or entertaining. The beef is best braised with a delicious, drinkable red wine. Serve over a helping of mashed potatoes or rice, or just as a delicious stew. And don't forget to enjoy with a big glass of the same wine! **AR**

SERVES: 6

Nonstick cooking spray, for pot

4 slices thick bacon

2 lb (905 g) top sirloin steak, trimmed of fat, sliced into chunks

1 medium white onion, diced

2 cloves garlic, minced

2 cups (260 g) peeled and chopped carrot

10 oz (280 g) sliced mushrooms

¼ cup (32 g) arrowroot starch

3 cups (700 ml) beef stock, divided

1 cup (237 ml) high-quality red wine (Burgundy or a bold cabernet)

1 tbsp (16 g) tomato paste

2 tbsp (30 ml) honey or (30 g) dark brown sugar

1 sprig rosemary

2 bay leaves

Salt

Freshly ground black pepper

Mashed potatoes (pages 403 or 404) or cooked rice, for serving (optional)

Select sauté on the Instant Pot, set to "medium," if possible. Spray the bottom of the pot with nonstick cooking spray and add the bacon. Cook for 2 to 3 minutes per side, until it is to your desired crispiness. Transfer the bacon to a paper towel–lined plate, but reserve the rendered fat in the pot.

Add the steak and onion to the bacon fat in the pot. Cook for 6 to 8 minutes, stirring occasionally, until the steak is browned. Select cancel. Toss in the garlic, carrot and mushrooms.

In a small bowl, whisk together the arrowroot starch with about ½ cup (120 ml) of the beef stock. Pour the mixture over the veggies and beef, then add the remaining stock to the pot. Add the wine, tomato paste, honey, rosemary and bay leaves.

Secure the lid and with the steam vent in the sealed position. Select meat/stew. Cook on high pressure for 40 minutes.

Use a natural release for at least 15 minutes, then release any remaining steam. Remove the lid.

Before serving, remove the bay leaf and rosemary sprig and season to taste with salt and black pepper. Serve warm over mashed potatoes or rice, or enjoy as a stew.

DAIRY-FREE OPTION · GLUTEN-FREE · GRAIN-FREE

SWEET & TANGY PINEAPPLE SHREDDED BEEF

Shredded beef is one of our favorites in my home. When my oldest was young, she called it "tree meat" because the little shreds are so tender and look like tree bark when it falls apart. The Instant Pot cooks this sweet and tangy meat so well. The end result is delicious served in tacos, sandwiches or wraps and is so good next to mashed potatoes (pages 403 or 404), veggie mashes (page 380), roasted or steamed veggies, homemade slaw or homemade potato salad. **ESV**

SERVES: 6 to 8

1 large pineapple, trimmed: top, bottom and outer skin removed

1 cup (237 ml) cider vinegar

⅓ cup (80 ml) coconut aminos

⅓ cup (80 ml) pure maple syrup or honey

1 tsp sea salt

3 tbsp (43 g) grass-fed butter, ghee or avocado oil

2 to 3 lb (905 g to 1.4 kg) grass-fed beef roast; e.g., chuck or rump

5 cloves garlic, chopped

1½ tsp (2 g) dried thyme

Slice the pineapple in half, then cut the halves in half. Remove the inner core and discard, then cut the pineapple flesh into 1- to 1½-inch (2.5- to 4-cm) chunks. Place the pineapple chunks in a blender, then add the vinegar, coconut aminos, your sweetener of choice and the salt. Blend on low speed until pureed and no pineapple chunks remain, about 20 seconds. Set aside.

Place your healthy fat of choice in the Instant Pot and press sauté. Once the fat has melted, add the roast and brown for about 3½ minutes per side. Remove the roast and transfer to a plate. Set aside. Add the garlic and thyme to the pot and sauté, stirring occasionally, for 2 minutes, or until fragrant. Add the pureed pineapple, giving the mixture a quick stir and scraping up any browned bits with a wooden spoon. Press keep warm/cancel.

Place the browned roast in the Instant Pot. Secure the lid with the steam vent in the sealed position. Press manual and set on high pressure for 35 minutes.

Once the timer sounds, press keep warm/cancel. Allow the Instant Pot to release pressure naturally for 15 minutes. Using an oven mitt, do a quick release. If there is any steam left over, allow it to release until the silver dial drops, then carefully open the lid.

Carefully remove the roast, place on a large plate or cutting board and pull apart into shredded pieces. Add the shredded beef back to the Instant Pot. Secure the lid with the steam vent in the sealed position. Press manual and set for 5 minutes.

Once the timer sounds, press keep warm/cancel. Using an oven mitt, do a quick release. When the steam venting stops and the silver dial drops, carefully open the lid.

To reduce the sauce, press sauté and allow the sauce and shredded beef to simmer for 5 to 10 minutes to thicken. Once the sauce has reduced, allow the shredded beef to sit and rest in the Instant Pot for about 15 minutes before serving.

Serve immediately or refrigerate for later use.

DAIRY-FREE GRAIN-FREE

SPICY & SWEET BABY BACK RIBS

Smoky, sweet and slightly spicy ribs fall off the bone when prepared in the Instant Pot! My little guy's favorite dinner in the world is ribs, and for years my husband would prepare them on the grill. On a cold day when we finally tried them in the Instant Pot, it quickly became everyone's favorite way of preparing ribs! **AR**

SERVES: 3 to 4

1 rack baby back pork ribs (about 3 lb [1.4 kg])

¼ cup (60 g) dark brown sugar

2 tbsp (14 g) smoked paprika

2 tsp (5 g) chili powder

1½ tsp (3 g) freshly ground black pepper

1½ tsp (9 g) sea salt

1 tsp garlic powder

1 tsp minced onion

½ tsp cayenne pepper

1 cup (237 ml) water

¼ cup (65 g) barbecue sauce, plus more for serving

Cut the rack of ribs into four equal parts.

In a small bowl, mix together the brown sugar, paprika, chili powder, black pepper, salt, garlic powder, minced onion and cayenne. Generously rub the meat side of the ribs with the mixture.

Pour the water into the Instant Pot and insert the steam trivet. Arrange the ribs on top of the trivet, standing them on their side to create a teepee formation.

Secure the lid with the steam vent in the sealed position. Select manual or pressure, and cook on high pressure for 30 minutes.

Meanwhile, preheat the oven to 425°F (220°C). Line a baking sheet with foil.

Use a quick release. Carefully transfer the ribs to the prepared baking sheet; they will be very tender and may break off the bone. Brush the ribs with the barbecue sauce and arrange meat side up.

Bake for 7 to 10 minutes, or until browned. Remove from the oven, pull out the bones and serve hot with additional barbecue sauce.

DAIRY-FREE   GF GLUTEN-FREE   GRAIN-FREE

SPICE-RUBBED APRICOT-GLAZED RIBS

Ribs are such a fun feast! These baby back ribs get a massage with a savory-sweet spice rub before they cook in the Instant Pot. They're finished in the oven with a lovely, tangy apricot glaze. **ESV**

SERVES: 3 to 4

SPICE RUB

1½ tsp (5 g) garlic granules or garlic powder

1½ tsp (4 g) onion powder

1½ tsp (4 g) chili powder

1 tsp smoked paprika

1½ tsp (2 g) dried thyme

1 tsp maple sugar

1 tsp sea salt

½ tsp freshly ground black pepper

Zest of 1 medium orange

1 rack baby back pork ribs (about 12 to 14 ribs)

1 cup (237 ml) water

½ cup (120 ml) cider vinegar

GLAZE

9 oz (255 g) sugar-free all-fruit apricot jam

¼ cup (60 ml) pure maple syrup or honey

1 tbsp (14 ml) coconut aminos

1 tsp finely minced or grated peeled fresh ginger

½ tsp finely chopped fresh thyme leaves

½ tsp finely chopped fresh rosemary leaves

Prepare the spice rub. In a small bowl, combine the garlic granules, onion powder, chili powder, smoked paprika, thyme, maple sugar, salt, black pepper and orange zest, then stir well. Set aside.

Remove the outer membrane on the ribs and discard. Rub the spice rub all over both sides of the ribs. Cut the rib rack in half to fit in the Instant Pot. Set aside.

Pour the water and cider vinegar into the Instant Pot and insert the steam trivet. Transfer the spice-rubbed ribs into the Instant Pot on top of the trivet, with the meat side facing outward.

Secure the lid with the steam vent in the sealed position. Press manual and set on high pressure for 25 minutes.

While the ribs are cooking, prepare the glaze: In a medium bowl, combine all the glaze ingredients, then stir well and set aside.

Preheat the oven to 400°F (200°C) and have ready a baking sheet.

Once the Instant Pot timer sounds, press keep warm/cancel. Allow the Instant Pot to release pressure naturally for 15 minutes. Using an oven mitt, do a quick release. If there is any steam left over, allow it to release until the silver dial drops, then carefully open the lid.

With tongs, carefully place the rib racks on the baking sheet. Using a basting brush, evenly distribute the apricot glaze mixture all over the tops of the ribs. Bake in the preheated oven for 25 minutes.

Serve immediately.

GF GLUTEN-FREE GRAIN-FREE

EASY BONELESS BEEF SHORT RIBS

Short ribs come out so tender in the Instant Pot! This version has a rich flavor from the red wine and balsamic vinegar. **KB**

SERVES: 4 to 6

2 tsp (10 ml) olive oil

2 lb (905 g) boneless beef short ribs

1 medium onion, chopped

1 medium carrot, diced

3 cloves garlic, minced

4 sprigs thyme

½ cup (120 ml) red wine

2 tbsp (30 ml) balsamic vinegar

2 tbsp (28 g) salted butter, cold

Coarse salt

Freshly ground black pepper

Press sauté to preheat the Instant Pot. When the word "hot" appears on the display, add the olive oil. When the oil is shimmering, add the short ribs and brown on all sides, about 10 minutes. Remove the ribs and set them aside.

Add the onion and carrot to the pot. Cook until the onion is starting to soften, about 5 minutes. Add the garlic and sauté for about another minute, stirring frequently. Add the thyme sprigs, wine and vinegar, stirring well to scrape up any browned bits from the bottom. Cook until the wine is reduced by half, about 5 minutes. Press cancel to turn off the Instant Pot.

Return the ribs to the pot. Secure the lid with the steam vent in the sealed position. Press manual and immediately adjust the timer to 40 minutes. Check that the display light is beneath high pressure.

When the timer sounds, quick release the pressure and carefully remove the lid. Remove the ribs and place on a serving platter.

Stir the butter into the liquid left in the pot and season to taste with salt and pepper. Pour the sauce over the ribs and serve.

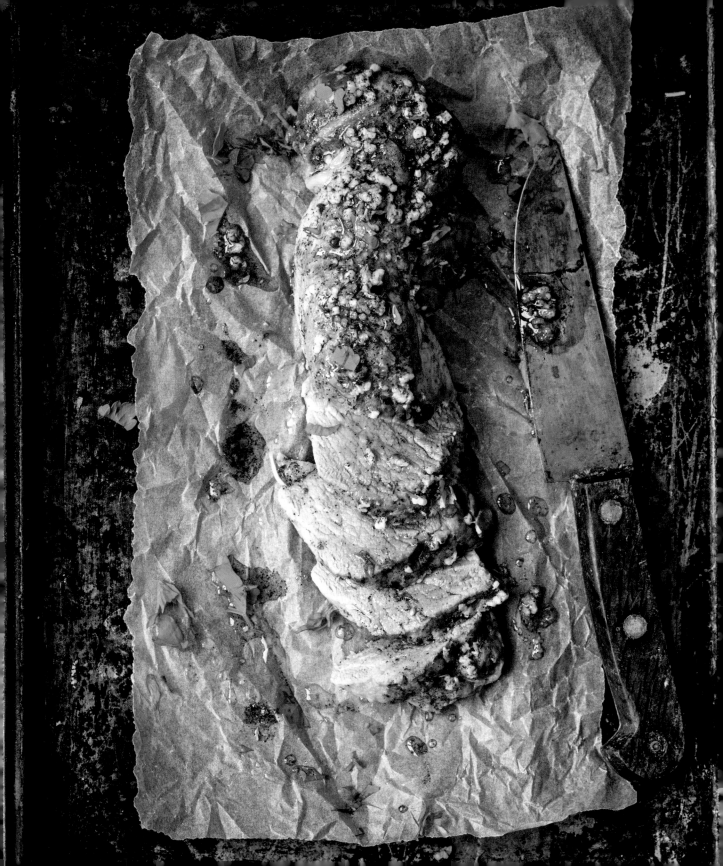

DAIRY-FREE GLUTEN-FREE GRAIN-FREE

GARLIC-HERB PORK LOIN

I like to stock up on pork loin when it's on sale just to make this easy weeknight recipe. Pork loin gets very tender in the Instant Pot and it's delicious served with the Blue Cheese Mashed Potatoes (page 404)! **KB**

SERVES: 4

2 tsp (10 ml) olive oil

3 cloves garlic, minced

2 tsp (4 g) Italian seasoning

1 tsp coarse salt

½ tsp freshly ground black pepper

1½ lb (680 g) pork tenderloin

1 cup (237 ml) water or chicken stock

In a small bowl, mix together the olive oil, garlic, Italian seasoning, salt and pepper. Rub the mixture all over the outside of the pork loin.

Pour the water or stock into the Instant Pot and insert the steam trivet. Place the pork loin on the trivet. Secure the lid with the steam vent in the sealed position. Press manual and immediately adjust the timer to 25 minutes. Check that the display light is beneath high pressure.

Once the timer sounds, allow the pressure to release naturally for 5 minutes, then quick release the pressure and carefully remove the lid. Remove the pork and allow it to rest on a carving board for 5 minutes, then slice and serve.

GF GLUTEN-FREE GRAIN-FREE

BACON-RANCH PORK CHOPS

Until the Instant Pot, I rarely cooked pork chops because of how quickly they can dry out. Now they come out fall-apart tender! This is the recipe that my kids still beg me to make at least once every few weeks. I always oblige because it's so simple and so flavorful! **KB**

SERVES: 4

5 strips bacon

4 (1" [2.5-cm]-thick) bone-in pork chops

1 cup (237 ml) chicken stock

4 tbsp (55 g) unsalted butter

1 (1-oz [28-g]) packet dried ranch seasoning mix

4 oz (115 g) cream cheese, softened

½ cup (115 g) sour cream

Press sauté to preheat the Instant Pot. When the word "hot" appears on the display, add the bacon. Cook until the bacon is browned and crispy, then remove it with a slotted spoon and place on paper towels to drain any excess fat.

In batches, if necessary, add the pork chops to the drippings in the pot and brown on both sides. Remove the chops and set aside. Press cancel to turn off the Instant Pot.

Add the chicken stock to the pot, taking care to scrape up any browned bits from the bottom of the pot. Return the pork chops to the pot and add the butter and ranch seasoning.

Secure the lid with the steam vent in the sealed position. Press manual and immediately adjust the timer to 20 minutes. Check that the display light is beneath high pressure.

Once the timer sounds, allow the pressure to release naturally for 10 minutes, then quick release the pressure and carefully remove the lid. Remove the pork chops and place on a serving platter.

Add the cream cheese and sour cream to the pot and stir well. Season to taste, then pour the sauce over the pork chops. Crumble the bacon and sprinkle over the top. Serve.

BALSAMIC-BROWN SUGAR PORK CHOPS

DAIRY-FREE GF GLUTEN-FREE GRAIN-FREE

Pork chops often get overlooked when thinking of showstopping main courses. Everybody thinks of steak or chicken. These pork chops have a great crust from the tangy balsamic vinegar and sweet brown sugar. They also are super tender, thanks to being cooked under pressure. Normally, to get that kind of tenderness, you have to cook the meat for a while. Not anymore, thanks to the Instant Pot. **SB**

SERVES: 4

4 (12-oz [340-g]) pork loin center cut chops

1 tbsp (15 ml) balsamic vinegar, divided

1 heaping tbsp (20 g) light brown sugar, divided

Salt

Freshly ground black pepper

1 tbsp (15 ml) canola oil

2 cups (475 ml) chicken stock

Press sauté on the Instant Pot. Let the pot heat up while you rub the pork chops evenly with 2½ teaspoons (13 ml) of the vinegar and 2½ teaspoons (13 g) of the brown sugar. Season each side of the chops additionally with salt and pepper.

Heat the oil in the hot pot. Sear the pork chops in batches for 5 minutes on each side. Remove from the pot and transfer to a separate plate.

Press cancel. Deglaze the bottom of the pot with the chicken stock, scraping up any browned bits.

Sprinkle the tops of each pork chop with the remaining ½ teaspoon each of the balsamic vinegar and brown sugar. Add salt and pepper as desired.

Insert the steam trivet into the Instant Pot. Arrange the pork chops on top of the trivet.

Secure the lid with the steam vent in the sealed position. Press pressure cook until the display light is beneath high pressure. Use the plus and minus buttons to adjust the time until the display reads "10 minutes."

When the timer sounds, quick release the pressure. Remove the lid and remove the pork chops, using tongs. Transfer to a serving platter or plates and top with a spoonful or two of the sauce in the pot.

GF GLUTEN-FREE GRAIN-FREE

PORK CHOPS & ONION GRAVY

These pork chops are wonderful served with the Blue Cheese Mashed Potatoes (page 404). The gravy is wonderful and rich. Perfect for a Sunday dinner! **KB**

SERVES: 4

4 (1" [2.5-cm]-thick) bone-in pork chops
Coarse salt
Freshly ground pepper
2 tsp (10 ml) olive oil
1 large onion, sliced
1 cup (237 ml) beef stock
¼ cup (60 ml) heavy cream
1 tbsp (8 g) cornstarch

Season the chops with salt and pepper. Press sauté to preheat the Instant Pot. When the word "hot" appears on the display, add the olive oil, then, working in batches, brown the chops on both sides, about 5 minutes. Remove the chops and set them aside.

Add the onion to the pot and cook until the onion is starting to soften, about 5 minutes. Add the beef stock, stirring to scrape up any browned bits from the bottom of the pot. Return the pork chops to the pot.

Secure the lid with the steam vent in the sealed position. Press manual and adjust the timer to 10 minutes. Check that the display light is beneath high pressure.

Once the timer sounds, allow the pot to release pressure naturally for 10 minutes, then quick release the pressure and carefully remove the lid. Remove the chops and tent with foil to keep warm.

In a small bowl, mix together the cream and cornstarch, then pour into the pot. Stir until the sauce is thickened, 2 to 3 minutes. Pour the sauce over the pork chops and serve.

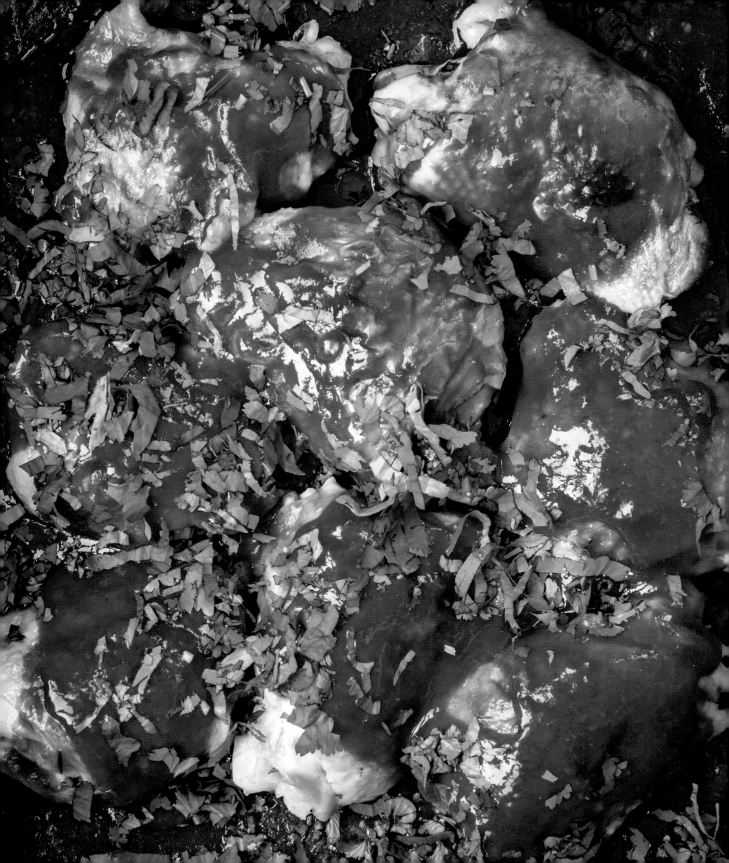

DAIRY-FREE

STICKY ORANGE CHICKEN THIGHS

This is the perfect meal when you want takeout but know you can make it better at home in the same amount of time. The sticky sauce goes so well with the tender chicken and crispy skin, and the sauce is so good you'll be licking your plate clean! **KB**

SERVES: 4

1 cup (237 ml) water or chicken stock

3 lb (1.4 kg) chicken thighs, skin on

1 cup (237 ml) fresh orange juice

¾ cup (180 g) ketchup

1 tbsp (15 ml) Worcestershire sauce

2 tbsp (28 g) light brown sugar

2 tsp (10 ml) white wine vinegar

2 tsp (10 ml) hot sauce

½ cup (20 g) chopped fresh cilantro

Pour the water or chicken stock into the pot, then add the chicken thighs.

Secure the lid with the steam vent in the sealed position. Press manual and immediately adjust the timer to 9 minutes. Check that the display light is beneath high pressure.

When the timer sounds, quick release the pressure and carefully remove the lid. Remove the chicken from the pot and place on a broiler pan. Broil until the chicken is browned and crispy, about 5 minutes.

Meanwhile, discard the liquid from the Instant Pot and wipe clean. Press sauté to turn on the pot.

Add the orange juice, ketchup, Worcestershire sauce, brown sugar, vinegar and hot sauce to the pot. Bring to a boil and simmer until thick and slightly reduced, 7 to 8 minutes.

Place the thighs on a serving dish and pour the sauce over them. Sprinkle with the cilantro and serve.

DAIRY-FREE GLUTEN-FREE

SWEET & TANGY THAI BASIL ORANGE CHICKEN

This wonderful chicken dish is brightly flavored with lots of sweet-peppery Thai basil and fresh spearmint. The tender chicken is out of this world paired with sharp-tasting orange, spicy ginger, floral honey and tangy vinegar. Serve it alongside steamed jasmine rice, sautéed riced cauliflower or sautéed veggies, such as baby bok choy. **ESV**

SERVES: 4 to 6

2 tbsp (28 g) grass-fed butter, ghee or avocado oil

1 large shallot, thinly sliced

5 cloves garlic, finely chopped

1" (2.5-cm) chunk fresh ginger, peeled and finely minced or grated

¾ tsp sea salt

¼ tsp red pepper flakes (optional)

¼ cup (60 ml) honey

¾ cup (175 ml) freshly squeezed orange juice

¼ cup (60 ml) cider vinegar

2 tbsp (30 ml) coconut aminos

2 tsp (10 ml) Asian fish sauce

2 lb (905 g) boneless, skinless chicken breast

1 cup (24 g) fresh Thai basil leaves, plus more for garnish (see note)

¼ cup (23 g) finely chopped fresh mint

Place your healthy fat of choice in the Instant Pot and press sauté. Once the fat has melted, add the shallot and sauté, stirring occasionally, for 3 minutes, or until fragrant. Add the garlic and ginger and sauté for 2 minutes, stirring occasionally. Press keep warm/cancel.

Add the salt, red pepper flakes (if using), honey, orange juice, vinegar, coconut aminos, fish sauce and chicken and give the mixture a stir, making sure the chicken is submerged in the liquid.

Secure the lid with the steam vent in the sealed position. Press manual and set on high pressure for 9 minutes.

Once the timer sounds, press keep warm/cancel. Using an oven mitt, do a quick release. When the steam venting stops and the silver dial drops, carefully open the lid.

With tongs or a large slotted spoon, transfer the chicken to a plate or cutting board. Cut the chicken into bite-size chunks, then set aside.

Press sauté and allow the liquid to come to a simmer, then simmer for about 5 minutes, or until the liquid slightly thickens. Press keep warm/cancel. Add the shredded chicken, Thai basil and mint, stir a few times until the fresh herbs have wilted into the sauce, then allow the mixture to rest for 10 minutes.

Serve immediately garnished with fresh Thai basil leaves.

NOTE: If you cannot find Thai basil, regular basil can be substituted.

DAIRY-FREE OPTION · GLUTEN-FREE OPTION · GRAIN-FREE OPTION

MUSHROOM-CHICKEN STROGANOFF

A creamy garlic and portobello mushroom sauce with chicken? Yes, please! You will love the bold and nutty flavors of this dish, which tastes fantastic over rice, potatoes or pasta. Pair with a glass of dry white wine for a fantastic Sunday evening dinner! **AR**

SERVES: 4

2 tbsp (30 ml) avocado oil or olive oil

1½ lb (675 g) chicken breast, cut into 1" to 2" (2.5- to 5-cm) chunks

2 tbsp (16 g) tapioca or arrowroot starch, plus more if needed

12 oz (340 g) portobello mushrooms, sliced

3 cloves garlic, minced

2 tbsp (30 ml) coconut aminos or soy sauce

1 tbsp (15 ml) cider vinegar

¾ cup (175 ml) chicken stock

½ cup (120 ml) full-fat canned coconut milk or coconut cream

Salt

Cooked rice, cauliflower rice or pasta, for serving

3 tbsp (8 g) chopped fresh basil or (12 g) parsley, for garnish (optional)

Select sauté on the Instant Pot. Once hot, add the oil.

In a lidded plastic storage container or resealable plastic bag, toss the chicken and tapioca starch together. Shake it up so that the chicken is completely covered, then add the chicken to the hot oil.

Sauté for 1 to 2 minutes per side, or until slightly browned. Toss in the mushrooms and garlic. Select cancel.

In a small bowl, stir together the coconut aminos, vinegar and chicken stock. Pour on top of the chicken mixture.

Secure the lid with the steam vent in the sealed position. Select manual or pressure, and cook on high pressure for 7 minutes.

Use a natural release for 15 minutes. Release any remaining steam and open the lid.

If the sauce seems too thin, add another tablespoon (8 g) of tapioca starch to the coconut milk. Pour the coconut milk into the Instant Pot and mix until well incorporated. Select cancel, then the sauté function. Let cook for another 10 minutes, or until the mixture is creamy. Select cancel. Season with salt to taste.

Spoon on top of rice, cauliflower rice or pasta and serve immediately, garnished with the fresh basil or parsley.

DAIRY-FREE GLUTEN-FREE GRAIN-FREE

CHICKEN TIKKA MASALA

Authentic Indian dishes often take hours (sometimes days) to prepare, but the Instant Pot is a valuable shortcut for getting that similar dish in just a fraction of the time! Such is the case with chicken tikka masala: delicious pieces of chicken braised in a spice-infused tomato sauce. We finish this dish with creamy coconut milk, making it a delicious and nutritious dinner! **AR**

SERVES: 5 to 6

2 tbsp (30 ml) avocado oil or extra-virgin olive oil

1 (1" [2.5-cm]) piece ginger, peeled and chopped

1 small onion, chopped

3 cloves garlic, minced

2 tsp (5 g) paprika

1 tsp garam masala

1 tsp ground turmeric

2 tsp (5 g) ground cumin

1 tsp ground coriander

¼ tsp cayenne pepper (optional)

½ cup (120 ml) chicken stock

1 (14.5-oz [411-g]) can diced tomatoes, with juice

1½ lb (680 g) boneless skinless chicken breast

½ cup (120 ml) canned coconut milk

1 tbsp (8 g) arrowroot starch (optional)

2 tbsp (30 ml) fresh lemon juice

Salt

Chopped fresh basil or cilantro (optional)

4 cups (744 g) cooked rice, for serving

Select sauté on the Instant Pot. Once the pot is hot, add the oil, ginger, onion and garlic. Cook, stirring, for 3 to 4 minutes, or until the onion is translucent. Select cancel.

Add the paprika, garam masala, turmeric, cumin, coriander and cayenne (if using), scraping the bottom of the pot to form a paste. Pour in the chicken stock to deglaze the pot; this also helps prevent burning when the dish comes to pressure. Add the tomatoes, then nestle the chicken on top.

Secure the lid with the steam vent in the sealed position. Select manual or pressure, and cook on high pressure for 7 minutes.

Use a quick release. Remove the lid and chop the chicken (a fork is fine, since it will be nice and tender). Return the chicken to the Instant Pot.

Select sauté and simmer for another 4 to 5 minutes. Add the coconut milk. If the mixture is too thin, add the arrowroot starch to the lemon juice before adding the juice to the mixture.

Season with salt to taste, and once the mixture is thick, serve immediately with fresh basil or cilantro (if using) over rice.

EASY CABBAGE ROLLS

These will always remind me of my childhood, and I still love them today. They take a bit more effort than my usual Instant Pot recipes, but it's so worth it! **KB**

SERVES: 4

1 head cabbage, core removed

1 lb (455 g) ground beef

½ medium onion, chopped

2 cloves garlic, minced

2 cups (340 g) cooked rice

1 (28-oz [800-g]) can crushed tomatoes

½ tsp salt

¼ tsp freshly ground black pepper

1 cup (237 ml) water

Microwave the cabbage, 1 minute at a time, removing leaves as you go, until you have 12 leaves (microwaving softens the outer layers of the cabbage, allowing them to be removed easily).

Press sauté to preheat the Instant Pot. When the word "hot" appears on the display, add the ground beef, onion and garlic, cooking until the ground beef is no longer pink, about 5 minutes. Drain the fat from the beef mixture, then stir in the cooked rice and tomatoes. Season with salt and pepper.

Stuff the cabbage leaves with the beef mixture and place in a cheesecake or lasagna pan made for the Instant Pot, or another Instant Pot–safe pan, and cover with foil.

Pour the water into the Instant Pot, scraping up anything stuck to the bottom of the pot. Insert the steam trivet, then set the cabbage roll pan on the trivet.

Secure the lid with the steam vent in the sealed position. Press manual and immediately adjust the timer to 25 minutes. Check that the display light is beneath high pressure.

Once the timer sounds, allow the pressure to release naturally.

DAIRY-FREE

CHICKPEA & LAMB
WITH PITAS

I don't want to call this a stew. It's more like chickpeas and lamb in a sauce. When you scoop it up with the pita bread, it's more like a sloppy joe or a meatball sub, except with tender lamb and chickpeas. Think of it as the Greek version of those sandwiches. When the lamb is pressure-cooked together with the spices, lemon and sauce, you get a hearty meal infused with meaty goodness. Make sure you don't skip the pita bread to absorb all that out-of-this-world flavor. **SB**

SERVES: 4 to 6

1 tbsp (15 ml) extra-virgin olive oil

4 (4-oz [115-g]) bone-in lamb shoulder chops

Salt

Freshly ground black pepper

1 yellow onion, diced

½ tsp ground fennel seeds

1 tsp smoked paprika

½ tsp dried oregano

¼ tsp crushed red pepper flakes

½ lemon

2 (15.5-oz [439-g]) cans chickpeas, drained and rinsed

¾ cup (175 ml) chicken or beef stock

1 (14.5-oz [411-g]) can fire-roasted diced tomatoes

1 (6-oz [170-g]) can tomato paste

12 (7" [18.5-cm]) pitas

Tzatziki, for serving (optional)

Place the oil in the pot. Press sauté and once the display says "hot," add the lamb. Season the top side with salt and black pepper. Sear the first side for 3 to 4 minutes. Flip the lamb and season that top side with salt and black pepper. Add the onion and sauté for 2 more minutes.

Add the fennel, more salt and black pepper, paprika, oregano, red pepper flakes and lemon half to the pot. Stir everything to combine.

Press cancel. Add the chickpeas, stock and diced tomatoes and stir to combine.

Secure the lid with the steam vent in the sealed position. Press pressure cook until the display light is beneath high pressure. Use the plus and minus buttons to adjust the time until the display reads "15 minutes."

When the timer sounds, quick release the pressure. Remove the lid. Use tongs to remove the lamb chops and transfer them to a cutting board. Remove the bones and dice the meat. Return the meat to the pot. Squeeze out the juice from the lemon half and discard the half.

Stir in the tomato paste and adjust the salt and black pepper, if needed. Serve with pita bread and tzatziki drizzled on top, if desired.

GLUTEN-FREE GRAIN-FREE

BEST-EVER CHICKEN WINGS

This method works well with just about any spice mixture. My favorites are lemon pepper and a sweet and spicy barbecue blend. Use your favorites; mix and match to make each family member happy! Perfect for an easy game day appetizer, too. **KB**

SERVES: 4

1 cup (237 ml) water or chicken stock

4 lb (1.8 kg) chicken wings

4 tbsp (55 g) unsalted butter, melted

2 tbsp (4 g) of your favorite seasoning mix

Pour the water or chicken stock into the pot and insert a steamer basket. Place the wings in the steamer basket.

Secure the lid with the steam vent in the sealed position. Press manual and immediately adjust the timer to 10 minutes. Check that the display light is beneath high pressure.

When the timer sounds, quick release the pressure and carefully remove the lid. Remove the chicken from the pot and place on a broiler pan. Broil until the chicken is browned and crispy, about 5 minutes.

In a small bowl, mix together the melted butter and seasoning mix. Brush the wings with the butter mixture and serve immediately.

DAIRY-FREE OPTION **GLUTEN-FREE** **GRAIN-FREE OPTION**

GREEK CHICKEN

When I dream up my ultimate Greek salad, all the ingredients in this dish are in it! This is a heartier dinner version of the perfect Greek salad, and would taste fantastic over a bed of greens. You can also serve over potatoes, rice or cauliflower rice for a more filling dish. **AR**

SERVES: 5 to 6

½ tsp salt, plus more for serving

¼ tsp freshly ground black pepper or lemon pepper, plus more for serving

2 lb (905 g) boneless, skinless chicken thighs

2 tbsp (15 ml) olive or avocado oil

3 cloves garlic, crushed

1 (8-oz [225-g]) jar marinated artichoke hearts, drained

1 (12-oz [340-g]) jar marinated roasted red peppers, drained and diced

1 cup (180 g) Kalamata olives

½ medium red onion, sliced

⅔ cup (160 ml) chicken stock

¼ cup (60 ml) red wine vinegar

Juice of ½ lemon

1 tsp dried oregano

1 tsp dried thyme

1 to 2 tbsp (8 to 16 g) arrowroot starch

Cooked potatoes, rice or cauliflower rice (optional)

3 tbsp (8 g) chopped fresh basil, for garnish

½ cup (75 g) crumbled feta (optional)

Select sauté on the Instant Pot. While the pot is heating, sprinkle the salt and black pepper on each side of the chicken thighs. Add the oil to the hot pot, then the garlic. Cook for 1 minute, then add the chicken. Sear the chicken on each side for about 2 minutes (no need to cook all the way through).

Arrange the artichoke hearts, roasted red peppers and olives around the chicken, filling in the gaps on the bottom of the Instant Pot (if there are any). It's okay to let some of those veggies sit on top of the chicken. Top with the sliced red onion.

In a bowl, stir together the chicken stock, vinegar, lemon juice, oregano and thyme. Pour on top of the chicken mixture.

Secure the lid with the steam vent in the sealed position. Select manual or pressure. Use the plus and minus buttons to adjust the time until the display reads "7 minutes."

Use a quick release. Remove the lid.

Spoon out some of the pan juices into a small bowl once the cooking is complete. Whisk the arrowroot starch into the juices and pour back into the Instant Pot. Allow the sauce to thicken for a few minutes before serving.

Serve over cooked potatoes, rice or cauliflower rice (if using). Garnish with the basil and sprinkle with additional salt, black pepper and feta (if using).

GF GLUTEN-FREE **GRAIN-FREE**

SMOKED PAPRIKA CHICKEN THIGHS

This is my favorite way to prepare chicken thighs! They come out so tender but still get a crispy skin from a quick run under the broiler. We love them with the Blue Cheese Mashed Potatoes (page 404)! **KB**

SERVES: 4

1 cup (237 ml) water or chicken stock

2 lb (905 g) chicken thighs, skin on

1 tsp smoked paprika

1 tsp ground cumin

1 tsp garlic powder

¼ tsp cayenne pepper

½ tsp coarse salt

½ tsp freshly ground black pepper

¼ cup (55 g) unsalted butter, melted

Pour the water or chicken stock into the pot, then add the chicken thighs.

Secure the lid with the steam vent in the sealed position. Press manual and immediately adjust the timer to 9 minutes. Check that the display light is beneath high pressure.

When the timer sounds, quick release the pressure and carefully remove the lid. Remove the chicken from the pot and place on a broiler pan. Broil until the chicken is browned and crispy, about 5 minutes.

In a small bowl, mix together the paprika, cumin, garlic powder, cayenne, salt and black pepper, then stir in the melted butter. Brush the thighs liberally with the butter mixture and serve immediately.

DAIRY-FREE OPTION **GF** **GLUTEN-FREE** **GRAIN-FREE OPTION**

CREAMY SOUTHWEST CHICKEN

The exact recipe you need on a weeknight: one pan, plus it's healthy, simple and downright delicious with a rich and creamy spicy sauce! This southwest chicken can be made dairy-free with coconut milk for a Paleo dinner. Easily served on a taco Tuesday over a bed of rice, cauliflower rice, vegetable noodles or pasta for the ultimate comfort dish! **AR**

SERVES: 6

1 tbsp (8 g) chili powder

2 tsp (5 g) paprika

1 tsp ground cumin

1 tsp ground coriander

1 tsp garlic powder

1 tsp sea salt, plus more to taste

½ tsp cayenne pepper

2 lb (905 g) boneless chicken thighs or breasts

2 tbsp (30 ml) avocado oil or extra-virgin olive oil

1 cup (237 ml) chicken stock

¼ cup (60 ml) fresh lime juice, plus more to taste

2 red bell peppers, seeded and sliced

½ cup (120 ml) full-fat canned coconut milk or half-and-half

1 tbsp (15 ml) water

1 tbsp (8 g) arrowroot starch, plus more if needed

Fresh cilantro, for garnish

Cooked rice, cauliflower rice, vegetable noodles or pasta, for serving

In a small bowl, mix together the chili powder, paprika, cumin, coriander, garlic powder, salt and cayenne. Rub the chicken with the spice mixture. Reserve any leftover spice mixture.

Select sauté on the Instant Pot, and once hot, coat the bottom of the pot with the oil. Add the chicken to the pot and cook on each side for about a minute or two to seal in the spices. Select cancel.

Place the chicken stock, lime juice, leftover spices and bell peppers on top of the chicken.

Secure the lid with the steam vent in the sealed position. Select manual or pressure, and cook on high pressure for 7 minutes.

Use a quick release. Open the lid and pour in the coconut milk.

In a small bowl, mix together the water and arrowroot starch and add to thicken the sauce. If you want an even thicker sauce, add another tablespoon (8 g) of arrowroot.

Add more salt to taste, and additional lime juice for more flavor. Garnish with fresh cilantro and serve over rice, cauliflower rice, vegetable noodles or pasta.

CHIPOTLE & SMOKED GOUDA MEAT LOAF

This meat loaf has amazing flavor! The pockets of smoky Gouda and the sweet and spicy glaze make it irresistible. Be sure to cut your carrots very small to ensure they cook through. **KB**

SERVES: 4 to 6

2 tbsp (30 ml) extra-virgin olive oil

1 carrot, diced

1 celery rib, diced

½ medium onion, diced

2 cloves garlic, minced

2 lb (905 g) ground beef

2 large eggs

½ cup (30 g) panko bread crumbs

1 chipotle pepper, chopped, plus 2 tbsp (30 ml) adobo sauce, from a can of chipotle peppers

1 tsp kosher salt

½ tsp freshly ground black pepper

1 cup (110 g) chopped smoked Gouda cheese

1 cup (237 ml) water

GLAZE

¾ cup (180 g) ketchup

⅓ cup (75 g) light brown sugar

2 tbsp (30 ml) adobo sauce, from a can of chipotle peppers

Press sauté to preheat the Instant Pot. When the word "hot" appears on the display, add the olive oil, then the carrot, celery and onion. Cook, stirring occasionally, until the onion starts to soften, about 5 minutes. Add the garlic and cook for about another minute, stirring frequently. Press cancel to turn off the Instant Pot.

Transfer the veggie mixture to a large mixing bowl. Add the ground beef, eggs, bread crumbs, chipotle pepper, adobo sauce, salt, black pepper and cheese. Using your hands, mix until everything is just incorporated. Gently form the mixture into a meat loaf shape.

Pour the water into the Instant Pot, then insert the steam trivet. Fold two large pieces of foil in half lengthwise, then overlap them in the middle to make a plus sign (+). Place the meat loaf in the center of the overlapped foil. Using the foil as handles, place the meat loaf on the steam trivet, leaving the foil in place and folding it over as needed so as not to obstruct placement of the lid.

Prepare the glaze: In a small bowl, mix together the ketchup, brown sugar and adobo sauce, then brush over the top and sides of the meat loaf.

Secure the lid with the steam vent in the sealed position. Press manual and adjust the timer to 30 minutes. Check that the display light is beneath high pressure.

When the timer sounds, quick release the pressure and carefully remove the lid. Allow the meat loaf to rest for about 5 minutes, then remove it from the pot, using the foil handles.

GF GLUTEN-FREE GRAIN-FREE

MINTED MEAT LOAF

One of my husband's favorite foods is meat loaf, so we make it often. We're always trying to come up with new ways to introduce lots of flavor into the classic meat loaf. One day, we were out of our usual fresh herbs but had lots of fresh mint, so my husband decided to use that instead. Serious flavor explosion! Hands down, this minted meat loaf is one of our favorites now and it cooks so quickly in the Instant Pot. **ESV**

SERVES: 4 to 6

2 tbsp (28 g) grass-fed butter, ghee or avocado oil, plus more for dish

1 small zucchini, grated

1 small carrot, peeled and grated

2 large celery ribs, diced

5 oz (140 g) frozen chopped spinach, thawed and moisture squeezed out

1 lb (455 g) ground beef

1 large egg

1 tsp sea salt

1 tsp garlic granules or garlic powder

1 tsp onion powder

1 tsp dried thyme

½ cup (48 g) chopped fresh mint

1 cup (115 g) shredded cheddar cheese

½ cup (50 g) grated Parmesan cheese

½ cup (125 g) ketchup or barbecue sauce

1 cup (237 ml) water

Place your healthy fat of choice in the Instant Pot and press sauté. Once the fat has melted, add the zucchini, carrot, celery and spinach and sauté for 5 minutes, stirring occasionally. Press keep warm/cancel.

Using a slotted spoon, carefully transfer the cooked vegetables to a large piece of cheesecloth or a clean kitchen towel. Wrap up the veggies and tightly squeeze out any excess liquid. Set aside.

Place a large piece of foil on a flat surface. Place a large piece of parchment paper on top of the foil. Set aside.

In a large bowl, combine the ground beef, cooked and drained veggies, egg, salt, garlic granules, onion powder, thyme, mint and cheeses. Gently mix until everything is well integrated. Transfer the mixture on top of the parchment paper and form into a meat loaf shape, being mindful of the size of the Instant Pot; the thickest part of the meat loaf should be no more than 3½ inches (9 cm) thick. Evenly slather the ketchup or barbecue sauce over the top of the meat loaf. Loosely form the parchment paper–lined foil up around the meat loaf, leaving a small opening at the top.

Pour the water into the Instant Pot and insert the steam trivet. Carefully place the meat loaf packet on the trivet.

Secure the lid with the steam vent in the sealed position. Press manual and set on high pressure for 25 minutes.

Once the timer sounds, press keep warm/cancel. Using an oven mitt, do a quick release. When the steam venting stops and the silver dial drops, carefully open the lid.

Using a meat thermometer, test the meat loaf to confirm that the internal temperature is at least 160°F (71°C) in the thickest part.

Carefully remove the meat loaf packet from the Instant Pot and gently unwrap the packet. Transfer to a serving plate and allow to rest for 10 to 15 minutes before slicing, then serve immediately.

GF
GLUTEN-FREE

BEEFY MEXICAN CASSEROLE

Mexican food is a staple at our house, so this casserole gets made often. The combination of chili powders give a deeper flavor, but you can replace them with regular chili powder if it's all you have on hand. The leftovers reheat nicely, so we can take it to school or work during the week, too. **KB**

SERVES: 4

2 tsp (10 ml) olive oil

1 medium onion, chopped

3 cloves garlic, minced

1 lb (455 g) ground beef

1 tbsp (8 g) chipotle chili powder

1 tbsp (8 g) ancho chili powder

1 tbsp (7 g) ground cumin

½ cup (120 ml) water

1 cup (195 g) uncooked long-grain white rice

1 red bell pepper, seeded and chopped

1 poblano pepper, chopped

1 jalapeño pepper, minced

1 (16-oz [455-g]) jar red salsa

1 (14.5-oz [411-g]) can fire-roasted diced tomatoes

2 cups (220 g) Mexican-blend shredded cheese

2 green onions, chopped

¼ cup (10 g) chopped fresh cilantro

Press sauté to preheat the Instant Pot. When the word "hot" appears on the display, add the oil and onion to the pot. Cook, stirring occasionally, until the onion is soft, about 5 minutes. Add the garlic, ground beef, chili powders and cumin. Cook the beef until no pink remains.

Add the water, taking care to scrape up any browned bits from the bottom of the pot. In this order, without stirring, add the rice, the bell, poblano and jalapeño peppers, and the salsa and tomatoes.

Secure the lid with the steam vent in the sealed position. Press manual and immediately adjust the timer to 9 minutes. Check that the display light is beneath high pressure.

When the timer sounds, quick release the pressure and carefully remove the lid. Stir in the cheese, then top with green onions and cilantro.

DAIRY-FREE GLUTEN-FREE GRAIN-FREE

MOLE CARNITAS

Once every two weeks, you can find me gently nestling a pork shoulder into the Instant Pot. We love carnitas tacos in our house. With the Instant Pot, in a matter of one hour, you can whip up a big batch of carnitas that will last a family of four through two different Taco Tuesdays. That's right, in one hour get that fall-off-the-bone, slow-cooked flavor that normally takes ten times as long. You will be enjoying the fruits of this hour of Instant Pot cooking in the form of tacos and burrito bowls for days! **SB**

SERVES: 4 to 8

3½ lb (1.6 kg) bone-in pork shoulder, cut into 3 pieces

1 tbsp (18 g) salt

1 tsp freshly ground black pepper

1 tbsp (7 g) ground cumin

1 tbsp (15 ml) extra-virgin olive oil

MOLE

1 tbsp (15 ml) extra-virgin olive oil

¼ cup (40 g) diced red onion

3 cloves garlic, grated

1 tsp ground cinnamon

2 tbsp (32 g) tomato paste

2 tbsp (32 g) creamy peanut butter

1 canned chipotle pepper

1½ cups (355 ml) low-sodium beef stock

1 (10-oz [280-g]) can red enchilada sauce

5 tbsp (35 g) dark unsweetened Dutch-processed cocoa powder

Liberally season all 3 pieces of pork shoulder with salt, black pepper and cumin. Rub the seasonings into the meat.

Place the oil in the Instant Pot. Press sauté and then add the seasoned pork shoulder pieces. Sear on multiple sides for about 10 minutes total. After 10 minutes, press cancel.

While the meat sears, prepare the mole: In a small saucepan, combine the olive oil, red onion and garlic. Sauté for 2 minutes over medium heat. Stir in the cinnamon, tomato paste, peanut butter, chipotle pepper, beef stock and enchilada sauce. Whisk to combine. Bring the mixture to a simmer and let cook for about 4 minutes.

Stir the cocoa powder into the sauce and then use an immersion blender to puree the sauce until smooth.

Add about half of the sauce directly on top of the seared pork.

Secure the lid with the steam vent in the sealed position. Press pressure cook until the display light is beneath high pressure. Use the plus and minus buttons to adjust the time until the display reads "60 minutes."

When the timer sounds, quick release the pressure. Remove the lid. Remove all the bones and large pieces of fat from the pork. Use two forks to shred the pork and mix it into the sauce.

The pork can be served right from the Instant Pot or can be transferred to a foil-lined baking sheet with some extra mole sauce and crisped up under a high broiler for 5 minutes.

SLOW COOKER METHOD: Follow all the steps from searing the pork to creating the sauce. Instead of pressure cook, press slow cook. Make sure the display light is beneath less. Use the plus and minus buttons to adjust the time until the display reads "12 hours."

DAIRY-FREE GLUTEN-FREE OPTION

SHREDDED CHICKEN MOLE

This Mexican dish works absolutely perfectly in the Instant Pot! Slightly spicy and smoky, with a hint of cocoa and cinnamon—such a delicious, flavorful dish! This shredded mole can be used for many things: tacos, burritos, enchiladas, or bowls of rice. I love this as a meal prep dish because it makes such a large amount that can last all week! **AR**

SERVES: 8

2 tbsp (30 ml) avocado oil or olive oil

1 large yellow onion, diced

3 cloves garlic, minced

1 (14.5-oz [411-g]) can fire-roasted diced tomatoes

2 chipotle peppers in adobo sauce

1 to 2 tbsp (15 to 30 ml) adobo sauce

⅓ cup (87 g) smooth peanut butter

2 tbsp (14 g) unsweetened cocoa powder

2 tbsp (15 g) chili powder

1 tsp ground cumin

1 tsp sea salt

½ tsp ground cinnamon

⅓ cup (50 g) raisins

1 cup (237 ml) chicken stock

3 lb (1.4 kg) chicken thighs, fat trimmed

Cooked rice or tortillas, for serving

Select sauté on the Instant Pot, set to "medium," if possible. Once hot, coat the bottom of the pot with the oil and toss in the onion and garlic. Cook for 3 to 4 minutes, or until fragrant. Select cancel.

Make your mole sauce: In a blender, combine the fire-roasted tomatoes, chipotle peppers, adobo sauce, peanut butter, cocoa powder, chili powder, cumin, salt, cinnamon, raisins, chicken stock and the onion mixture. Pulse until smooth.

Place the chicken inside the Instant Pot. Pour the mole sauce on top.

Secure the lid with the steam vent in the sealed position. Select manual or pressure, and cook on high pressure for 8 minutes.

Use a quick release. Once the steam is released, open the lid and remove the chicken. Shred the chicken with a fork and return it to the sauce.

Serve hot over a bed of rice or in a tortilla.

MEXICAN "LASAGNA"

My girls helped me come up with this recipe one night when we didn't have any lasagna noodles. They loved it so much that it's become one of our regular easy recipes. It's a good way to use up leftover chicken, too. **KB**

SERVES: 4

Nonstick cooking spray, for pan

2 cups (520 g) salsa, divided

4 (6" [15-cm]) flour tortillas

1 cup (238 g) refried beans

1 jalapeño pepper, minced

1¼ cups (138 g) shredded Mexican-blend cheese

2 cups (280 g) cooked, shredded chicken

1 cup (237 ml) water

¼ cup (10 g) chopped fresh cilantro

½ cup (115 g) sour cream

Spray a 7-inch (18.5-cm) round baking pan with nonstick cooking spray. Spread a thin layer of the salsa on the bottom of the pan. Add a tortilla, followed by a third each of the refried beans, salsa, jalapeño, cheese and chicken. Continue layering twice more, starting with a tortilla and ending with a bit of salsa and cheese on the top and pressing down gently each time you add a new tortilla.

Pour the water into the Instant Pot and insert the steam trivet. Make a sling out of foil—a long piece of foil folded twice lengthwise. Center the baking pan on top of the foil. Cover the baking pan with additional foil, then, using the sling, carefully place the pan on the steam trivet, folding down any foil so that it doesn't interfere with closing the lid.

Close the lid, press manual and adjust the timer to 15 minutes. Check that the display light is beneath high pressure.

When the timer sounds, quick release the pressure and carefully remove the lid. Using the foil sling as handles, carefully remove the baking pan from the Instant Pot.

Remove the foil and pop the lasagna under the broiler for a few minutes to brown the cheese. Allow the lasagna to rest for 10 minutes before serving, then serve with the fresh cilantro and sour cream.

DAIRY-FREE · GLUTEN-FREE OPTION · GRAIN-FREE OPTION

SWEET & SPICY PARTY MEATBALLS

My friends call these the "Disappearing Meatballs." This is the appetizer I bring to every party, and it's quickly gone before we all get enough! Adults and kids all go crazy over the flavor combo: spicy buffalo sauce combined with sweetness from honey and jam. Easily thrown together in your Instant Pot for ultimate ease and perfect for holidays, football season or any potluck! **AR**

SERVES: 8

⅔ cup (160 ml) buffalo wing sauce

⅓ cup (80 ml) soy sauce or gluten-free tamari

⅓ cup (80 ml) honey

1 tbsp (11 g) Dijon mustard

½ cup (160 g) raspberry preserves

⅓ cup (80 ml) hot water

2½ lb (1.1 kg) frozen meatballs (see note)

In a medium bowl, whisk together the buffalo wing sauce, soy sauce, honey, Dijon mustard, raspberry preserves and hot water.

Place the frozen meatballs in the Instant Pot. Pour the sauce on top and gently toss to coat the meatballs.

Secure the lid with the steam vent in the sealed position. Select manual or high pressure, and cook for 5 minutes.

Use a quick release. Remove the lid once the steam is released and give the meatballs a good stir to cover completely in sauce.

Serve hot!

NOTE: I use mini meatballs, about 1 inch (2.5 cm) in diameter, which are fully cooked and frozen. This size works perfectly for serving and makes this recipe so easy to make!

DAIRY-FREE GLUTEN-FREE GRAIN-FREE

CORNED BEEF & CABBAGE

Corned beef in the Instant Pot comes out so amazingly tender. Although it's typically made for St. Patrick's Day, we enjoy it year-round since it's so simple to make and tastes amazing! **KB**

SERVES: 4

1 cup (237 ml) beef stock

3 lb (1.4 kg) corned beef

1 lb (455 g) baby potatoes, quartered

1 lb (455 g) baby carrots

1 head cabbage, thickly sliced, core removed

In the Instant Pot, combine the beef stock and the corned beef along with the contents of its seasoning packet.

Secure the lid with the steam vent in the sealed position. Press manual and immediately adjust the timer to 80 minutes. Check that the display light is beneath high pressure.

When the timer sounds, quick release the pressure and carefully remove the lid. Remove the corned beef and place on a serving platter. Tent with foil to keep warm and prevent the beef from drying out.

Add the potatoes, carrots and cabbage to the pot. Secure the lid with the steam vent in the sealed position. Press manual and immediately adjust the timer to 4 minutes. Check that the display light is beneath high pressure.

When the timer sounds, quick release the pressure and carefully remove the lid. Transfer the potatoes, carrots and cabbage to the serving platter, then drizzle some of the juice from the pot over everything. Serve immediately.

DAIRY-FREE OPTION GLUTEN-FREE

CHICKEN BIRYANI

Traditional Indian food is one of my favorite things to eat, and with the Instant Pot, it comes together so quickly! This classic Indian dish is packed full of spices, textures and flavors, and is ready in about 30 minutes. **AR**

SERVES: 4 to 5

2 tbsp (30 ml) ghee, avocado oil or extra-virgin olive oil

1 medium yellow onion, diced

3 cloves garlic, minced

2 tbsp (23 g) finely diced fresh ginger

1½ lb (680 g) chicken breast, cut into 1" (2.5-cm) pieces

1 cup (240 g) canned diced tomatoes, with juices

2 tsp (12 g) sea salt, plus more to taste

2 tsp (4 g) garam masala

1 tsp paprika

1 tsp coriander powder

½ tsp ground turmeric

½ tsp ground cumin

1 cup (195 g) uncooked basmati rice

1½ cups (355 ml) chicken stock

½ cup (75 g) raisins

½ cup (70 g) roasted and salted cashews

¼ cup (10 g) chopped fresh cilantro (optional)

Select sauté on the Instant Pot. Once hot, coat the bottom of your pot with the ghee. Add the onion and cook for 2 to 3 minutes, then toss in the garlic and ginger. Cook for another 2 minutes, then select cancel.

Toss the chicken and tomatoes into the pot.

In a small bowl, mix together the salt, garam masala, paprika, coriander, turmeric and cumin. Pour the spice mixture into the pot and stir.

Add the basmati rice, then pour the chicken stock on top. Don't stir. Secure the lid with the steam vent in the sealed position. Select manual or pressure, and cook on high pressure for 8 minutes.

Use a quick release. Stir in the raisins and cashews.

Serve hot and top with fresh cilantro (if using) and additional salt to taste.

CORN & GREEN CHILE CASSEROLE

A dear friend of mine's mom from southern Illinois makes the best corn casserole. I tried this casserole for the first time in college while visiting her family during holiday break. It's normally fluffy corn bread studded with corn kernels. But, since I can never leave things well enough alone, I had to spice it up a bit with a can of green chiles. The added spiciness really completes the dish. Making this in the Instant Pot keeps the casserole very moist and fluffy. I love to serve it alongside my BBQ Chicken Jalapeño Sliders (page 97). **SB**

SERVES: 4 to 6

12 oz (340 g) frozen corn, thawed

1 (8.5-oz [240-g]) box corn muffin mix, Jiffy brand preferred

¼ tsp ground cumin

1 tsp salt

½ tsp freshly ground black pepper

4 tbsp (55 g) unsalted butter, melted

2 large eggs

¼ cup (60 ml) heavy cream

¾ cup (172 g) light sour cream

1 (4.5-oz [130-g]) can mild diced green chiles

Butter or oil, for dishes

1 cup (237 ml) water

In a large bowl, whisk together the corn, muffin mix, cumin, salt and black pepper. Add the butter, eggs, cream, sour cream and chiles. Mix until a yellow batter is formed and no dry bits are visible.

Butter two 7-inch (18.5-cm) round baking dishes.

Divide the batter between the two prepared dishes. Cover each dish with foil.

Pour the water into the Instant Pot and insert the steam trivet. Place one dish at a time on the trivet.

Secure with the steam vent in the sealed position. Press pressure cook until the display light is beneath high pressure. Use the plus and minus buttons to adjust the time until the display reads "30 minutes."

When the timer sounds, quick release the pressure. Remove the lid. Use oven mitts to carefully grip the dish and remove it from the Instant Pot.

Place the other dish in the Instant Pot and cook the same way.

DAIRY-FREE OPTION · GLUTEN-FREE · GRAIN-FREE

TURKEY MEATBALLS & SPAGHETTI SQUASH

My entire family are huge spaghetti and meatball fans. The best sauce is one that simmers for hours, but with the Instant Pot, it can be done without stirring and a lot quicker! I love this version because I can cook my beloved spaghetti squash all in one pot. Broiling meatballs makes them cook much faster. If that is unavailable to you, you can ground the turkey in the Instant Pot and create a traditional meat sauce. **AR**

SERVES: 4

MEATBALLS

1 lb (455 g) ground turkey

⅓ cup (33 g) almond flour

2 tsp (4 g) Italian seasoning

1 tsp garlic powder

1 large egg, beaten

½ tsp sea salt

Nonstick cooking spray, for pan

SAUCE

1 tbsp (15 ml) avocado oil or olive oil

1 medium yellow onion, diced

3 cloves garlic, minced

¼ cup (60 ml) red wine

¼ cup (60 ml) red wine vinegar

½ cup (120 ml) water

1 (28-oz [800-g]) can San Marzano whole tomatoes

1 (14.5-oz [411-g]) can pureed tomatoes

1½ tsp (9 g) salt

1 medium spaghetti squash

½ cup (40 g) shredded Parmesan cheese, for garnish (optional)

Fresh basil, for garnish

Salt

Prepare the meatballs: Set the oven to broil. In a medium bowl, mix together all the meatball ingredients, except for the nonstick cooking spray. Mix well with your hands and roll into 1-inch (2.5-cm) balls. Lightly spray a baking sheet with nonstick cooking spray and place the meatballs on the pan. Transfer to the oven and broil for about 4 minutes. The meatballs need to be browned on the outside so they maintain their shape once placed in the Instant Pot. It is okay if they are not cooked all the way.

Prepare the sauce: Select sauté on the Instant Pot. Once hot, coat the bottom of the pan with the oil, then toss in the onion and garlic. Once fragrant and lightly browned, select cancel. Pour in the wine, vinegar and water and deglaze the pot with the liquid. Add the whole and pureed tomatoes and the salt.

Pierce the spaghetti squash numerous times with a fork. Place the whole squash on top of the spaghetti sauce. Place the meatballs around the squash, on top of the sauce.

Secure the lid with the steam vent in the sealed position. Select manual or pressure, and cook on high pressure for 30 minutes.

Use a quick release, ensuring the steam is released before removing the lid. Remove the spaghetti squash with tongs and set aside to cool for about 10 minutes. Once cool, slice in half. Scoop out and discard the seeds, and use a fork to pull out the spaghetti squash strands.

Pour the sauce and meatballs on top of the squash strands. Top with Parmesan cheese (if using), fresh basil and additional salt to taste.

DAIRY-FREE OPTION GLUTEN-FREE

GRAIN-FREE PALEO

BBQ APRICOT PULLED PORK

Bold, saucy and full of flavor, that's how pulled pork is meant to be. This easy-to-make shredded meat is jam-packed with sweet apricot flavor, vibrant herbs and a little kick of mildly spicy barbecue sauce. It's extra tasty served in wraps or lettuce wraps topped with homemade cabbage coleslaw. **ESV**

SERVES: 6 to 8

3 tbsp (43 g) grass-fed butter, ghee or avocado oil

1 (2- to 3-lb [905-g to 1.4-kg]) pork roast

1 small yellow onion, thinly sliced

5 cloves garlic, chopped

½ tsp chopped fresh thyme leaves

½ tsp chopped fresh rosemary leaves

1 cup (250 g) sugar-free homemade or store-bought barbecue sauce

½ cup (120 ml) cider vinegar

9 oz (255 g) sugar-free all-fruit apricot jam

¼ cup (60 ml) pure maple syrup or honey

1 tsp sea salt

NOTES: Keep the size of your Instant Pot in mind when purchasing the pork roast.

There are some great Paleo-friendly barbecue sauces on the market these days—you can find them at most natural food stores and online; just make sure to check the ingredients.

Place your healthy fat of choice in the Instant Pot and press sauté. Once the fat has melted, add the roast and brown for about 3½ minutes per side. Remove the roast and transfer to a plate. Set aside. Add the onion, garlic, thyme and rosemary to the pot and sauté, stirring occasionally, for 4 minutes, or until fragrant. Add the barbecue sauce, vinegar, jam, your sweetener of choice and salt, giving the mixture a quick stir and scraping up any browned bits with a wooden spoon. Press keep warm/cancel.

Place the browned roast in the Instant Pot. Secure the lid with the steam vent in the sealed position. Press manual and set on high pressure for 35 minutes.

Once the timer sounds, press keep warm/cancel. Allow the Instant Pot to release pressure naturally for 15 minutes. Using an oven mitt, do a quick release. If there is any steam left over, allow it to release until the silver dial drops, then carefully open the lid.

Carefully remove the roast, place on a large plate or cutting board and pull apart into shreds. Add the shredded pork back to the Instant Pot and stir to combine, making sure all the pork gets coated. Secure the lid with the steam vent in the sealed position. Press manual and set on high pressure for 5 minutes.

Once the timer sounds, press keep warm/cancel. Using an oven mitt, do a quick release. When the steam venting stops and the silver dial drops, carefully open the lid.

Give the shredded pork several stirs until everything is fully incorporated. Pour the shredded pork into a shallow dish and allow the juices to set up and absorb into the meat for 15 minutes.

Serve immediately or refrigerate for later use.

DAIRY-FREE GLUTEN-FREE

CHICKEN & SAUSAGE JAMBALAYA

This easy recipe is packed with flavor yet it comes together in no time flat. Leftovers reheat nicely, too, so we'll take it for lunch all week long. **KB**

SERVES: 4 to 6

2 tsp (10 ml) extra-virgin olive oil

1 lb (455 g) andouille sausage, cut into ¼" (6-mm)-thick slices

2 boneless, skinless chicken breasts, cut into bite-size pieces

1 yellow onion, chopped

1 red bell pepper, seeded and chopped

2 celery ribs, chopped

3 cloves garlic, minced

2 tsp (5 g) Cajun or Creole seasoning

½ tsp coarse salt

1 tsp Italian seasoning

2 cups (475 ml) low-sodium chicken stock

1½ cups (300 g) uncooked long-grain white rice

1 (14.5-oz [411-g]) can fire-roasted diced tomatoes, undrained

Press sauté to preheat the Instant Pot. When the word "hot" appears on the display, add the olive oil. When the oil is shimmering, add the sausage and chicken, cooking until they're browned, about 4 to 5 minutes. Remove the sausage and chicken and set aside.

Add the onion, bell pepper and celery to the pot. Cook until the onion is soft, about 5 minutes, stirring frequently. Add the garlic, Cajun seasoning, salt and Italian seasoning and cook for 1 more minute. Add the chicken stock, stirring well to scrape up any browned bits from the bottom. Press cancel to turn off the Instant Pot.

Add the rice, then add the sausage and chicken back to the pot on top of the rice. Pour the fire-roasted tomatoes over all.

Secure the lid with the steam vent in the sealed position. Press manual and immediately adjust the timer to 5 minutes. Check that the display light is beneath high pressure. When the timer sounds, quick release the pressure and carefully remove the lid. Gently stir and serve immediately.

DAIRY-FREE **GF GLUTEN-FREE** **GRAIN-FREE OPTION**

CHICKEN VINDALOO
WITH POTATOES

The tangy and spicy flavors of chicken vindaloo make it one of my absolute favorite dishes! The closest variation I can get to my favorite Indian restaurant is by cooking in the Instant Pot. The flavors meld beautifully and the complete cook time is less than 40 minutes! You can eat this as is, especially since potatoes are also included, or serve over a bed of rice. **AR**

SERVES: 4

2 tbsp (30 ml) avocado oil or extra-virgin olive oil

1 large yellow onion, diced

1 (6" [15-cm]) piece fresh ginger, peeled and chopped

6 cloves garlic, minced

1 hot red chili pepper, seeded and chopped (see note)

1 (14.5-oz [411-g]) can diced tomatoes

2 tbsp (32 g) tomato paste

⅓ cup (80 ml) white wine vinegar

1¼ cups (295 ml) chicken stock

1 tbsp (6 g) garam masala

2 tsp (4 g) ground coriander

2 tsp (4 g) ground turmeric

1 tsp mustard powder

1 tsp ground cinnamon

1½ tsp (9 g) sea salt, plus more to taste

2 lb (905 g) raw chicken breast, cut into 1" to 2" (2.5- to 5-cm) pieces

4 medium Yukon gold potatoes, cut into chunks

Cooked rice, for serving (optional)

Chopped fresh cilantro, for garnish

Select sauté on the Instant Pot. Once hot, coat the bottom of the pot with the oil, then add the onion, ginger, garlic and chili pepper. Sauté for 3 to 4 minutes, or until fragrant and lightly browned. Select cancel.

Transfer the onion mixture to a blender. Add the tomatoes, tomato paste, vinegar, chicken stock, garam masala, coriander, turmeric, mustard powder, cinnamon and salt. Blend until smooth, 1 to 2 minutes.

Clean the Instant Pot to ensure no onion mixture is sticking to the bottom. Return the pot to its base and pour the sauce into the pot. Add the chicken and potatoes.

Secure the lid with the steam vent in the sealed position. Select manual or pressure, and cook on high pressure for 10 minutes.

Use a quick release, and remove the lid once the steam is completely released.

Serve plain or over a bed of rice. Season with additional salt to taste and garnish with fresh cilantro.

NOTE: You can adjust the spicy factor on this dish by adding an additional hot red chili pepper or leaving the seeds in the pepper. This variation is mild, but with a small amount of heat.

DAIRY-FREE GF GLUTEN-FREE GRAIN-FREE

CABERNET BALSAMIC POT ROAST
WITH POTATOES & CARROTS

A tender, melt-in-your-mouth pot roast makes the best Sunday night dinner! This complete meal has a delicious cabernet gravy that tastes amazing over the potatoes and carrots. Simple to make in the Instant Pot, and also elegant enough for a holiday feast. **AR**

SERVES: 6

4 lb (1.8 kg) chuck beef roast, cut into 4 pieces, fat trimmed

2 tsp (12 g) sea salt, plus more to taste

1 tsp paprika

1 tsp dried rosemary

1 tsp dried basil

1 tsp dried thyme

1 tsp onion powder

1 tsp garlic powder

3 tbsp (45 ml) olive or avocado oil

1 small yellow onion, diced

1 cup (237 ml) cabernet sauvignon wine

1½ cups (355 ml) beef stock

¼ cup (60 ml) balsamic vinegar

2 tbsp (30 ml) gluten-free tamari or coconut aminos

4 large carrots, peeled and cut into 2" to 3" (5- to 7.5-cm) pieces

12 oz (340 g) sliced bella mushrooms or button mushrooms

1½ lb (680 g) baby potatoes

3 tbsp (24 g) tapioca starch

Select sauté on the Instant Pot. Pat the beef dry. In a medium bowl, mix together the salt, paprika, rosemary, basil, thyme, onion powder and garlic powder. Generously rub the mixture on each side of the beef pieces.

Coat the bottom of the pot with oil, then toss in the onion. Cook for 2 to 3 minutes, then add the meat, a few pieces at a time. Cook for about 2 minutes per side, and repeat until all of the pieces have been seared. Select cancel. Remove the beef from the pot and set aside.

Deglaze the pot by pouring in the wine and beef stock. Scrape the bottom for any leftover browned bits. Pour in the vinegar and gluten-free tamari. Place the beef on top of the liquid mixture, then top with the carrots, mushrooms and potatoes.

Secure the lid with the steam vent in the sealed position. Select manual or pressure, and cook on high pressure for 40 minutes.

Use a natural release for at least 10 minutes, then release any remaining steam. Gently remove the vegetables and then the beef. Set both aside separately, tented with foil to keep warm.

Transfer about ¼ cup (60 ml) of the cooking liquid into a small bowl, whisk in the tapioca starch, then return the liquid to the pot and stir. Select sauté, and allow the sauce to thicken, 5 to 7 minutes.

While the sauce is cooking, shred or cut the beef. Place back in the pot. Spoon the beef and sauce over the vegetables and serve warm.

GLUTEN-FREE GRAIN-FREE

SMOKY & SPICY CHICKEN BREASTS

I tend to shy away from cooking chicken breasts because they always dry out so easily. The Instant Pot makes them so tender that I'm now a convert! I especially love that a quick run under the broiler gets the skin nice and crispy. **KB**

SERVES: 4

1 cup (237 ml) water or chicken stock

2 lb (905 g) chicken breasts, skin-on

2 tsp (5 g) smoked paprika

½ tsp cayenne pepper

¼ tsp garlic powder

1 tsp onion powder

¼ tsp coarse salt

¼ tsp freshly ground black pepper

4 tbsp (55 g) unsalted butter, melted

Pour the water or chicken stock into the pot, then add the chicken breasts.

Secure the lid with the steam vent in the sealed position. Press manual and immediately adjust the timer to 8 minutes. Check that the display light is beneath high pressure.

When the timer sounds, quick release the pressure and carefully remove the lid. Remove the chicken from the pot and place on a broiler pan. Broil until the chicken is browned and crispy, about 5 minutes.

In a small bowl, mix together the paprika, cayenne, garlic and onion powders, salt and black pepper, then stir in the melted butter. Brush the breasts liberally with the butter mixture and serve immediately.

DAIRY-FREE OPTION   GLUTEN-FREE   GRAIN-FREE

POMEGRANATE CHICKEN

If you're a fan of pomegranates, you're going to love this boldly spiced, sweet and sticky chicken. It's packed with beautiful flavors from sweet spices—cloves, allspice, cinnamon and cardamom; lots of fresh herbs; and of course, pomegranate. **ESV**

SERVES: 4

2 tbsp (28 g) grass-fed butter, ghee or avocado oil

2 lb (905 g) boneless, skinless chicken thighs, quartered

1 medium yellow onion, thinly sliced

5 cloves garlic, finely chopped

1 tsp sea salt

1 tsp chili powder

¼ tsp ground cloves

¼ tsp ground allspice

¼ tsp ground cinnamon

¼ tsp ground cardamom

¼ cup (60 ml) sugar-free 100% pomegranate juice

2 large celery ribs with leaves, thinly sliced

¼ cup (15 g) finely chopped fresh flat-leaf parsley, plus more for garnish

1 tbsp (2 g) finely chopped fresh rosemary

1 tbsp (2 g) finely chopped fresh mint

2 tsp (2 g) finely chopped fresh thyme leaves

¼ cup (60 ml) honey

1 tbsp (15 ml) quality blackstrap molasses

¾ cup (175 ml) chicken or vegetable stock

½ cup (87 g) pomegranate arils, for garnish

Place your healthy fat of choice in the Instant Pot and press sauté. Once the fat has melted, add the chicken and brown for about 3½ minutes per side—you may need to do this in two batches if the chicken is too cramped in the Instant Pot. Remove the chicken and transfer to a plate. Set aside. Add the onion to the pot and sauté, stirring occasionally, for 5 minutes, or until fragrant. Then, add the garlic, salt, chili powder, cloves, allspice, cinnamon and cardamom and sauté for 1 minute, stirring occasionally. Add the pomegranate juice and deglaze the pot, scraping up any browned bits with a wooden spoon. Press keep warm/cancel.

Add the celery, parsley, rosemary, mint, thyme, honey, molasses, browned chicken and stock, giving the mixture a stir and making sure the chicken is submerged in the liquid.

Secure the lid with the steam vent in the sealed position. Press manual and set on high pressure for 12 minutes.

Once the timer sounds, press keep warm/cancel. Allow the Instant Pot to naturally pressure release for 15 minutes. Using an oven mitt, do a quick release. When the steam venting stops and the silver dial drops, carefully open the lid.

With tongs or a large slotted spoon, transfer the chicken to a plate or cutting board. Chop the chicken into bite-size chunks, then set aside.

Press sauté and allow the liquid to come to a simmer, then simmer for about 5 minutes, or until the liquid slightly thickens. Press keep warm/cancel. Add the chicken, give the mixture a stir, taste for seasoning and adjust the salt to taste. Allow it to rest for 10 minutes.

Serve immediately, garnished with fresh pomegranate arils and chopped fresh flat-leaf parsley.

NOTES: Use a chili powder that is a blend of such ingredients as chile, cumin, oregano, coriander, garlic, allspice and cloves, preferably an organic brand.

DAIRY-FREE GLUTEN-FREE GRAIN-FREE

HEALTHY LEMON CHICKEN

I'll make this easy chicken and serve it with potatoes and a vegetable, or slice it to add to my salads throughout the week. It's light, flavorful and healthy! **KB**

SERVES: 2

½ cup (120 ml) water

2 lemons (zest from 1, juice from both)

2 cloves garlic, crushed

1 tsp dried oregano

1 lb (455 g) boneless, skinless chicken breast

Pour the water into the Instant Pot. Add the lemon zest and juice, garlic and oregano, then add the chicken to the pot.

Secure the lid with the steam vent in the sealed position. Press manual and immediately adjust the timer to 7 minutes. Check that the display light is beneath high pressure.

When the timer sounds, quick release the pressure and carefully remove the lid. Carefully remove the chicken, slice and serve.

DAIRY-FREE GLUTEN-FREE

STEAMED TAMALES

Tamales have been on my cooking bucket list for a while. I finally gave it a shot and lived to tell about it. Tamales are so easy. The only thing is that the process of stuffing them is time consuming. However, this recipe yields a lot of tamales, so you won't be making them that often. Steaming the tamales to perfection is so easy with the Instant Pot. The masa filling stays fluffy and flavorful. Cross it off your cooking bucket list, too! **SB**

MAKES: 20 to 25 tamales

1 (6-oz [170-g]) package corn husks

6 cups (682 g) masa de harina

2 tsp (12 g) salt

1 tsp ground cumin

1 tsp ground coriander

1 tsp baking powder

5 cups (1 L) vegetable stock

¾ cup (175 ml) canola oil

2 to 3 cups (400 to 450 g) leftover Mole Carnitas (page 322)

1 cup (237 ml) water

Place about 30 husks in a shallow pan and then cover with water. Place a small bowl on top to weigh the husks down. Allow the husks to soak for at least 30 minutes.

In an electric stand mixer fitted with the paddle attachment, mix together the masa, salt, cumin, coriander and baking powder.

With the mixer on low speed, add the stock 1 cup (237 ml) at a time. Once the cup has been incorporated, add another, until all the stock has been added. Then, mix in the canola oil.

Peel a strip off the end of a soaked husk to use as a tie for the tamale. Use an ice-cream scoop to scoop the masa onto the husk. Wet your fingers and press out the masa into a large rectangle. Add 1 or 2 tablespoons (13 to 25 g) of mole carnitas to the center of the masa rectangle. Fold each side into the center to form almost a tube of masa around the filling. Wrap one side over the other and then fold the bottom of the tamale upward. Use the strip of husk to tie the tamale together. Continue that process for all the tamales. Discard the soaking water.

Pour the cup (237 ml) of water into the Instant Pot and insert the steam trivet. Fold a piece of foil into a 7-inch (18.5-cm) square and poke several holes in the foil. Place the foil on top of the trivet.

Arrange as many tamales, folded end down, as will fit in the Instant Pot on top of the foil.

Secure the lid with the steam vent in the sealed position. Press steam. Use the plus and minus buttons to adjust the time until the display reads "20 minutes."

When the timer sounds, quick release the pressure. Remove the lid. Use tongs to remove the tamales. Serve immediately.

Wrap the tamales in foil and freeze for up to 3 months. To reheat, steam in the Instant Pot the same way as before.

DAIRY-FREE   GLUTEN-FREE OPTION   GRAIN-FREE OPTION

ASIAN PEANUT BUTTER CHICKEN

When I want to make my kids really excited for dinner, I serve peanut butter chicken! This Asian-inspired dish has the most delicious peanut sauce, and works perfectly with shredded chicken served over rice or cauliflower rice. Feel free to swap out for another nut or seed butter to accommodate allergies; any variation will taste delicious! **AR**

SERVES: 6

½ cup (130 g) smooth peanut butter

¼ cup (60 ml) soy sauce or gluten-free tamari

¼ cup (60 ml) honey

¼ cup (60 ml) rice vinegar

⅔ cup (160 ml) chicken stock

3 cloves garlic, minced

2 lb (905 g) chicken breast

⅓ cup (80 ml) full-fat canned coconut milk

3 to 4 cups (558 to 744 g) cooked rice or (330 to 440 g) cauliflower rice, for serving

3 tbsp (8 g) chopped fresh cilantro (optional)

3 tbsp (27 g) chopped peanuts (optional)

Salt

Freshly ground black pepper

In a bowl, whisk together the peanut butter, soy sauce, honey, vinegar, chicken stock and garlic.

Place the chicken in the bottom of the Instant Pot. Pour the peanut butter sauce on top.

Secure the lid with the steam vent in the sealed position. Select manual or pressure, and cook on high pressure for 8 minutes.

Use a quick release. Once the steam is completely released, open the lid and pour in the coconut milk. You can cut or shred the chicken into smaller pieces, or keep as a larger breast.

Serve warm over rice or cauliflower rice. Garnish with fresh cilantro and peanuts (if using). Sprinkle with salt and pepper to taste.

GF
GLUTEN-FREE

CREAMY MUSHROOM-HERB CHICKEN

The elegant flavor of caramelized mushrooms in a creamy white wine sauce and generous bites of chicken brings home the best real food version of your childhood: canned mushroom soup–baked chicken casserole. It's delicious served as is or alongside jasmine rice and roasted vegetables. **ESV**

SERVES: 2 to 3

2 tbsp (28 g) grass-fed butter or ghee

1 medium yellow onion, thinly sliced

1½ lb (680 g) mushrooms, cut into thirds, woody ends removed

5 cloves garlic, chopped

½ cup (120 ml) dry white wine

2 large celery ribs with leaves, thinly sliced

1 tsp sea salt

¼ cup (15 g) finely chopped fresh flat-leaf parsley, plus more for garnish

1 tbsp (2 g) finely chopped fresh rosemary

1 tbsp (4 g) finely chopped fresh dill

2 tsp (2 g) finely chopped fresh thyme leaves

2 boneless, skinless chicken breasts

¾ cup (175 ml) chicken or vegetable stock

¾ cup (175 ml) heavy cream

2 tbsp (15 g) gluten-free all-purpose flour

¼ cup (20 g) shredded Parmesan cheese, plus more for garnish

Place your healthy fat of choice in the Instant Pot and press sauté. Once the fat has melted, add the onion and mushrooms and sauté, stirring occasionally, for 7 minutes, or until caramelized. Then, add the garlic and sauté for 1 minute, stirring occasionally. Add the wine and deglaze the pot, scraping up any browned bits with a wooden spoon. Press keep warm/cancel.

Add the celery, salt, parsley, rosemary, dill, thyme, chicken and stock, making sure the chicken is submerged in the liquid.

Secure the lid with the steam vent in the sealed position. Press manual and set on high pressure for 9 minutes.

While the chicken is cooking, place the cream in a large measuring cup or medium bowl, then sprinkle the flour on the top, whisking until the flour is mostly incorporated. Set aside.

Once the timer sounds, press keep warm/cancel. Using an oven mitt, do a quick release. When the steam venting stops and the silver dial drops, carefully open the lid.

With tongs, transfer the chicken to a plate or cutting board. Chop the chicken into bite-size chunks, then set aside.

Press sauté and add the cream mixture and the Parmesan to the Instant Pot, allowing the mixture to come to a simmer, then quickly stir until the cream and Parmesan are fully mixed in. Simmer for about 5 minutes, or until the liquid slightly thickens. Press keep warm/cancel. Add the chicken, give the mixture a stir, taste for seasoning and adjust the salt to taste. Allow it to rest for 10 minutes.

Serve immediately, garnished with shredded Parmesan and chopped fresh parsley.

LEMON-ARTICHOKE CHICKEN

DAIRY-FREE · GLUTEN-FREE OPTION · GRAIN-FREE OPTION

Although this recipe screams "spring," it can be enjoyed year-round. Chicken thighs or breast are cooked in a zesty and tangy lemon sauce with artichoke hearts and spices. This simple and delicious meal can be served over rice, cauliflower rice or pasta. **AR**

SERVES: 4

½ tsp sea salt, plus more to taste

½ tsp freshly ground black pepper

1½ lb (680 g) boneless, skinless chicken breast or thighs

1 cup (237 ml) dry white wine, e.g., chardonnay; or chicken stock

Juice of 1 large lemon (about ¼ cup [60 ml])

2 tsp (4 g) garam masala

1 tsp ground turmeric

1 clove garlic, crushed

1 (6-oz [170-g]) can hearts of palm, drained

1 (6-oz [170-g]) jar artichoke hearts, drained

3 sprigs thyme

1 lemon, sliced

2 tsp (4 g) lemon pepper

3 tbsp (24 g) arrowroot starch

2 tbsp (30 ml) water

Cooked rice, cauliflower rice, pasta or cooked vegetables, for serving

Salt and pepper both sides of your chicken. Place in the Instant Pot.

In a small bowl, stir together the wine, lemon juice, garam masala, turmeric and garlic. Pour on top of the chicken.

Cover the chicken with the hearts of palm, artichoke hearts, thyme and lemon slices and sprinkle with the lemon pepper.

Secure the lid with the steam vent in the sealed position. Select manual or pressure, and cook on high pressure for 9 minutes.

Use a quick release, ensuring the steam is completely released before opening the lid. In a small bowl, whisk together the arrowroot starch and the water and add to the sauce. Continue to stir until thickened. Remove the thyme sprigs.

Serve the chicken on top of rice, cauliflower rice or pasta, or with vegetables.

GLUTEN-FREE

LOADED BACON CHEESEBURGER QUINOA

Remember when I said that Macaroni & Beer Cheese (page 247) was the frontrunner for my favorite recipe in the book? Well, it was dethroned by this beauty. It was the pickles that did it for me. Or maybe the little secret sauce mixed in at the end. Actually, I love everything about this. Sautéing the beef and onions with a little mustard and onion powder in the Instant Pot before pressure-cooking with the quinoa really brings that cheeseburger flavor home. It's like biting into a bunless burger! You're gonna love it. **SB**

SERVES: 4 to 6

4 slices raw bacon, diced

1 yellow onion, diced

1 lb (455 g) 90% lean ground beef

½ tsp ground mustard powder

½ tsp onion powder

1 tsp salt

½ tsp freshly ground black pepper

1 (14.5-oz [411-g]) can fire-roasted diced tomatoes

1 cup (173 g) uncooked quinoa

1 cup (237 ml) water

1 tbsp (14 g) mayonnaise

1 tbsp (16 g) barbecue sauce

1 tbsp (11 g) prepared yellow mustard

2 tbsp (30 g) ketchup

1 cup (115 g) shredded cheddar cheese

½ cup (73 g) diced kosher dill pickles

½ cup (90 g) diced Roma tomatoes

Press sauté on the Instant Pot and let the pot heat up for 2 minutes. Add the bacon and cook until crisp. Remove with a slotted spoon and transfer to a paper towel–lined plate.

Add the onion, beef, mustard powder, onion powder, salt and pepper. Break apart the beef using a wooden spoon. Once the onion begins to turn translucent, about 3 minutes, press cancel.

Stir in the can of tomatoes, quinoa and water.

Secure the lid with the steam vent in the sealed position. Press pressure cook until the display light is beneath high pressure. Use the plus and minus buttons to adjust the time until the display reads "1 minute."

When the timer sounds, release the pressure naturally for 10 minutes. Remove the lid.

Press sauté. Stir in the mayonnaise, barbecue sauce, mustard and ketchup. Sauté for 2 minutes while stirring.

Press cancel. Transfer the quinoa to a serving bowl and top with the cheese, pickles and tomatoes.

ORANGE CHICKEN & BROCCOLI

This simple Asian dish is reminiscent of your favorite takeout meal, without the junk ingredients! Orange juice and ginger provide the right amount of sweetness in an all-natural way. Serve over a bed of quinoa, rice or cauliflower rice! **AR**

SERVES: 4

1½ lb (680 g) chicken, cut into bite-size pieces

1½ tbsp (12 g) arrowroot starch

½ cup (120 ml) coconut aminos or gluten-free tamari

⅓ cup (80 ml) fresh orange juice

2 tsp (4 g) orange zest

¼ cup (60 ml) rice vinegar

2 tsp (10 ml) sesame oil

3 cloves garlic, crushed, divided

1 tbsp (8 g) finely chopped fresh ginger, divided

1 tsp crushed red pepper flakes (optional)

1 tbsp (15 ml) avocado oil

3 cups (273 g) chopped broccoli

4 cups cooked (740 g) quinoa, (744 g) rice or (440 g) cauliflower rice, for serving

2 tsp (5 g) sesame seeds, for garnish (optional)

2 tbsp (12 g) chopped green onion, for garnish (optional)

Place the chicken and arrowroot starch in a resealable plastic bag or lidded plastic container. Shake around until the chicken is well coated.

In a small bowl, whisk together the coconut aminos, orange juice and zest, vinegar, sesame oil, two-thirds of the garlic, two-thirds of the ginger and the red pepper flakes (if using).

Select sauté on the Instant Pot. Once hot, add the avocado oil and the remaining garlic and ginger. Stir, then add the chicken. Cook for 1 to 2 minutes, or until the chicken is slightly browned. Select cancel.

Pour the orange sauce on top of the chicken.

Secure the lid with the steam vent in the sealed position. Select manual or pressure, and cook on high pressure for 7 minutes.

Use a quick release. Remove the lid once the steam has been released, and toss in the chopped broccoli. Stir, then replace the lid. Let the broccoli steam and cook for another 3 to 4 minutes.

Serve over quinoa, rice or cauliflower rice, garnished with the sesame seeds and green onion (if using).

GF GLUTEN-FREE GRAIN-FREE

CHICKEN-BROCCOLI-CHEDDAR CASSEROLE

I grew up in the '80s with my mom's chicken casserole, which was loaded with a creamy mayo-based filling and topped with potato chips. Don't get me wrong, I loved it, but as an adult I wanted something a bit healthier for my family, with the same flavors. This casserole is inspired by that nostalgic classic, with a real-food spin. **ESV**

SERVES: 4

1 cup (237 ml) water

2½ cups (228 g) broccoli florets, cut into bite-size pieces

2 tbsp (28 g) grass-fed butter or ghee

1 medium yellow onion, finely diced

5 cloves garlic, chopped

2 large celery ribs with leaves, thinly sliced

2 medium carrots, peeled and finely diced

1 tsp sea salt

¼ cup (15 g) finely chopped fresh flat-leaf parsley, plus more for garnish

1 tbsp (4 g) finely chopped fresh dill

1 tsp finely chopped fresh thyme leaves

2 boneless, skinless chicken breasts

1 cup (237 ml) chicken or vegetable stock

1½ cups (345 g) sour cream

1½ cups (173 g) shredded cheddar cheese

Place the water in the Instant Pot and insert a steamer basket. Layer the broccoli florets in the steamer basket.

Secure the lid with the steam vent in the sealed position. Press manual and set on high pressure for 1 minute.

Once the timer sounds, press keep warm/cancel. Using an oven mitt, do a quick release. When the steam venting stops and the silver dial drops, carefully open the lid.

Immediately remove the steamer basket and broccoli, using caution because both are very hot. Set aside. Discard the water in the Instant Pot.

Place your healthy fat of choice in the Instant Pot and press sauté. Once the fat has melted, add the onion and sauté for 5 minutes, stirring occasionally. Then, add the garlic and sauté for 1 minute, stirring occasionally. Press keep warm/cancel.

Add the celery, carrots, salt, parsley, dill, thyme, chicken and stock to the Instant Pot, making sure the chicken is submerged in the liquid. Secure the lid with the steam vent in the sealed position. Press manual and set on high pressure for 9 minutes.

Once the timer sounds, press keep warm/cancel. Using an oven mitt, do a quick release. When the steam venting stops and the silver dial drops, carefully open the lid. With tongs, transfer the chicken to a plate or cutting board. Chop the chicken into bite-size chunks, then set aside.

Press sauté. Allow the liquid in the Instant Pot to come to a simmer; allow it to simmer for about 5 minutes, or until the liquid reduces. Return the chicken to the pot and add the broccoli, sour cream and cheese, quickly stirring until the sour cream and cheese are fully mixed in. Press keep warm/cancel. Taste for seasoning and adjust the salt to taste. Allow the casserole to rest for 10 minutes.

Serve immediately, garnished with chopped fresh parsley.

DAIRY-FREE   GF GLUTEN-FREE OPTION   GRAIN-FREE OPTION

SAUCY TURKEY TACOS

Taco Tuesday is my family's favorite night of the week! I make tacos many ways, and these stand out for their flavor and ease. Meal prep this ground turkey on a weekend and enjoy throughout the week! It works perfectly in a salad, wrapped in tortilla or on top of a bowl of rice or cauliflower rice. **AR**

SERVES: 6

2 tbsp (30 ml) avocado oil or olive oil

1 yellow onion, diced

2 lb (905 g) ground turkey

1 tbsp (8 g) chili powder

2 tsp (5 g) ground cumin

2 tsp (5 g) paprika

1½ tsp (8 g) sea salt

1 tsp dried oregano

1 tsp chipotle powder (optional)

1 (14.5-oz [411-g]) can fire-roasted tomatoes

1 (4-oz [115-g]) can diced green chiles

2 tbsp (32 g) tomato paste

2 tbsp (30 ml) cider vinegar

¾ cup (175 ml) water

¼ cup (10 g) fresh cilantro, for garnish

1 avocado, peeled, pitted and diced, for garnish

Tortillas, cooked rice or cauliflower rice, for serving (optional)

Select sauté on the Instant Pot, set to "medium," if possible. Once the pot is hot, coat the bottom of the pot with the oil. Add the onion and sauté for 2 to 3 minutes, then add the ground turkey. Cook until the turkey is mostly cooked through, about another 8 minutes. Select cancel.

In a small bowl, mix together the chili powder, cumin, paprika, salt, oregano and chipotle powder (if using). Add the spice mixture to the turkey and give the mixture a good stir.

Add the fire-roasted tomatoes, green chiles, tomato paste, vinegar and water to the pot and stir.

Secure the lid with the steam vent in the sealed position. Select manual or pressure, and cook on high pressure for 7 minutes.

Use a quick release.

Serve hot with fresh cilantro, avocado and tortillas, rice or cauliflower rice (if using).

GARLIC-LEMON-ROSEMARY TURKEY BREAST

Sometimes, during off-holiday times, I get a hankering for a big old slice of turkey breast. Mainly for sandwiches, but still. I don't want to roast an entire turkey for a few sandwiches. I discovered that even though it may not look as if it will fit, you can quickly cook an entire turkey breast in the Instant Pot. Not only is it quick, it is so juicy and infused with all that garlic and lemon flavor. If you are using the turkey as a main course, I highly recommend the added step of crisping the skin in the oven. If you just want a sandwich, slice up that turkey breast and quiet that craving. **SB**

SERVES: 4 to 6

1 tbsp (15 ml) extra-virgin olive oil

2 tbsp (28 g) unsalted butter, at room temperature

1 (3-lb [1.4-kg]) turkey breast, spine and neck removed

2 tbsp (3 g) chopped fresh rosemary

Zest of 1 lemon

2 cloves garlic, grated

Salt

Freshly ground black pepper

1 cup (237 ml) water

Pour the olive oil onto the turkey. Rub the butter all over and even under the skin of the turkey breast.

Sprinkle the rosemary, lemon zest, garlic and generous amounts of salt and pepper all over the turkey breast. Use your hands to rub the seasonings all over the turkey and under the skin.

Pour the water into the Instant Pot and insert the steam trivet. Place the turkey on top of the trivet, breast/skin side up and bone side down.

Secure the lid with the steam vent in the sealed position. Press pressure cook until the display light is beneath high pressure. Use the plus and minus buttons to adjust the time until the display reads "25 minutes."

If you are choosing to crisp up the skin, preheat the oven to 450°F (230°C) during this time. Line a large baking sheet with foil.

When the timer sounds, quick release the pressure. Remove the lid. Use two sets of tongs to carefully transfer the turkey breast to the prepared baking sheet.

Bake the turkey breast in the oven until the skin is nice and golden and crispy, about 15 minutes.

Let the turkey rest for 10 minutes before removing the meat from the bones and then slicing.

DAIRY-FREE OPTION GLUTEN-FREE GRAIN-FREE PALEO

SHREDDED HONEY-GARLIC CHICKEN

This Asian-inspired shredded chicken is similar to teriyaki chicken, but this version has a lot more honey-garlic flavor that coats the tender chicken perfectly. Salty, sweet and with a little bit of tang, this chicken is sure to be a family favorite. **ESV**

SERVES: 4 to 6

2 tbsp (28 g) grass-fed butter, ghee or avocado oil

1 medium yellow onion, thinly sliced

7 cloves garlic, finely chopped

½ tsp sea salt

1 tsp chili powder

1 tsp ground ginger

¼ cup (15 g) finely chopped fresh flat-leaf parsley, plus more for garnish (optional)

1 tsp finely chopped fresh thyme leaves

⅓ cup (80 ml) honey

¼ cup (60 ml) coconut aminos

2 tbsp (30 ml) cider vinegar

2 lb (905 g) boneless, skinless chicken breast

¾ cup (175 ml) chicken or veggie stock

1 scallion, white and light green parts only, thinly sliced, for garnish (optional)

Place your healthy fat of choice in the Instant Pot and press sauté. Once the fat has melted, add the onion and sauté, stirring occasionally, for 5 minutes, or until fragrant. Then, add the garlic and sauté for 1 minute, stirring occasionally. Press keep warm/cancel.

Add the salt, chili powder, ginger, parsley, thyme, honey, coconut aminos, vinegar, chicken and stock to the Instant Pot, giving the mixture a stir, making sure the chicken is submerged in the liquid.

Secure the lid with the steam vent in the sealed position. Press manual and set on high pressure for 10 minutes.

Once the timer sounds, press keep warm/cancel. Allow the Instant Pot to naturally pressure release for 15 minutes. Using an oven mitt, do a quick release. When the steam venting stops and the silver dial drops, carefully open the lid.

With tongs or a large slotted spoon, transfer the chicken to a plate or cutting board. Shred the chicken into bite-size chunks, then set aside.

Press sauté and allow the liquid in the pot to come to a simmer, then simmer for about 5 minutes, or until the liquid slightly thickens. Press keep warm/cancel. Add back the shredded chicken, give the mixture a stir and allow it to rest for 10 minutes.

Serve immediately, garnished with chopped fresh flat-leaf parsley and/or thinly sliced scallion (if using).

DAIRY-FREE   GLUTEN-FREE   GRAIN-FREE

CHICKEN SALTIMBOCCA
WITH DATES

Ever eaten bacon-wrapped dates? This is exactly like that, except with chicken. Sweet dates and salty prosciutto are a match made in heaven. I like to serve this over a big plate of noodles. The chicken cooks in the Instant Pot and makes the most perfect caramelized sauce. Instead of waiting to make those salty date appetizers, whip this together for a quick weeknight meal. **SB**

SERVES: 4

4 boneless, skinless chicken cutlets

Salt

Freshly ground black pepper

Big pinch of crushed red pepper flakes

4 to 6 slices prosciutto

2 tbsp (30 ml) extra-virgin olive oil

1 tsp red wine vinegar

½ cup (120 ml) low-sodium chicken stock

1 clove garlic, grated

1 tsp balsamic vinegar

½ tsp light brown sugar

1 cup (150 g) chopped pitted dates

3 sprigs thyme

Chili-Garlic Bow Ties (page 126), to serve (optional)

Season the chicken with salt, black pepper and red pepper flakes. Wrap the chicken in prosciutto.

Press sauté on the Instant Pot and wait 2 minutes for the pot to heat. Add the oil to the pot. Sauté the chicken for 3 minutes per side.

When both sides of the chicken are crisped, remove from the pot and transfer to a plate.

Deglaze the pan with the red wine vinegar and chicken stock. Scrape any bits off the bottom of the pot.

Press cancel. Add the garlic to the pot. Stir to combine. Stir in the balsamic vinegar, brown sugar, dates and thyme. Nestle the chicken breasts back into the pot.

Secure the lid with the steam vent in the sealed position. Press pressure cook until the display light is beneath high pressure. Use the plus and minus buttons to adjust the time until the display reads "5 minutes."

When the timer sounds, quick release the pressure. Remove the thyme sprigs. Transfer the chicken to plates, then top with the dates and sauce. Add more salt, black pepper or red pepper flakes, if needed. Serve with Chili-Garlic Bow Ties, if desired.

DAIRY-FREE GLUTEN-FREE GRAIN-FREE OPTION

COCONUT RED CURRY SHRIMP

For those evenings when you crave a restaurant-quality dinner without having to leave your house, this shrimp dish will do the trick! Its creamy, flavorful Thai curry sauce is perfectly spiced without being spicy. And so easy to make in the Instant Pot! **AR**

SERVES: 6

1 (13.5-oz [400-ml]) can plus ¼ cup (60 ml) coconut milk, divided

1 tsp ground cumin

1 tsp paprika

2 tsp (4 g) curry powder

3 tbsp (45 ml) fresh lime juice

1½ tsp (9 g) sea salt, divided, plus more to taste

1 tbsp (8 g) grated fresh ginger, divided

3 cloves garlic, minced, divided

2 lb (905 g) large shrimp, peeled and deveined

2 tbsp (30 ml) coconut oil or olive oil

1 small white onion, diced

1 (28-oz [800-g]) can diced tomatoes

3 tbsp (45 g) Thai red curry paste

⅓ cup (13 g) chopped fresh cilantro, for garnish (optional)

4 cups (744 g) cooked rice or (440 g) cauliflower rice, for serving

In a large bowl, combine ¼ cup (60 ml) coconut milk and the cumin, paprika, curry powder, lime juice, ½ teaspoon of the salt, 1 teaspoon of the ginger and one-third of the garlic. Whisk together, then add the shrimp. Toss to coat and let sit while you prepare the sauce.

Select sauté on the Instant Pot. Once hot, coat the bottom of the pot with the coconut oil. Add the onion, remaining ginger and remaining garlic. Sauté for a few minutes, then select cancel. Add the tomatoes, curry paste, the remaining 13.5 ounces (400 ml) of coconut milk and the remaining teaspoon of salt.

Secure the lid with the steam vent in the sealed position. Select manual or pressure, and cook on high pressure for 7 minutes.

Use a quick release, and remove the lid once the steam has been released.

Select cancel, then the sauté function. Toss in the shrimp, plus its marinade.

Simmer until the shrimp is cooked through and no longer pink, 2 to 5 minutes. Serve, garnished with chopped fresh cilantro (if using) and salt to taste, over rice or cauliflower rice.

CHICKEN CACCIATORE

This hearty dish could not be more nutritious! It's packed with vegetables and herbs, but still maintains a robust and comfort food flavor that makes everyone happy. This traditional Italian dish is generally served over pasta, but it is also delicious with a bed of vegetable noodles. **AR**

SERVES: 8

1 tsp salt, plus more to season chicken

Freshly ground black pepper

2 lb (905 g) chicken breast or thighs

2 tbsp (30 ml) avocado oil or extra-virgin olive oil, plus more if needed

1 medium yellow onion, diced

2 cloves garlic, minced

1 tsp dried oregano

1 tsp paprika

1 tsp dried rosemary

1 tsp dried thyme

1 (14.5-oz [411-g]) can diced or pureed tomatoes

3 tbsp (48 g) tomato paste

¼ cup (60 ml) red wine vinegar

1 large green bell pepper, seeded and diced

8 oz (225 g) sliced mushrooms

½ cup (150 g) diced marinated artichoke hearts

¼ cup (60 ml) chicken stock

½ cup (120 ml) red wine

1 tbsp (2 g) fresh thyme, for garnish (optional)

2 tbsp (3 g) fresh basil, for garnish (optional)

Cooked pasta or vegetable noodles, for serving

Select sauté on the Instant Pot. While it heats, salt and pepper the chicken. Cover the bottom of the pot with the oil, then add the chicken. Cook on each side for 1 to 2 minutes. Remove the chicken from the pot. Add more oil, if needed, then toss in the onion. Cook for about 2 minutes, then add the garlic and cook for another minute. Select cancel.

In a small bowl, mix together the oregano, paprika, rosemary, thyme and salt. Add the tomatoes, tomato paste and vinegar. Give it a quick stir and transfer the mixture to the Instant Pot.

Top the sauce with the chicken and the bell pepper, mushrooms and artichoke hearts. Cover the mixture with the stock and wine.

Secure the lid with the steam vent in the sealed position. Select manual, and cook on high pressure for 8 minutes.

Use a quick release. Once the steam is completely released, remove the lid and stir.

You can let the dish sit for several minutes on warm, so that it thickens up. Or serve immediately with thyme or basil, if desired, over pasta or vegetable noodles.

SIDES

GF GLUTEN-FREE GRAIN-FREE

LOADED MASHED CAULIFLOWER

My kids will gobble up their cauliflower with this recipe and the adults love it just as much. It's a great potluck dish since it still tastes great at room temperature. It's great for keto followers, too! **KB**

SERVES: 6

½ lb (225 g) bacon

1 cup (237 ml) water

2 medium heads cauliflower, cut into florets and core removed

1½ cups (173 g) shredded sharp cheddar cheese, divided

4 tbsp (55 g) unsalted butter, at room temperature

½ cup (120 ml) heavy cream

2 green onions, chopped

Press sauté to preheat the Instant Pot. When the word "hot" appears on the display, add the bacon. Cook until the bacon is browned and crispy, then remove it with a slotted spoon and place on paper towels to drain any excess fat. Press cancel to turn off the Instant Pot. Discard the drippings and wipe the pot clean.

Pour the water into the pot and insert a steamer basket. Place the cauliflower in the steamer basket.

Secure the lid with the steam vent in the sealed position. Press manual and immediately adjust the timer to 4 minutes. Check that the display light is beneath high pressure.

When the timer sounds, quick release the pressure and carefully remove the lid. Carefully transfer the cauliflower to a large bowl and mash until very smooth. Add 1 cup (115 g) of the shredded cheese plus the butter and cream, stirring to combine.

Place the cauliflower mixture into a 7 x 11–inch (18.5 x 28–cm) baking dish. Sprinkle the remaining ½ cup (58 g) of cheese on top, the broil until the cheese is melted, about 5 minutes. Crumble the bacon and sprinkle over the top along with the green onions.

WHIPPED CELERY ROOT-CAULIFLOWER MASH
WITH CARAMELIZED ONION

A comforting alternative to mashed potatoes, this smooth veggie-packed mash gets topped with caramelized onions. While perfect on its own, it's also delicious topped with homemade Nourishing Mushroom Gravy (page 488). **ESV**

SERVES: 6 to 8

6 tbsp (85 g) grass-fed butter or ghee, divided

1 yellow onion, sliced

¾ tsp sea salt, divided

1 cup (237 ml) water

4 small celery roots, peeled and cut into large cubes

1 small head cauliflower, cut into florets

2 small parsnips, peeled and cut into large cubes

2 tbsp (30 ml) chicken or vegetable stock, or bone broth

Leaves from 2 sprigs thyme

½ tsp garlic granules or powder

Place 2 tablespoons (28 g) of your healthy fat of choice in the Instant Pot and press sauté. Once the fat has melted, add the onion and ¼ teaspoon of the salt and sauté, stirring occasionally, for 7 minutes, or until the onion is light golden brown and caramelized. Press keep warm/cancel, transfer the caramelized onion to a bowl or plate, then set aside.

Pour the water into the Instant Pot and insert a steamer basket. Layer the celery roots, cauliflower and parsnips in the steamer basket.

Secure the lid with the steam vent in the sealed position. Press manual and set on high pressure for 5 minutes.

Once the timer sounds, press keep warm/cancel. Allow the Instant Pot to release pressure naturally for 10 minutes. Using an oven mitt, do a quick release. If there is any steam left over, allow it to release until the silver dial drops, then carefully open the lid.

Using a large slotted spoon, carefully remove the vegetables and place them in a blender or food processor. Add the remaining 4 tablespoons (57 g) of your healthy fat of choice plus the stock, thyme, remaining ½ teaspoon of salt and the garlic granules. Pulse or blend for 30 seconds to 1 minute, or until completely smooth.

Serve the mash immediately, topped with the reserved caramelized onions.

NOTE: Heavy cream can be substituted for the stock for a creamier mash.

DAIRY-FREE GLUTEN-FREE GRAIN-FREE

CORNED BEEF & CABBAGE SLAW

This is a recipe I love to make and keep in the fridge for easy lunches all week long. Corned beef gets so tender in the Instant Pot and it tastes just like a Reuben! You could even put some between a few slices of rye bread; it makes a killer grilled sandwich. **KB**

SERVES: 6

1 cup (237 ml) beef stock

3 lb (1.4 kg) corned beef

1¼ cups (295 g) mayonnaise

2 tsp (10 ml) cider vinegar

¼ tsp celery seeds

1 small head green cabbage, sliced thinly, core removed

1 cup (110 g) diced Swiss cheese

In the Instant Pot, combine the beef stock and the corned beef along with the contents of its seasoning packet.

Secure the lid with the steam vent in the sealed position. Press manual and immediately adjust the timer to 85 minutes. Check that the display light is beneath high pressure.

When the timer sounds, quick release the pressure and carefully remove the lid. Remove the corned beef and place on a cutting board to cool.

Meanwhile, in a small bowl, mix together the mayonnaise, vinegar and celery seeds. Chop the corned beef into bite-size pieces. In a large bowl, combine the beef, mayonnaise mixture, cabbage and cheese and stir.

Refrigerate for at least 1 hour before serving.

CARAMELIZED ONION & VEGGIE-PACKED STUFFING

Who doesn't love stuffing?! It's one of those classic dishes that everyone seems to love, especially for the holidays. This version is brimming with veggies and a touch of seasonal fruit for a little sweetness. Making your stuffing in the Instant Pot is so easy and as a bonus, during the holidays, it will free up the oven space for other cooking and baking. **ESV**

SERVES: 6 to 8

1 (1-lb [455-g]) loaf gluten-free sourdough bread, cubed

6 tbsp (85 g) grass-fed butter, ghee or avocado oil, plus more for casserole dish

1 small yellow onion, diced

2 celery ribs, diced

1 small fennel bulb, diced

½ cup (50 g) cauliflower rice

2 cloves garlic, finely chopped

1 small sweet apple, cored, peeled and diced (I like Fuji, Gala or Honeycrisp apples)

¼ cup (30 g) dried cranberries or raisins (optional)

1 tbsp (3 g) chopped fresh sage

1 tbsp (2 g) chopped fresh thyme

1 tbsp (4 g) chopped fresh flat-leaf parsley

1¼ tsp (8 g) sea salt

1 cup (237 ml) chicken or vegetable stock, or bone broth

1 cup (237 ml) water

Toast the bread cubes: You can do this on a dry baking sheet in a 350°F (180°C) oven for 25 minutes. Transfer the toasted bread cubes to a very large bowl and set aside.

Use your healthy fat of choice to grease a 1½-quart (1.5-L) casserole dish that fits inside the Instant Pot. Set it aside.

Place your healthy fat of choice in the Instant Pot and press sauté. Once the fat has melted, add the onion and sauté, stirring occasionally, for 7 minutes, or until light golden brown. Add the celery and fennel and sauté, stirring occasionally, for 3 minutes. Add the riced cauliflower and garlic and sauté, stirring constantly, for 2 minutes. Add the apple, dried fruit (if using), sage, thyme, parsley and salt, stirring just to combine. Press keep warm/cancel.

Carefully transfer the vegetable mixture and stock into the bowl that contains the toasted bread cubes and gently stir to combine for about 30 seconds, allowing some of the stock to absorb into the bread. Pour the stuffing mixture into the prepared casserole dish, patting down as needed. Cover the casserole dish with its glass lid. If your casserole dish doesn't have a glass lid, you can cover the top of the dish with unbleached parchment paper, then top it with foil and secure it around the edges.

Pour the water into the Instant Pot and insert the steam trivet. Carefully set the covered casserole dish on top of the trivet.

Secure the lid with the steam vent in the sealed position. Press manual and set on high pressure for 23 minutes.

Once the timer sounds, press keep warm/cancel. Using an oven mitt, do a quick release. When the steam venting stops and the silver dial drops, carefully open the lid.

Using an oven mitt, carefully remove the casserole dish and place on a wire rack. Carefully remove the hot lid without dripping any condensation onto the stuffing. Allow the stuffing to cool on a wire rack at room temperature for 20 minutes before serving.

GF GLUTEN-FREE GRAIN-FREE

HERB BUTTERNUT SQUASH & ROOT VEGETABLES

Looking for an easy hands-off side dish for dinner? You'll love this hearty vegetable recipe! Pairs perfectly with anything from the grill, a roasted chicken or even a steak. This medley of fall vegetables can be enjoyed any time of the year. **AR**

SERVES: 4

2 tbsp (28 g) unsalted butter

2 cloves garlic, minced

1 cup (140 g) cubed butternut squash (1" [2.5-cm] cubes)

1 cup (130 g) sliced carrot

1 cup (150 g) cubed turnip (1" [2.5-cm] cubes)

1 large fennel bulb, cut into ½" (1.3-cm) pieces

¼ tsp baking soda

1 tbsp (1.7 g) herbes de Provence

½ tsp sea salt, plus more to taste

¾ cup (175 ml) chicken or vegetable stock

1 tbsp (2 g) fresh rosemary, for garnish

1 tbsp (2 g) fresh thyme, for garnish

Select sauté on the Instant Pot. Once hot, add the butter and garlic. Cook for about 1 minute, then add the butternut squash. Cook for another 4 to 5 minutes, or until the squash is lightly browned. Select cancel.

Add the carrot, turnip and fennel. Sprinkle the vegetables with the baking soda, herbes de Provence and salt. Pour the stock on top of the vegetable mixture.

Secure the lid with the steam vent in the sealed position. Select manual, and cook on high pressure for 6 minutes.

Use a quick release, and ensure all the steam is released before removing the lid.

Serve warm, garnished with the rosemary, thyme and additional salt to taste.

GF
GLUTEN-FREE

CREAMY MUSHROOM RISOTTO

The bold flavor of mushrooms permeates this creamy risotto. Spice up your rice fancy style with herbs, dry white wine and caramelized mushrooms and enjoy as a side next to your favorite main course or as is— just grab yourself a bowl, a big spoon and enjoy! **ESV**

SERVES: 6 to 8

4 tbsp (55 g) grass-fed butter or ghee, divided

1 medium yellow onion, diced

1½ lb (680 g) mushrooms, woody ends removed, thinly sliced

5 cloves garlic, finely chopped

½ cup (120 ml) dry white wine

1 cup (195 g) uncooked arborio or other short-grain white rice

1 large celery rib with leaves, thinly sliced

1 tsp sea salt

2 cups (475 ml) chicken or vegetable stock

¼ cup (60 ml) heavy cream

½ cup (40 g) shredded Parmesan cheese, plus more for garnish

¼ cup (15 g) finely chopped fresh flat-leaf parsley, plus more for garnish

1 tsp finely chopped fresh thyme leaves

Place 2 tablespoons (28 g) of your healthy fat of choice in the Instant Pot and press sauté. Once the fat has melted, add the onion and mushrooms and sauté, stirring occasionally, for 7 minutes, or until caramelized. Then, add the garlic and sauté for 1 minute, stirring occasionally. Add the wine and deglaze the pot, scraping up any browned bits with a wooden spoon. Add the rice, then give everything a stir to combine, stirring for 1 minute. Press keep warm/cancel.

Add the celery, salt and stock, then give everything a quick stir.

Secure the lid with the steam vent in the sealed position. Press manual and set on high pressure for 6 minutes.

Once the timer sounds, press keep warm/cancel. Allow the Instant Pot to naturally pressure release for 10 minutes. Using an oven mitt, do a quick release. When the steam venting stops and the silver dial drops, carefully open the lid.

Add the cream, the remaining 2 tablespoons (28 g) of your healthy fat, and the Parmesan, parsley and thyme, then quickly stir until the cream and Parmesan are fully mixed in. Allow the mixture to rest for 10 minutes.

Serve immediately, garnished with shredded Parmesan and chopped fresh flat-leaf parsley.

GF
GLUTEN-FREE

PARMESAN-LEMON CHICKEN RISOTTO

This Italian creamy rice dish is full of the traditional risotto ingredients, including butter, onion, dry white wine and Parmesan. To make this more filling, bites of chicken are added with a little extra flavor from vibrant lemon zest and fresh parsley. It's the perfect cozy side! **ESV**

SERVES: 6 to 8

4 tbsp (55 g) grass-fed butter or ghee, divided

1 lb (455 g) boneless, skinless chicken breast, cut into 1" (2.5-cm) cubes

1 medium yellow onion, diced

5 cloves garlic, finely chopped

½ cup (120 ml) dry white wine

2 tbsp (30 ml) fresh lemon juice

1 cup (195 g) uncooked arborio or other short-grain white rice

1 tsp sea salt

2 cups (475 ml) chicken or vegetable stock

¼ cup (60 ml) heavy cream

¾ cup (75 g) shredded Parmesan cheese, plus more for garnish

¼ cup (15 g) finely chopped fresh flat-leaf parsley, plus more for garnish

Zest of 2 small lemons

Place 2 tablespoons (28 g) of your healthy fat of choice in the Instant Pot and press sauté. Once the fat has melted, add the chicken and sauté, stirring occasionally, for 5 to 7 minutes, or until the pink color is gone. Transfer to a plate and set aside.

Add the onion and sauté, stirring occasionally, for 7 minutes, or until caramelized. Then, add the garlic and sauté for 1 minute, stirring occasionally. Add the wine and lemon juice to deglaze the pot, scraping up any browned bits with a wooden spoon. Add the rice, then give everything a stir to combine, stirring for 1 minute. Press keep warm/cancel.

Add the salt, stock and sautéed chicken, then give everything a quick stir.

Secure the lid with the steam vent in the sealed position. Press manual and set on high pressure for 6 minutes.

Once the timer sounds, press keep warm/cancel. Allow the Instant Pot to naturally pressure release for 10 minutes. Using an oven mitt, do a quick release. When the steam venting stops and the silver dial drops, carefully open the lid.

Add the cream, the remaining 2 tablespoons (28 g) of your healthy fat, and the Parmesan, parsley and lemon zest, then quickly stir until the cream and Parmesan are fully mixed in. Allow the mixture to rest for 10 minutes.

Serve immediately, garnished with shredded Parmesan and chopped fresh flat-leaf parsley.

GF
GLUTEN-FREE

CREAMY & EXTRA-CHEESY POLENTA

Creamy polenta has been one of my favorites since I was a kid. I used to eat it at my Italian neighbors' home often and my dad used to make it a lot as I got older. Similar to grits, this Italian version is a thick, lovely porridge made with coarsely ground cornmeal. Between its cheese, lots of butter and a bit of cream, you're going to be enjoying every bite. **ESV**

SERVES: 4

4 cups (946 ml) filtered water

½ cup (120 ml) chicken or vegetable stock

1 cup (160 g) polenta (not quick-cooking)

1 tsp sea salt

½ tsp dried thyme

4 tbsp (55 g) grass-fed butter

¼ cup (60 ml) heavy cream

6 oz (170 g) shredded Parmesan cheese, plus more for garnish

¼ cup (30 g) shredded mild cheddar cheese

Press sauté on the Instant Pot and combine the water, stock, polenta, salt and thyme in the pot, whisking to mix the polenta into the water.

Secure the lid with the steam vent in the sealed position. Press manual and set on high pressure for 9 minutes.

Once the timer sounds, press keep warm/cancel. Using an oven mitt, do a quick release. When the steam venting stops and the silver dial drops, carefully open the lid.

Add the butter, cream and shredded cheeses, stirring until fully incorporated.

Transfer to a serving bowl and garnish with grated or shredded Parmesan cheese.

GF
GLUTEN-FREE GRAIN-FREE

STEAMED ARTICHOKES
WITH LEMON-GARLIC BUTTER

Although artichokes may seem intimidating to cook at first glance, the Instant Pot makes it so easy! These gorgeous vegetables are so nutritious, packed with antioxidants and taste absolutely delicious when the hearts are dipped in a lemon-garlic butter. These make a perfect starter dish or veggie side to a spring dinner. **AR**

SERVES: 4

4 medium to large globe artichokes

Juice of 1 lemon, divided

1 cup (237 ml) water

1 tsp Dijon mustard

1 clove garlic

¼ tsp sea salt, plus more to taste

4 tbsp (55 g) unsalted butter or ghee, melted

Prepare your artichokes. Remove the outer leaves, trim about ½ inch (1.3 cm) from the top and remove the stem so each artichoke can sit upright. Brush each artichoke with lemon juice, reserve the remaining lemon juice and set aside.

Pour the water into the Instant Pot and insert the steam trivet. Arrange the artichokes, stem side down, on the trivet so they sit upright.

Secure the lid with the steam vent in the sealed position. Select manual or pressure, and cook on high pressure for 12 to 15 minutes (12 for medium artichokes, 15 for large ones). Use a quick release.

Meanwhile, prepare the lemon-garlic butter. In a small bowl, stir the Dijon, remaining lemon juice, garlic and salt into the butter.

Serve warm with the lemon-garlic butter on the side for dipping. Sprinkle with additional salt to taste.

GF
GLUTEN-FREE

GRAIN-FREE
OPTION

CHEESY HERB SCALLOPED POTATOES

These scalloped potatoes are the perfect side dish to serve alongside an elegant dinner, holiday meal or simply when you want some comfort food. Rich and creamy, they're seasoned with herbs and lots of shredded cheese. **ESV**

SERVES: 6 to 8

Grass-fed butter, ghee or olive oil, for casserole dish

5 medium russet potatoes, peeled and thinly sliced

¾ cup (175 ml) heavy cream

¾ cup (175 ml) milk

½ cup (115 g) sour cream

2 tbsp (15 g) gluten-free all-purpose flour blend or grain-free cassava flour

1 tbsp (4 g) chopped fresh flat-leaf parsley

1 tsp sea salt

1½ tsp (5 g) garlic granules or garlic powder

1 tsp dried thyme

1¾ cups (140 g) shredded Italian cheese blend (equal parts provolone, Romano and Parmesan), divided

1½ cups (355 ml) water

Use your healthy fat of choice to grease a 1½-quart (1.5-L) casserole dish that fits inside the Instant Pot. Set aside.

Place the sliced potatoes in a large bowl. Set aside.

In another large bowl or large measuring cup, whisk together the cream, milk, sour cream, flour, parsley, salt, garlic granules and thyme until mostly combined (there will be a few small lumps; that's okay). Pour this mixture over the potatoes, then add 1½ cups (120 g) of the shredded cheese and give it a good stir to combine. Pour into the prepared casserole dish and sprinkle the top with the remaining ¼ cup (20 g) of shredded cheese. Cover the casserole dish with its glass lid. If your casserole dish doesn't have a glass lid, you can cover the top of the dish with unbleached parchment paper, then top it with foil and secure it around the edges.

Pour the water into the Instant Pot and insert the steam trivet. Carefully set the covered casserole dish on top of the trivet. Secure the lid with the steam vent in the sealed position. Press manual and set on high pressure for 50 minutes.

Once the timer sounds, press keep warm/cancel. Allow the Instant Pot to release pressure naturally for 15 minutes. Using an oven mitt, do a quick release. If there is any steam left over, allow it to release until the silver dial drops, then carefully open the lid.

Using an oven mitt, carefully remove the casserole dish and place on a wire rack to rest. If you prefer a golden brown cheesy top, place the uncovered casserole dish on a baking sheet and place in the oven under a preheated broiler for about 2 minutes, or just until the cheese becomes light golden brown.

Allow to rest for 20 minutes before serving.

DAIRY-FREE GLUTEN-FREE

GRAIN-FREE VEGAN

LEMON-GARLIC SMASHED POTATOES

Baby red potatoes with a lemon-garlic flavor make a delicious companion to any dinner! The potatoes are cooked perfectly (and lightning fast) in the Instant Pot, then finished off in the oven to get that crispy texture. **AR**

SERVES: 4

1½ lb (680 g) baby red potatoes

1 cup (237 ml) water

2 tbsp (30 ml) avocado oil or extra-virgin olive oil

3 cloves garlic, minced

½ tsp sea salt, plus more to taste

½ tsp freshly ground black pepper

2 tbsp (30 ml) fresh lemon juice

Turn on the oven to broil.

Wash and dry the potatoes. Pour the water into the Instant Pot and insert the steam trivet. Place the potatoes on the trivet.

Secure the lid with the steam vent in the sealed position. Select manual or pressure, and cook on high pressure for 6 minutes.

Use a quick release. Remove the potatoes and place on a large baking sheet. Using a glass or the back of a spoon, gently press down on the potatoes, or smash them.

In a small bowl, whisk together the oil and garlic. Brush over each of the potatoes, then sprinkle with salt and pepper.

Transfer the potatoes to the oven. Broil for 4 to 5 minutes, or until crispy.

Remove from the oven and drizzle with the lemon juice. Sprinkle with additional salt to taste. Serve hot.

GF GLUTEN-FREE GRAIN-FREE

FULLY LOADED MASHED POTATOES

Think: loaded potato skins but in mashed potato form—these fully loaded mashed potatoes are out of this world! The Instant Pot steams the potatoes perfectly, helping to make the most delicious mashed potatoes full of cheese, sour cream, crispy bacon bits and scallions. They're always a crowd-pleaser! **ESV**

SERVES: 4 to 6

1 cup (237 ml) water

5 medium russet potatoes, peeled and cut into 2" (5-cm) cubes

4 tbsp (55 g) grass-fed butter

1 cup (230 g) sour cream

½ cup (120 ml) milk or heavy cream

1 tsp sea salt

1 cup (115 g) shredded cheddar cheese

¾ cup (80 g) shredded Italian cheese blend (equal parts provolone, Romano and Parmesan)

6 oz (170 g) precooked crispy bacon or turkey bacon, crumbled

1 scallion, white and light green parts only, sliced

Pour the water into the Instant Pot and insert a steamer basket. Layer the potatoes in the steamer basket.

Secure the lid with the steam vent in the sealed position. Press manual and set on high pressure for 10 minutes.

Once the timer sounds, press keep warm/cancel. Using an oven mitt, do a quick release. When the steam venting stops and the silver dial drops, carefully open the lid.

Carefully remove the potatoes and steamer basket, setting the potatoes aside. Pour out and discard the water that remains in the pot, then return the potatoes to the pot; alternatively, transfer the potatoes to a very large bowl.

Add the butter, allowing it to melt over the potatoes. Once the butter has melted, add the sour cream, milk and salt, then use a potato masher to start mixing everything together—do not overmix, just mash until there are no more lumps. Gently fold in the cheeses, 4 ounces (115 g) of the crumbled crispy bacon bits and the scallions (or if you prefer, reserve the scallions for garnish only) until all of the cheese has melted into the hot potatoes and everything is incorporated; do not overmix.

Serve immediately, garnished with the remaining 2 ounces (55 g) of crumbled crispy bacon bits.

NOTES: If possible, use organic potatoes since potatoes are on the EWG's "Shopper's Guide to Pesticides in Produce" Dirty Dozen list.

Six ounces (170 g) of bacon ends up being about 6 slices. Look for quality, humanely raised, antibiotic-free, natural or organic bacon or turkey bacon.

GF GLUTEN-FREE GRAIN-FREE

BLUE CHEESE MASHED POTATOES

I love mashed potatoes, but they don't always have a lot of flavor. Blue cheese adds a wonderful flavor twist and they're so easy with the Instant Pot. And there's no peeling the potatoes or even draining them! **KB**

SERVES: 6

1 cup (237 ml) chicken stock

3 lb (1.4 kg) red potatoes, quartered

4 oz (115 g) cream cheese, softened

⅔ cup (150 g) unsalted butter, very soft

½ cup (120 ml) half-and-half or heavy cream, at room temperature

⅓ cup (40 g) crumbled blue cheese

Pour the chicken stock into the Instant Pot, then add the potatoes.

Secure the lid with the steam vent in the sealed position. Press manual and immediately adjust the timer to 8 minutes. Check that the display light is beneath high pressure.

When the timer sounds, quick release the pressure and carefully remove the lid. Add the cream cheese, butter and half-and-half. Mash with a potato masher until smooth. Stir in the blue cheese until just starting to melt.

Keep the potatoes on the warm setting until ready to serve.

GF GLUTEN-FREE   GRAIN-FREE

BUTTERY SOUR CREAM CABBAGE

This side dish is so simple and easy to prepare! It's a family recipe that my mom used to make for me when I was a little girl. With only a few ingredients, this tasty cabbage gets quickly steamed, then sautéed with butter, sour cream and sea salt. Top it with crumbled crispy bacon bits, if you'd like; otherwise, just devour on its own. **ESV**

SERVES: 4 to 6

1 cup (237 ml) water

1 medium-large green or savoy cabbage, sliced

4 tbsp (55 g) grass-fed butter

½ cup (115 g) sour cream

¾ tsp sea salt

4 oz (114 g) precooked crispy bacon or turkey bacon, crumbled, for garnish (optional)

Pour the water into the Instant Pot and insert a steamer basket. Layer the sliced cabbage in the steamer basket.

Secure the lid with the steam vent in the sealed position. Press manual and set on high pressure for 2 minutes.

Once the timer sounds, press keep warm/cancel. Using an oven mitt, do a quick release. When the steam venting stops and the silver dial drops, carefully open the lid.

Carefully remove the cabbage and steamer basket, setting the cabbage aside. Pour out and discard the water that remains in the pot.

Place the butter in the Instant Pot and press sauté. Once the butter has melted, return the cabbage to the pot and sauté for 1 minute, stirring occasionally. Add the sour cream and salt and sauté for 2 minutes, stirring occasionally. Press keep warm/cancel.

Serve immediately, garnished with the crumbled crispy bacon (if using).

NOTE: Four ounces (114 g) of bacon ends up being about 4 slices. Look for quality, humanely raised, antibiotic-free, natural or organic bacon or turkey bacon.

ASIAN GINGER-GARLIC BOK CHOY

Kale, spinach and chard are great, but other greens that are just as nourishing and delicious often get forgotten, such as bok choy. This beautiful leafy green is one of the most requested veggies in my home—yes, kids love it, too! We like to cook it quickly with traditional Asian flavors, which are the perfect complement for this veggie. **ESV**

SERVES: 4

3 tbsp (43 g) grass-fed butter or ghee

1 (¾-inch [2-cm]) piece fresh ginger, peeled and finely minced

3 cloves garlic, minced

¾ tsp sea salt

3 tbsp (45 ml) coconut aminos

½ cup (120 ml) filtered water

7 baby bok choy, cut in half down the middle

1 scallion, white and light green parts only, sliced on a bias

1 tsp toasted sesame oil, for garnish

Place your healthy fat of choice in the Instant Pot and press sauté. Once the fat has melted, add the ginger and garlic and sauté for 2 minutes, stirring occasionally. Press keep warm/cancel.

Add the salt, coconut aminos and water, then add the bok choy and scallion and give the mixture a gentle stir.

Secure the lid with the steam vent in the sealed position. Press manual and set on high pressure for 3 minutes.

Once the timer sounds, press keep warm/cancel. Allow the Instant Pot to release pressure naturally for 5 minutes. Using an oven mitt, do a quick release. If there is any steam left over, allow it to release until the silver dial drops, then carefully open the lid.

Serve immediately, drizzled with the toasted sesame oil.

SPAGHETTI SQUASH
WITH BROWNED BUTTER & GARLIC

When craving some yummy pasta with garlic, this spaghetti squash will do the trick! Such a simple lunch, or a fantastic accompaniment to marinara and meatballs. **AR**

SERVES: 2

1 (4-lb [1.8-kg]) spaghetti squash

½ tsp sea salt, plus more to taste

1 cup (237 ml) water

4 tbsp (55 g) unsalted butter

3 cloves garlic, minced

3 tbsp (15 g) shredded Parmesan cheese (optional)

Cut the spaghetti squash in half along its equator. Remove and discard the seeds and sprinkle the squash with the salt.

Pour the water into the Instant Pot and insert the steam trivet. Place the spaghetti squash, cut side up, on the trivet.

Secure the lid with the steam vent in the sealed position. Select manual or pressure, and cook on high pressure for 7 minutes.

Use a quick release, and ensure all the steam is released before removing the lid. Using tongs or pot holders, remove the spaghetti squash and let cool for a few minutes. Using a fork, slowly pull out the spaghetti squash strands and place in a bowl or plate.

Empty the water from the Instant Pot. Select sauté. Once hot, add the butter and cook for about 1 minute, or until lightly browned. Add the garlic and sauté for another 2 to 3 minutes, or until the butter is golden.

Pour the butter on top of the spaghetti squash. Sprinkle with additional salt to taste and Parmesan cheese (if using).

GF
GLUTEN-FREE
OPTION

V
VEGAN

ASIAN QUINOA

I made quinoa for years a few times a week on the stovetop, well before I owned an Instant Pot. Oh, how the Instant Pot makes things so much easier! This is a perfect side or lunch dish that you can make ahead and enjoy throughout the week. **AR**

SERVES: 2 to 3

1 cup (180 g) uncooked quinoa, rinsed

1½ cups (355 ml) water

½ tsp sea salt, plus more to taste

¼ cup (60 ml) avocado oil or extra-virgin olive oil

2 tbsp (30 ml) rice vinegar

2 tsp (10 ml) sesame oil

2 tsp (10 ml) soy sauce or tamari

½ tsp garlic powder

3 tbsp (24 g) diced green onion

1 cup (130 g) diced or matchstick-cut carrot

1 cup (150 g) seeded and diced red or orange bell pepper

¼ cup (10 g) chopped fresh cilantro

¼ cup (35 g) chopped almonds or peanuts (optional)

In the Instant Pot, combine the quinoa, water and salt.

Secure the lid with the steam vent in the sealed position. Select manual or high pressure, and cook on high pressure for 1 minute.

Use a natural release. After about 15 minutes, release any remaining steam and remove the lid.

Meanwhile, make the dressing: In a small bowl or jar, combine the avocado oil, vinegar, sesame oil, soy sauce and garlic powder. Give it a good stir or shake.

Once the quinoa is completely done cooking, transfer to a large bowl. Mix in the green onion, carrot, bell pepper and cilantro. Toss with the dressing.

Serve or store in the fridge for up to 5 days. Garnish with almonds or peanuts (if using) before serving.

CHIPOTLE BAKED BEANS

Here's my twist on traditional baked beans. The chipotle adds an irresistible smoky spiciness! I love how quickly you can make them in an Instant Pot. **KB**

SERVES: 6

2 cups (475 ml) water

1 medium onion, chopped

2 tsp (6 g) garlic powder

1 cup (250 g) barbecue sauce

¾ cup (110 g) light brown sugar

2 to 4 chipotle peppers, minced

1 lb (455 g) dried great northern beans

1 ham bone

In a medium bowl, whisk together the water, onion, garlic powder, barbecue sauce, brown sugar and chipotle peppers. Pour into the Instant Pot, then stir in the beans. Nestle the ham bone into the bean mixture.

Press sauté to preheat the Instant Pot. When the word "hot" appears on the display, press manual and immediately adjust the timer to 40 minutes. Check that the display light is beneath high pressure.

When the timer sounds, quick release the pressure and carefully remove the lid. Remove the ham bone and allow to cool slightly, then remove any meat from the bone and return it to the pot. Stir well and serve.

DAIRY-FREE OPTION   GLUTEN-FREE

GRAIN-FREE   PALEO

BACON BRUSSELS SPROUTS

Bacon and Brussels sprouts go so well together and they cook to perfection in the Instant Pot! This easy side dish tastes like Thanksgiving with the hints of garlic and vibrant fresh thyme. **ESV**

SERVES: 8 to 10

1 cup (237 ml) water

2 lb (905 g) Brussels sprouts, trimmed and halved

4 tbsp (55 g) grass-fed butter, ghee or avocado oil

3 cloves garlic, minced

1 tsp finely chopped fresh thyme leaves

1 tsp sea salt

4 oz (114 g) precooked crispy bacon or turkey bacon, crumbled

Place the water in the Instant Pot and insert a steamer basket. Layer the Brussels sprouts in the steamer basket.

Secure the lid with the steam vent in the sealed position. Press manual and set on high pressure for 2 minutes.

Once the timer sounds, press keep warm/cancel. Allow the Instant Pot to release pressure naturally for 10 minutes. Using an oven mitt, do a quick release. If there is any steam left over, allow it to release until the silver dial drops, then carefully open the lid.

Carefully remove the Brussels sprouts and steamer basket, setting the Brussels sprouts aside. Pour out and discard the water that remains in the pot.

Place your healthy fat of choice in the Instant Pot and press sauté. Once the fat has melted, add the garlic and thyme and sauté for 1 minute, stirring occasionally. Add the Brussels sprouts back to the pot along with the salt and sauté until they start to turn golden brown, about 4 minutes. Add the crumbled bacon and give everything a stir, then sauté for 1 minute to warm the bacon. Press keep warm/cancel.

Serve immediately.

NOTE: Four ounces (114 g) of bacon ends up being about 4 slices. Look for quality, humanely raised, antibiotic-free, natural or organic bacon or turkey bacon.

GF GLUTEN-FREE   GRAIN-FREE

CHEESY CAULIFLOWER AU GRATIN

I grew up loving the flavor of Gruyère cheese because my mom used it in fancier dishes that she'd make for company, such as in scalloped potatoes and veggie au gratins. While the ingredients were simple, this cheese made easy dishes seem gourmet and extra special. Gruyère shines as the star in this rich, delectable cauliflower au gratin. **ESV**

SERVES: 4 to 6

Grass-fed butter, ghee or avocado oil, for casserole dish

½ cup (115 g) cream cheese, softened

¼ cup (60 ml) milk or heavy cream

¾ cup (60 g) shredded Gruyère cheese, divided

½ cup (40 g) shredded Parmesan cheese, divided

¼ cup (28 g) shredded Swiss cheese, divided

1 tsp sea salt

½ tsp garlic granules or garlic powder

½ tsp dried thyme

2 tbsp (8 g) chopped fresh flat-leaf parsley, plus more for garnish (optional)

1 large head cauliflower, chopped into bite-size florets

1½ cups (355 ml) water

Use your healthy fat of choice to grease a 1½-quart (1.5-L) casserole dish that fits in the Instant Pot. Set aside.

In a very large bowl, combine the cream cheese and milk and give it a stir. Add three-quarters of the cheeses (reserving the rest) and the salt, garlic, thyme, parsley and cauliflower florets and gently toss until everything is combined. Transfer to the prepared casserole dish and sprinkle with the remaining quarter of the cheeses. Cover the casserole dish with its glass lid. If your casserole dish doesn't come with a glass lid, you can cover the top of the dish with unbleached parchment paper, then top it with foil and secure it around the edges

Pour the water into the Instant Pot and insert the steam trivet. Carefully set the covered casserole dish on the trivet.

Secure the lid with the steam vent in the sealed position. Press manual and set on high pressure for 10 minutes.

Once the timer sounds, press keep warm/cancel. Allow the Instant Pot to release pressure naturally for 15 minutes. Using an oven mitt, do a quick release. If there is any steam left over, allow it to release until the silver dial drops, then carefully open the lid.

Carefully remove the casserole dish from the Instant Pot and remove the lid. Place the casserole dish on a baking sheet and place in the oven under a preheated broiler for 2 to 3 minutes, just until the cheese becomes light golden brown, then remove from the broiler and allow to rest for 15 minutes before serving.

Serve as is or garnished with chopped fresh flat-leaf parsley.

DAIRY-FREE OPTION · GLUTEN-FREE (GF) · GRAIN-FREE · VEGAN OPTION (V)

SUMMER RATATOUILLE

Just being a little biased here; this is one of my favorite recipes of all time! I do love vegetables, and when flavored with a lemon-basil sauce and cooked perfectly, this ratatouille is out-of-this-world delicious. So easy to make with the Instant Pot! Although the title implies that you eat it during the summer, it can easily be made year-round. It does taste best when using vegetables picked at their prime! **AR**

SERVES: 6

⅓ cup (80 ml) avocado oil or olive oil, divided

1 large white onion, diced

⅓ cup (80 ml) fresh lemon juice

3 cloves garlic, minced

2 tbsp (32 g) tomato paste

1 cup (40 g) loosely packed fresh basil, plus more for garnish

2 tbsp (30 ml) white wine vinegar

1 tsp sea salt, plus more to taste

1 small eggplant, diced (see note)

2 medium zucchini, diced

2 medium yellow summer squash, diced

1 lb (455 g) cherry or grape tomatoes

3 tbsp (15 g) grated fresh Parmesan, for garnish (optional)

Select sauté on the Instant Pot, set to "medium," if possible. Coat the bottom of the pot with 2 tablespoons (30 ml) of the oil, then add the onion. Sauté for 3 minutes, or until translucent and fragrant. Select cancel.

Meanwhile, prepare the lemon-basil sauce: In a food processor, combine the remaining oil, lemon juice, garlic, tomato paste, basil, vinegar and salt. Pulse until smooth.

Place the eggplant, zucchini, squash and tomatoes in the Instant Pot. Pour the lemon-basil sauce over the vegetable mixture.

Secure the lid with the steam vent in the sealed position. Select manual or pressure, and cook on high pressure for 8 minutes.

Use a natural release.

Serve hot with Parmesan cheese (if using) and more basil for garnish, and additional salt to taste.

NOTE: Eggplants can have a bitter taste. To eliminate, slice the eggplant into chunks and sprinkle with sea salt. Let it sit for 5 to 10 minutes. The eggplant will "sweat." Use a paper towel to soak up the juice, to prevent the bitter taste.

GF

GLUTEN-FREE

SWEET HONEY CORN BREAD

I grew up eating corn bread often; it was one of those frugal foods that filled the belly but also tasted like incredible comfort food. It's such a versatile side that can go with lots of meals, such as chili, soups, stew and even hearty savory dishes and breakfast. This version is similar to the sweet one I grew up with, except it's gluten-free and made with healthier ingredients. **ESV**

SERVES: 8 to 10

6 tbsp (85 g) grass-fed butter, divided, plus more for casserole dish

6 tbsp (90 ml) light-colored honey, divided (see note)

2 cups (275 g) fine- or medium-ground cornmeal

1 tsp baking powder

1 tsp baking soda

½ tsp sea salt

1 large egg, beaten

1½ cups (345 g) sour cream

1½ cups (355 ml) water

Butter a 1½-quart (1.5-L) casserole dish that fits inside the Instant Pot and line the bottom of the dish with a circle of parchment paper. Set it aside.

In a small saucepan, melt together 4 tablespoons (55 g) of the butter and 4 tablespoons (60 ml) of honey over medium-low heat. Remove from the heat and set aside to cool.

In a medium bowl, combine the cornmeal, baking powder, baking soda and salt, then give it a stir. Set aside.

In a large bowl, combine the egg, melted butter mixture and sour cream, then stir well. Add the cornmeal mixture to the egg mixture and stir just until incorporated; do not overmix.

Pour the batter into the prepared casserole dish. Cover the casserole dish with its lid. If your casserole dish doesn't come with a glass lid, you can cover the top of the dish with unbleached parchment paper, then top it with foil and secure it around the edges.

Pour the water into the Instant Pot and insert the steamer trivet. Carefully set the covered casserole dish on the trivet.

Secure the lid with the steam vent in the sealed position. Press manual and set on high pressure for 37 minutes.

Once the timer sounds, press keep warm/cancel. Allow the Instant Pot to release pressure naturally for 15 minutes. Using an oven mitt, do a quick release. If there is any steam left over, allow it to release until the silver dial drops, then carefully open the lid.

While the corn bread is naturally releasing pressure, melt the remaining 2 tablespoons (28 g) of butter and 2 tablespoons (30 ml) of honey in a small saucepan. Remove from the heat and set aside.

Carefully lift the trivet and the casserole dish out of the Instant Pot. Use oven mitts or towels because the Instant Pot and dish will be extremely hot. Carefully remove the hot lid, taking care not to drip any of the condensation on the top of the bread. Test with a toothpick to make sure the center is fully cooked; no more than a few moist crumbs should be on the toothpick. If it needs more time, re-cover with the lid (make sure to wipe off any condensation first) and return to the Instant Pot to cook on manual for another 5 minutes, then do a quick pressure release.

Evenly pour the melted butter mixture over the top of the hot corn bread. Allow the corn bread to fully cool at room temperature sitting on top of the trivet (as a cooling rack). Gently run a knife around the edges of the corn bread to loosen it when you're ready to remove it from the dish. Turn the dish upside down on a plate to release the corn bread. Cut the corn bread into thick wedges and serve immediately. Enjoy it with extra pats of butter or even a drizzle of honey!

NOTE: I do not recommend using wildflower honey because it tends to be too overpowering in flavor. Instead, use a lighter-colored honey, such as clover.

GF
GLUTEN-FREE

DELECTABLE SWISS FONDUE

Hands down, fondue was my favorite thing that my mom made when I was a little girl. She made the best, better than any I've ever had at a restaurant! It wasn't something that we had often, but was more of a special-occasion food or a meal when we both just needed some comfort food. This is my mom's version — adapted to cook in the Instant Pot. **ESV**

SERVES: 4 to 6

1½ cups (165 g) shredded Gruyère cheese

1½ cups (165 g) shredded Emmental or Swiss cheese

1 cup (115 g) shredded white cheddar or Gouda cheese

2 tbsp (15 g) gluten-free all-purpose flour

1 cup (237 ml) milk

1 cup (237 ml) quality dry white wine

1 tbsp (15 ml) fresh lemon juice

1 tsp Dijon mustard

1 tsp garlic powder

¾ tsp sea salt

In a large bowl, combine the shredded cheeses and sprinkle the flour on the top. Use a spoon to stir until the cheeses are coated with the flour. Set aside.

Pour the milk and wine into the Instant Pot.

Secure the lid with the steam vent in the sealed position. Press manual and set on high pressure for 2 minutes.

Once the timer sounds, press keep warm/cancel. Using an oven mitt, do a quick release. When the steam venting stops and the silver dial drops, carefully open the lid.

Add the cheese mixture, lemon juice, Dijon, garlic powder and salt, whisking or stirring constantly until everything is fully incorporated and the cheeses have melted into a smooth fondue consistency. Allow to rest, uncovered, for 5 minutes before serving.

Stir and serve immediately with your favorite fondue dipping ingredients, such as cubed gluten-free bread or steamed and then blanched veggies, such as broccoli, cauliflower and so on.

NOTE: If you need to keep the fondue warm, keep it on the warming setting or if you need to quickly reheat the fondue, return the fondue to the Instant Pot and press sauté, stirring constantly until the mixture heats up.

QUICK & CRISPY BROCCOLINI

This title may be deceiving. It isn't really crispy fried broccolini. It is more like perfectly steamed broccolini topped with crispy panko bread crumbs that coat the broccolini, thanks to the Parmesan cheese. You still get that crispy bite that you would from baking or frying, but in half the time by using the Instant Pot. **SB**

SERVES: 4

1 cup (237 ml) water

1 lb (455 g) broccolini

½ cup (30 g) panko bread crumbs

1 tbsp (14 g) unsalted butter, at room temperature

½ tsp salt

¼ tsp freshly ground black pepper

¼ tsp smoked paprika

1 tsp fresh lemon juice

2 tbsp (5 g) finely grated fresh Parmesan cheese

Pour the water into the Instant Pot and insert the steam trivet. Place the broccolini on the trivet.

Secure the lid with the steam vent in the sealed position. Press steam. Use the plus and minus buttons to adjust the time until the display reads "1 minute."

While the broccolini steams, toast the panko bread crumbs in a small, dry skillet over medium heat for 2 minutes, stirring continuously to prevent burning.

When the timer sounds, quick release the pressure of the Instant Pot. Remove the lid and use tongs to transfer the broccolini to a bowl.

Toss the broccolini with the butter, salt, pepper, paprika and lemon juice. Transfer the broccolini to a serving platter.

Sprinkle the grated cheese on top of all the broccolini, then sprinkle the toasted bread crumbs on top.

SPINACH-ARTICHOKE-STUFFED MUSHROOMS

Everyone loves stuffed mushrooms served as an appetizer. They're great at parties or small gatherings, but they can also be served as a snack or side dish. These stuffed mushrooms cook very quickly in the Instant Pot and are overflowing with a classic spinach and artichoke filling. **ESV**

MAKES: 12 small mushrooms

12 cleaned small white button or cremini mushrooms, stems removed

2.5 oz (70 g) frozen chopped spinach, thawed and moisture squeezed out

1 oz (28 g) cream cheese, softened

¼ cup (30 g) shredded mozzarella cheese

¼ cup (20 g) shredded Parmesan cheese

Zest of 1 lemon

½ tsp sea salt

1 tsp garlic granules or garlic powder

1 small scallion, white and light green parts only, finely chopped

¼ cup (15 g) chopped fresh flat-leaf parsley

1 tsp dried dill

¼ tsp dried thyme

1 cup (237 ml) water

Place all the mushrooms, bottom up, on a cutting board or large plate.

In a large bowl, combine the thawed spinach, cream cheese, mozzarella, Parmesan, lemon zest, salt, garlic granules, scallion, parsley, dill and thyme, stirring well. Stuff each mushroom with a spoonful of the mixture—depending on the size of your mushrooms, this will be about 2 teaspoons (10 g) to 1 heaping tablespoon (15 g). Set aside.

Pour the water into the Instant Pot and insert the steam trivet or a steamer basket. Set the stuffed mushrooms on the trivet or in the steamer basket—12 should fit snugly; however, if there is not enough room based on the size of your mushrooms, you may need to do this in two batches.

Secure the lid with the steam vent in the sealed position. Press manual and set on high pressure for 5 minutes.

Once the timer sounds, press keep warm/cancel. Using an oven mitt, do a quick release. When the steam venting stops and the silver dial drops, carefully open the lid.

With tongs, carefully remove the stuffed mushrooms and transfer them to a serving plate.

Serve immediately.

NOTE: If you prefer a browned top, place the stuffed mushrooms on a baking sheet and place under a preheated broiler for 2 to 3 minutes, just until the filling becomes light golden brown, then remove from the broiler and serve immediately.

GF
GLUTEN-FREE   GRAIN-FREE   PALEO

BUTTERY HERBED CARROTS & PARSNIPS

Carrots and parsnips are a lovely pair and even more tempting when paired with herbs such as dill and thyme. This simple root veggie side dish cooks up in just seven minutes and is enjoyable served alongside any savory meat dish. **ESV**

SERVES: 4 to 6

1 cup (237 ml) water

4 large carrots, peeled and thickly sliced on the diagonal

3 medium parsnips, peeled and sliced on the diagonal

3 tbsp (43 g) grass-fed butter or ghee

2 cloves garlic, minced

1 tsp sea salt

1 tsp dried thyme

1 tsp dried dill

Pour the water into the Instant Pot and insert a steamer basket. Layer the carrots and parsnips in the steamer basket.

Secure the lid with the steam vent in the sealed position. Press manual and set on high pressure for 3 minutes.

Once the timer sounds, press keep warm/cancel. Using an oven mitt, do a quick release. When the steam venting stops and the silver dial drops, carefully open the lid.

Carefully remove the carrots and parsnips and steamer basket, setting the carrots and parsnips aside. Pour out and discard the water that remains in the pot.

Place your healthy fat of choice in the Instant Pot and press sauté. Once the fat has melted, add the garlic and sauté for 1 minute, stirring occasionally. Add the carrots and parsnips back to the pot along with the salt, thyme and dill. Give everything a stir, then sauté for 3 minutes, stirring occasionally. Press keep warm/cancel.

Serve immediately.

GARLIC-BUTTER-BACON GREEN BEANS

Grab some green beans when they're in season and make these well-seasoned, garlicky, buttered bacon beans. This is a wonderful dish to prepare to go alongside any meal. The warm green beans are also delicious on top of a salad! **ESV**

SERVES: 4 to 6

1 cup (237 ml) water

1½ lb (680 g) green beans, ends trimmed

3 tbsp (43 g) grass-fed butter or ghee

4 cloves garlic, minced

1 tsp sea salt

4 oz (114 g) precooked crispy bacon or turkey bacon, crumbled

Pour the water into the Instant Pot and insert a steamer basket. Layer the green beans in the steamer basket.

Secure the lid with the steam vent in the sealed position. Press manual and set on high pressure for 2 minutes.

Once the timer sounds, press keep warm/cancel. Allow the Instant Pot to release pressure naturally for 10 minutes. Using an oven mitt, do a quick release. If there is any steam left over, allow it to release until the silver dial drops, then carefully open the lid.

Carefully remove the green beans and steamer basket, setting the green beans aside. Pour out and discard the water that remains in the pot.

Place your healthy fat of choice in the Instant Pot and press sauté. Once the fat has melted, add the garlic and sauté for 2 minutes, stirring occasionally. Add the green beans back to the pot along with the salt and crumbled bacon. Give everything a stir, then sauté for 1 minute to warm the bacon. Press keep warm/cancel.

Serve immediately.

NOTE: Four ounces (114 g) of bacon ends up being about 4 slices. Look for quality, humanely raised, antibiotic-free, natural or organic bacon or turkey bacon.

GF GLUTEN-FREE **GRAIN-FREE**

GREEN BEANS
WITH BACON & WALNUTS

Let me introduce you to the hit at my last Thanksgiving dinner: tender green beans served with crispy bacon and walnuts. The beans are steamed inside the Instant Pot in the bacon fat and butter. Forget that green bean casserole; this is that indulgent side dish you need at your next gathering. **SB**

SERVES: 4

5 strips raw bacon, chopped

1 tbsp (14 g) unsalted butter

¼ cup (60 ml) low-sodium chicken stock

12 oz (340 g) washed and trimmed green beans

Salt

Freshly ground black pepper

2 oz (55 g) walnuts

Press sauté on the Instant Pot. Add the chopped bacon. Cook for 5 to 6 minutes, or until crispy. Remove the crisp bacon with a slotted spoon and transfer to a paper towel–lined plate.

Press cancel. Stir the butter and stock into the bacon fat. Use a wooden spoon to scrape up any browned bacon bits from the bottom of the pot.

Add the green beans to the pot. Season with salt and pepper to taste. Toss to evenly coat the beans.

Secure the lid with the steam vent in the sealed position. Press steam. Use the plus and minus buttons to adjust the time until the display reads "1 minute."

While the beans steam, heat a small, dry skillet over medium heat. Add the walnuts and toast them for 2 minutes. Remove from the heat and chop.

When the timer sounds, quick release the pressure. Remove the lid and toss the beans with tongs.

Transfer the beans and sauce to a plate. Top with the bacon and walnuts.

MEXICAN STREET CORN SALAD

DAIRY-FREE GLUTEN-FREE

If you've ever had Mexican street corn, you will love this salad. I like to slightly undercook the corn so it retains a bit of crunch that's perfect with the creamy dressing. **KB**

SERVES: 4

1 cup (237 ml) water

4 ears corn

2 tbsp (28 g) mayonnaise

Juice of ½ lime (start with half of the juice and add the rest if it needs more)

⅛ tsp ground chipotle pepper

¼ cup (10 g) chopped fresh cilantro

¼ cup (28 g) crumbled Cotija cheese

Coarse salt

Freshly ground black pepper

Pour the water into the Instant Pot and insert the steam trivet. Place the corn on the trivet.

Secure the lid with the steam vent in the sealed position. Press manual and adjust the timer to 3 minutes. Check that the display light is beneath high pressure.

When the timer sounds, quick release the pressure and carefully remove the lid. Allow the corn to cool completely.

Remove the kernels from the corn cobs and place in a medium bowl. In a small bowl, mix together the mayonnaise, lime juice, chipotle pepper, cilantro and cheese, seasoning to taste with salt and pepper. Mix into the cooked corn. Chill the salad for at least 30 minutes before serving.

DAIRY-FREE OPTION

GF GLUTEN-FREE

GRAIN-FREE

PALEO

V VEGAN OPTION

HERB-CITRUS BLISTERED OLIVES

These little bites are the perfect party food hors d'oeuvre! Who knew piping hot olives with hints of herbs and citrus could be so satisfying? This appetizer is so easy to put together plus everyone loves them; they'll be gone in no time! **ESV**

SERVES: 16

1 cup (237 ml) water

1 lb (455 g) any variety green olives

1 lb (455 g) any variety marinated black olives (not canned black olives)

2 lemons, sliced

1 orange, sliced

3 tbsp (43 g) grass-fed butter, ghee or avocado oil

4 cloves garlic, minced

2 tsp (2 g) fresh thyme leaves

1 tsp fresh rosemary leaves, finely chopped

2 tbsp (30 ml) pure maple syrup

Pour the water into the Instant Pot and insert the steamer basket. Layer the olives and citrus slices in the steamer basket.

Secure the lid with the steam vent in the sealed position. Press manual and set on high pressure for 1 minute.

Once the timer sounds, press keep warm/cancel. Using an oven mitt, do a quick release. When the steam venting stops and the silver dial drops, carefully open the lid.

Carefully remove the olives, citrus slices and steamer basket, setting the olives and citrus slices aside. Pour out and discard the water that remains in the pot.

Place your healthy fat of choice in the Instant Pot and press sauté. Once the fat has melted, add the garlic and sauté for 2 minutes, stirring occasionally. Add the olives and citrus slices back to the pot along with the thyme, rosemary and maple syrup. Give everything a stir, then sauté for 3 minutes, stirring occasionally. Press keep warm/cancel.

Serve immediately.

NOTE: A mixture of olives (more than two) can be used. Some great varieties to choose from are Picholine, Castelvetrano, Manzanilla, Liguria, Ponentine, Gaeta, Kalamata and Niçoise, among others. Look for pitted olives, if possible. Garlic-stuffed green olives are great, too!

GF
GLUTEN-FREE   GRAIN-FREE

SOUTHERN BUTTERED BACON DEVILED EGGS

Deviled eggs are a great protein-rich snack and fun appetizer when served at gatherings. You won't find any mayonnaise in these—sour cream is used instead—and this version has my southern grandma's special touch of adding melted butter to the yolk mixture. It adds the most delicious, creamy touch. **ESV**

MAKES: 24 deviled eggs

1 cup (237 ml) water

12 large eggs, preferably pasture-raised or organic

Lots of ice and cold water

¼ cup (60 g) sour cream

4 tbsp (55 g) grass-fed butter, melted and cooled

1 tbsp (11 g) Dijon mustard

¾ tsp sea salt

1 large celery rib with leaves, finely diced

1 scallion, white and light green parts only, finely sliced

5 tbsp (20 g) chopped fresh flat-leaf parsley

4 oz (114 g) precooked crispy bacon or turkey bacon, crumbled

Place the water in the Instant Pot and insert a steamer basket. Carefully layer the eggs into the steamer basket.

Secure the lid with the steam vent in the sealed position. Press manual and set on high pressure for 5 minutes.

While the eggs cook, prepare a large bowl of ice water for the eggs to have an ice bath. Set aside.

Once the timer sounds, press keep warm/cancel. Using an oven mitt, do a quick release. When the steam venting stops and the silver dial drops, carefully open the lid.

Carefully remove the eggs and steamer basket. Using a spoon or tongs, immediately place the eggs in the ice bath to stop the cooking, letting them soak and cool for at least 5 minutes.

When the eggs have cooled, peel them and slice them in half lengthwise, setting the halved eggs, yolk up, on a large plate. Using a teaspoon, scoop out the cooked yolks and place them in a large bowl. Add the sour cream, melted butter, Dijon and salt. Mix well, smashing the egg yolks with a fork and making sure no chunks are left. Next, add the celery, scallion, parsley and crumbled bacon, giving the mixture a good stir until everything is combined.

Use a teaspoon, a piping bag or a makeshift piping bag from a small resealable plastic bag with a corner cut off to fill the egg white halves until you have used up all of the egg yolk mixture.

Serve immediately or refrigerate and fully chill for later.

NOTE: Four ounces (114 g) of bacon ends up being about 4 slices. Look for quality, humanely raised, antibiotic-free, natural or organic bacon or turkey bacon.

GF GLUTEN-FREE   **✿** GRAIN-FREE

SAUSAGE DEVILED EGGS

You'll love this twist on deviled eggs. It's always the first thing to go at our summer barbecues. The sausage adds such an unexpected flavor! **KB**

SERVES: 4

2 tsp (10 ml) extra-virgin olive oil

½ (12-oz [340-g]) package chicken sausage, any flavor

1 cup (237 ml) water

1 dozen large eggs

⅓ cup (75 g) mayonnaise

¼ cup (60 g) sour cream

1 tsp Dijon mustard

½ tsp hot sauce

½ tsp coarse salt

Press sauté to preheat the Instant Pot. When the word "hot" appears on the display, add the oil, then the sausage. Cook until the sausage is lightly browned, about 5 minutes. Remove with a slotted spoon.

Pour the water into the pot and scrape up any browned bits from the bottom, then insert the steam trivet. Place the eggs on the trivet. Secure the lid with the steam vent in the sealed position. Press manual and immediately adjust the timer to 5 minutes. Check that the display light is beneath high pressure.

Once the timer sounds, allow the pressure to release naturally for 5 minutes, then quick release the pressure and carefully remove the lid. Run the eggs immediately under cold water and peel.

Slice the eggs in half lengthwise and remove the yolks. In a medium bowl, mix together the yolks, mayonnaise, sour cream, mustard, hot sauce and salt until very smooth, using a fork to vigorously break up the yolks, if necessary.

Fill each egg white half with a few pieces of sausage, then top with the yolk mixture. (I like to use a piping bag; it makes them so pretty.)

DAIRY-FREE OPTION   GLUTEN-FREE

GRAIN-FREE   PALEO   VEGAN OPTION

CITRUS BEETS

Beets are one of the easiest sides to make in the Instant Pot. They steam perfectly, making the outer skin so easy to peel off—this method is so much better than cooking them on the stovetop. This version is very simple, too, with just a hint of sweet orange. They're delicious served hot, but can also be served cold or room temperature to go with salads or other veggies. **ESV**

SERVES: 4 to 6

1 cup (237 ml) water

5 medium beets, about 2" (5 cm) in diameter, leaves removed

2 tbsp (28 g) grass-fed butter, ghee or avocado oil

¾ tsp sea salt

Zest of 1 orange

Juice of 1 orange

Pour the water into the Instant Pot and insert a steamer basket. Place the beets in the steamer basket.

Secure the lid with the steam vent in the sealed position. Press manual and set on high pressure for 20 minutes.

Once the timer sounds, press keep warm/cancel. Allow the Instant Pot to release pressure naturally for 15 minutes. Using an oven mitt, do a quick release. If there is any steam left over, allow it to release until the silver dial drops, then carefully open the lid.

Carefully remove the beets and steamer basket, setting the beets aside on a cutting board or large plate. Pour out and discard the water that remains in the pot.

Slice off the tops of the beets and carefully slide or cut off the skin—it should come off very easily—then discard the tops and peeled-off skin. Using a sharp knife, slice the beets into round slices about ¼ inch (6 mm) thick.

Place your healthy fat of choice in the Instant Pot and press sauté. Once the fat has melted, add the beets back to the pot along with the salt and the orange zest and juice, gently stirring occasionally for 2 minutes to warm the citrus. Press keep warm/cancel.

Serve immediately.

NOTE: If you're using larger beets, you're going to need to increase the cook time anywhere from 25 minutes for large beets to 35 minutes for extra-large beets.

DESSERT

GF GLUTEN-FREE · **GRAIN-FREE**

SPICED PUMPKIN CHEESECAKE

Pumpkin pie and cheesecake lovers, this special dessert is for you! Thick and creamy cheesecake joins the classic spices and flavors of pumpkin pie in this delectable treat that the Instant Pot cooks perfectly every single time. **ESV**

SERVES: 8 to 10

CRUST

2 tbsp (28 g) grass-fed butter or ghee, melted, plus more butter for pan

2 tbsp (19 g) maple sugar

1 cup (100 g) superfine blanched almond flour

CHEESECAKE

16 oz (455 g) cream cheese, softened

1 cup (245 g) pure pumpkin puree

2 large eggs, at room temperature

½ cup (76 g) maple sugar

1 tbsp (8 g) cassava flour

1 tsp pure vanilla extract

Zest of 1 orange

2 tsp (5 g) ground cinnamon

½ tsp ground ginger

½ tsp ground cloves

½ tsp ground allspice

¼ tsp sea salt

1 cup (237 ml) water

Homemade whipped cream or coconut whipped cream, for garnish (optional)

Ground cinnamon, for garnish (optional)

Prepare the crust. Butter a 6- or 7-inch (15- or 18.5-cm) round springform pan that fits in the Instant Pot. Set aside.

In a bowl, combine all the crust ingredients and mix with clean hands until completely incorporated. Dump the mixture into the prepared springform pan and press down to form a packed crust at the bottom. Don't allow too much to go up the sides of the pan. Transfer the pan to the freezer to chill for 15 minutes.

Prepare the cheesecake. In a blender, combine the cream cheese, pumpkin, eggs, maple sugar, cassava flour, vanilla, orange zest, cinnamon, ginger, cloves, allspice and salt. Process on low speed until smooth and fully blended. Pour the cheesecake filling into the frozen crust.

Pour the water into the Instant Pot and insert the steam trivet. Gently place the springform pan on the trivet and cover with a casserole dish glass lid. Secure the lid with the steam vent in the sealed position. Press manual and set on high pressure for 45 minutes.

Once the timer sounds, press keep warm/cancel. Allow the Instant Pot to release pressure naturally for 15 minutes. Using an oven mitt, do a quick release. If there is any steam left over, allow it to release until the silver dial drops, then carefully open the lid.

Remove the lid and carefully lift the trivet and the springform pan out of the Instant Pot. Use oven mitts or towels because the Instant Pot and springform pan will be extremely hot. Allow the cheesecake to cool to room temperature with the glass lid still on. Once it has cooled, remove the lid, taking care not to drip any of the condensation on the top of the cheesecake. Gently run a knife around the edges of the cheesecake to loosen it for when you're ready to remove it from the pan. Wipe off all the condensation from the lid and place it back on top of the cheesecake. Transfer to the refrigerator for at least 6 hours, or until completely chilled, preferably overnight.

Serve chilled. Garnish, if you wish, with homemade whipped cream or coconut whipped cream, or dust with ground cinnamon.

MINI COOKIES & CREAM CHEESECAKE

On my son's birthday, he demanded cheesecake. He had never eaten a cheesecake. He assured me he would eat the cheesecake. Turned out, he didn't. But that's okay. It took me little to no work to whip this baby together. Cheesecake in the oven can be tricky to keep warm and moist so it doesn't crack. The Instant Pot keeps everything nice and cozy, yet it keeps that crust crisp. And nobody ever complains about having extra cheesecake. **SB**

SERVES: 4

CRUST

2 cups (180 g) finely ground chocolate sandwich cookies, preferably Oreos

1 tbsp (13 g) sugar

Pinch of salt

3 tbsp (43 g) unsalted butter, melted

CHEESECAKE

16 oz (455 g) cream cheese, softened

1⅓ cups (268 g) sugar

1 tbsp (5.6 g) finely ground chocolate sandwich cookies, preferably Oreos

1 tsp pure vanilla extract

2 large eggs

½ cup (120 ml) heavy cream

1 cup (237 ml) water

Prepare the crust. In a medium bowl, mix together the cookie crumbs, sugar, salt and butter. Press the mixture into the bottom of a 7-inch (18.5-cm) leakproof round springform pan.

Prepare the cheesecake. In the bowl of an electric stand mixer fitted with the paddle attachment, cream the cream cheese and sugar together until light and fluffy. Scrape down the sides.

Add the cookie crumbs and vanilla. Mix until combined. Add 1 egg at a time and mix until combined, scraping down the bowl, if needed. Mix in the heavy cream.

Pour the cheese mixture over the crust in the springform pan.

Pour the water into the Instant Pot and insert the steam trivet. Place the springform pan on the trivet.

Secure the lid with the steam vent in the sealed position. Press pressure cook until the display light is beneath high pressure. Use the plus and minus buttons to adjust the time until the display reads "25 minutes."

When the timer sounds, allow the pressure to naturally release.

When the float valve falls, remove the springform pan from the pot. Transfer the cake to the fridge and chill overnight before slicing.

PUMPKIN CHEESECAKE
WITH A GRANOLA CRUST

The granola crust on this cheesecake adds so much flavor with minimal effort. I make this all the time in the fall, and it's fun to watch everyone try to guess what the crust is made with! Freezes well. **KB**

SERVES: 6

1 cup (237 ml) water

Nonstick cooking spray, for pan

1½ cups (183 g) granola

4 tbsp (55 g) unsalted butter, melted

2 (8-oz [225-g]) packages cream cheese, softened

½ cup (100 g) sugar

2 large eggs

½ cup (123 g) pure pumpkin puree

1½ tsp (3 g) pumpkin pie spice

½ tsp pure vanilla extract

Pour the water into the Instant Pot and insert the steam trivet.

Spray a 7-inch (18.5-cm) cheesecake pan with a removable bottom with nonstick cooking spray. Using a food processor or high-powered blender, grind the granola into large crumbs. Mix the granola crumbs and melted butter together, then press firmly into the bottom of the pan.

In a medium bowl, beat together the cream cheese and sugar until smooth. Add the eggs, 1 at a time, until they're fully incorporated. Add the pumpkin puree, pumpkin pie spice and vanilla and mix until smooth.

Pour the batter into the cheesecake pan, then cover it with foil. Make a foil sling—a long piece of foil folded twice lengthwise. Center the pan on top of the foil then, using the sling, carefully place the pan on the steam trivet, taking care to fold the sling "handles" down so they don't interfere with closing the pot.

Secure the lid with the steam vent in the sealed position. Press manual and immediately adjust the timer to 30 minutes. Check that the display light is beneath high pressure.

Once the timer sounds, allow the pressure to release naturally for 15 minutes, then quick release the pressure and carefully remove the lid. Carefully remove the cheesecake, using the sling, then let it cool completely on a wire rack (gently dab any condensation from the top of cheesecake before cooling). Chill for at least 4 hours.

MINI CINNAMON CRUNCH MONKEY BREADS

How did it take me so long to discover monkey bread? If you are new to this supereasy and oh-so-sticky sweet dessert, let me fill you in. It is canned biscuit dough cut up and rolled into sugars and, in this recipe, crushed cinnamon crunch cereal. The cereal adds extra crunchiness. I like the fact that these are mini. It means you can totally pop more than one in your mouth and get away with it! **SB**

SERVES: 4

1 (1-lb [455-g]) can buttermilk biscuits

⅓ cup (68 g) granulated sugar

Pinch of salt

½ cup (20 g) crushed cinnamon crunch cereal, divided, plus more for sprinkling

¼ cup (60 ml) melted unsalted butter

1 cup (237 ml) water

1 cup (120 g) confectioners' sugar

2 tbsp (30 ml) milk

Cut each biscuit into 6 pieces.

In a bowl, combine the granulated sugar, salt and half of the crushed cereal. Add the cut biscuit pieces to the bowl. Toss to evenly coat.

Place about 2 heaping tablespoons (35 g) of the coated biscuits, along with a spoonful of the cereal mixture, in each well of a silicone egg bite mold. Top each pile of coated dough with melted butter.

Pour the water into the Instant Pot and insert the steam trivet. Place the filled mold on top of the trivet.

Secure the lid with the steam vent in the sealed position. Press pressure cook until the display light is beneath high pressure. Use the plus and minus buttons to adjust the time until the display reads "20 minutes."

When the timer sounds, quick release the pressure. Remove the lid and take out the silicone mold. Let the monkey breads cool in the mold.

Meanwhile, in a medium bowl, mix together the confectioners' sugar and milk until smooth.

Remove the monkey breads from the mold. Drizzle each monkey bread with icing. Top with a sprinkle of crushed cereal.

POMEGRANATE BREAD PUDDING

Creamy bread pudding made from challah bread and studded with pretty pomegranate arils. This is such a pretty dessert that you can whip together in under 20 minutes. People will think this took you way longer. Plus, the upside to not only being quick is that it doesn't require the oven or stovetop. I highly recommend making this for a dinner party or holiday dessert because it is truly a small but mighty showstopper. **SB**

SERVES: 4

1 cup (237 ml) whole milk

1 cup (237 ml) heavy cream

2 tbsp (30 g) unsalted butter, melted, plus more for pan

1 tsp pure vanilla extract

⅓ cup (67 g) plus 1 tsp granulated sugar, plus more for sprinkling

Pinch of salt

2 large eggs, beaten

½ loaf challah bread, cut into 2" (5-cm) cubes

½ cup (87 g) pomegranate arils, divided

1 cup (237 ml) water

Confectioners' sugar

In a large bowl, combine the milk, cream, melted butter, vanilla, sugar, salt and eggs. Whisk until smooth. Add the challah cubes to the bowl. Mix until all the bread is coated. Let the bread sit in the liquid for a few minutes, then mix in three-quarters of the pomegranate arils.

Butter a 7-inch (18.5-cm) heatproof bowl. Transfer the challah mixture to the prepared bowl. Add the remaining pomegranate seeds to the top of the challah mixture. Sprinkle with granulated sugar.

Pour the water into the Instant Pot and insert the steam trivet. Place the pudding bowl on the center of the trivet.

Secure the lid with the steam vent in the sealed position. Press pressure cook until the display light is beneath high pressure. Use the plus and minus buttons to adjust the time until the display reads "15 minutes."

When the timer sounds, quick release the pressure. Remove the lid and carefully remove the bowl. Lightly dust with confectioners' sugar.

GF GLUTEN-FREE GRAIN-FREE

MEXICAN CHOCOLATE GELATIN PUDDING CUPS

Chocolaty deliciousness with hints of cinnamon, orange and chiles—the bold flavors of Mexican hot chocolate come to life in these fun gelatin pudding cups. Grab a jar and enjoy this afternoon snack or special treat by the spoonful! **ESV**

SERVES: 5

1½ cups (355 ml) heavy cream

½ cup (120 ml) milk

¾ cup (131 g) chocolate chips or chopped chocolate

2 large eggs

¼ cup (60 ml) pure maple syrup or honey

1½ tbsp (11 g) unsweetened cocoa powder

2 tbsp (28 g) grass-fed butter, ghee or coconut oil, melted, divided

1 tbsp (15 ml) pure vanilla extract

½ tsp organic orange extract

½ tsp ground cinnamon

⅛ tsp ground cayenne

⅛ tsp sea salt

1 tsp grass-fed bovine gelatin

1 cup (237 ml) water

Homemade whipped cream, for garnish (optional)

Shaved or chopped organic stone-ground Mexican chocolate, for garnish (optional)

In a small saucepan, over medium-low heat, gently warm the cream, milk and chocolate, whisking until melted. Remove from the heat and set aside.

In a blender, combine the eggs, sweetener of choice, cocoa powder, melted fat of your choice, vanilla, orange extract, cinnamon, cayenne and salt. Process on low speed for 30 seconds until fully blended. While the blender is still blending, remove the vent lid and add the chocolate mixture then the gelatin, and continue to blend for 30 seconds until fully combined.

Evenly pour the custard mixture into five half-pint (250-ml) glass jars, leaving at least a ½-inch (1.3-cm) headspace at the top. Cover and secure the jars with lids.

Pour the water into your Instant Pot and insert the steam trivet. Set all five jars on the trivet. They should fit perfectly inside the Instant Pot. Secure the lid with the steam vent in the sealed position. Press manual, then low pressure and set for 5 minutes.

Once the timer sounds, press keep warm/cancel. Using an oven mitt, do a quick release. When the steam venting stops and the silver dial drops, carefully open the lid.

Using an oven mitt or tongs, carefully remove the jars and remove their lids. Give each pudding cup a good stir until the mixture becomes smooth, then allow them to cool at room temperature. Once they have cooled, transfer them to the refrigerator to set. Let them chill for a minimum of 6 hours, best overnight for the most authentic solid texture.

Serve chilled as is or garnished, if desired, with homemade whipped cream and/or shaved or chopped organic stone-ground Mexican chocolate (I highly recommend the vanilla or cinnamon Mexican chocolate versions).

NOTE: Sustainably sourced grass-fed bovine gelatin is sold at most natural food stores and widely available online.

DAIRY-FREE OPTION **GF** **GLUTEN-FREE**

CHAI-SPICED RICE PUDDING

On days when I need a break from a coffee or espresso drink, I love to switch things up with a chai-spiced drink. There has never been a more cozy combination of spices. Cinnamon, cardamom, allspice, cloves and ginger are the perfect complement to a creamy rice pudding. To switch things up and add a little color, I mixed in golden raisins. On cozy nights in, fire up the Instant Pot for five minutes and enjoy a little dessert. **SB**

SERVES: 4

1 cup (195 g) uncooked arborio rice

1½ cups (355 ml) water

Pinch of salt

2 cups (475 ml) whole milk or almond milk, divided

½ cup (100 g) sugar

2 large eggs

½ tsp pure vanilla extract

½ tsp ground cardamom

½ tsp ground allspice

2 tsp (5 g) ground cinnamon

¼ tsp ground cloves

1 tbsp (6 g) ground ginger

½ cup (75 g) golden raisins

In the Instant Pot, combine the rice, water and salt. Stir well.

Secure the lid with the steam vent in the sealed position. Press pressure cook until the display light is beneath high pressure. Use the plus and minus buttons to adjust the time until the display reads "3 minutes."

Allow the pressure to naturally release for 10 minutes. After 10 minutes, quick release any remaining pressure.

Remove the lid. Add ½ cup (120 ml) of the milk and the sugar. Stir to combine.

In a small bowl, mix together the eggs and the remaining 1½ cups (355 ml) of milk along with the vanilla, cardamom, allspice, cinnamon, cloves, ginger and raisins.

Press sauté. Pour the egg through a mesh strainer into the Instant Pot. Stir to combine.

Once the pudding starts to simmer, press cancel. Stir in the raisins.

The pudding can be served warm or cooled completely in the refrigerator.

GF GLUTEN-FREE   GRAIN-FREE

CHOCOLATE FLOURLESS CAKE

This is my ultimate perfect dessert—dense and fudgy, rich and unbelievably decadent! Being the chocoholic that I am, I love nothing more than simple chocolate cake. This particular cake is my absolute favorite and I love serving it to guests! I also love how easy it is to make, mixing together just a few ingredients. **AR**

SERVES: 6

5 oz (140 g) high-quality unsweetened chocolate

6 tbsp (85 g) unsalted butter

1 tbsp (15 ml) pure vanilla or chocolate extract

1 cup (200 g) sugar

4 large eggs, whisked

½ cup (55 g) unsweetened cocoa powder

Nonstick cooking spray, for pan

1 cup (237 ml) water

½ cup (65 g) raspberries, for serving (optional)

In a microwave or double boiler, melt the chocolate and butter together, then let cool for a few minutes.

Stir the vanilla, sugar, eggs and cocoa powder into the chocolate mixture and mix until smooth.

Lightly spray a 6-inch (15-cm) springform pan with nonstick cooking spray. Alternatively, you can use a 6- to 7-inch (15- to 18.5-cm) round cake pan, but create a sling with foil for ease when removing the cake. Pour the batter into the pan, then cover with foil.

Pour the water into the Instant Pot, insert the steam trivet and place the cake pan on top.

Secure the lid with the steam vent in the sealed position. Select manual or pressure, and cook on high pressure for 35 minutes.

Use a quick release. Remove the lid, then use potholders to remove the cake pan.

Chill for 1 to 2 hours before removing from the pan and slicing. Serve chilled or at room temperature with berries (if using).

DAIRY-FREE   GLUTEN-FREE   GRAIN-FREE

GRAIN-FREE BANANA BREAD
WITH CHOCOLATE CHIPS

I love the idea of using the Instant Pot for baked goods! This recipe came in particularly handy during a kitchen renovation when I had to use up some very ripe bananas. It's hard for me to not include chocolate chips in my banana bread; they certainly add that special element! This variation is gluten-free and Paleo, but still moist and buttery tasting! **AR**

SERVES: 6

1½ cups (150 g) blanched almond flour

2 tbsp (14 g) coconut flour

2 tsp (5 g) ground cinnamon

Pinch of ground nutmeg

¾ tsp baking soda

½ tsp sea salt

¼ cup (60 ml) melted coconut oil

2 medium very ripe bananas, mashed

2 large eggs

2 tbsp (30 ml) pure maple syrup

1 tsp pure vanilla extract

½ cup (88 g) chocolate chips

Nonstick cooking spray, for dish or pan

In a small bowl, stir together the almond flour, coconut flour, cinnamon, nutmeg, baking soda and salt.

In a large bowl, using an electric mixer on low speed, beat together the coconut oil, bananas, eggs, maple syrup and vanilla until mostly smooth. Fold in the flour mixture and continue to beat until no dry pockets remain. Fold in the chocolate chips.

Spray a 7-inch (18.5-cm) heatproof round glass dish or 6- to 7-inch (15- to 18.5-cm) springform pan with nonstick cooking spray. Pour the batter into the prepared dish, then cover the dish with foil.

Pour the water into the Instant Pot and insert the steam trivet. Place the dish on the trivet.

Secure the lid with the steam vent in the sealed position. Select manual or pressure, and cook on high pressure for 35 minutes.

Use a quick release. Carefully remove the dish from the Instant Pot, using pot holders. Allow the banana bread to completely cool before slicing.

PEAR & SWEET POTATO APPLESAUCE

Any other parents out there spend a small fortune on those pouches of pureed applesauce? Ya know, the ones with secret veggies snuck in so your picky kids get all their nutrients and vitamins? It's an easy way to get some fruits and veggies on the go. Making a big batch in the Instant Pot will allow you to freeze some of this slightly sweet and oh so snackable applesauce for later. You will never be faced with running out and having to make a store run to replenish their fave snack. **SB**

SERVES: 4 to 6

5 Honeycrisp apples, cored and chopped

1 sweet potato, peeled and chopped

1 Bartlett pear, cored and chopped

Pinch of salt

1 cup (237 ml) water

½ tsp cinnamon

1 tbsp (15 ml) pure maple syrup

In the Instant Pot, combine all the ingredients and mix well.

Secure the lid with the steam vent in the sealed position. Press pressure cook until the display light is beneath high pressure. Use the plus and minus buttons to adjust the time until the display reads "10 minutes."

When the timer sounds, quick release the pressure. Remove the lid and use an immersion blender to puree until smooth.

DAIRY-FREE GLUTEN-FREE GRAIN-FREE

HEALTHY BROWNIES

I know what you might be thinking: Why make these in the Instant Pot if I could make them in the oven? Well, I can think of many reasons! Maybe you live in a college dorm, are on a camping trip or have a cramped apartment. Or maybe you don't have a working oven or don't want to turn on your oven. Just know that you don't have to be deprived of one of the best desserts ever: brownies! The pumpkin adds a subtle flavor and nutrients, and keeps these brownies nice and moist. **AR**

SERVES: 6

1 cup (245 g) pure pumpkin puree

¼ cup (65 g) almond butter

2 large eggs

1 tbsp (30 ml) pure vanilla extract

1 cup (225 g) coconut sugar

½ cup (50 g) almond flour

½ cup (55 g) unsweetened cocoa powder

½ tsp baking powder

½ tsp sea salt

½ cup (88 g) chocolate chips

Nonstick cooking spray, for pan

2 cups (475 ml) water

In a medium bowl, using an electric mixer, beat together the pumpkin, almond butter, eggs, vanilla and coconut sugar.

In a smaller bowl, whisk together the almond flour, cocoa powder, baking powder and salt. Pour the dry ingredients into the wet and continue to beat until no dry pockets remain. Fold in the chocolate chips.

Prepare a 7-inch (18.5-cm) round springform or cake pan by coating with nonstick cooking spray. Pour the batter into the pan and smooth it out (it should be thick). Cover the pan with a paper towel, then cover with foil. This will help keep the moisture out.

Pour the water into the Instant Pot and insert the steam trivet. Place the pan on the trivet. Secure the lid with the steam vent in the sealed position. Select manual or pressure, and cook on high pressure for 35 minutes.

Use a natural release for at least 15 minutes, then release any remaining steam. Remove the lid and use pot holders to remove the pan.

Let sit for at least 15 minutes to cool before removing the brownies from the pan.

STUFFED APPLES

For those times when you find yourself with an abundance of apples and want a simple yet light apple dessert, stuffed apples are perfect! In the Instant Pot, these apples become softened with a delicious buttery, cinnamon and sweet taste. Serve plain or top with a scoop of vanilla ice cream! **AR**

SERVES: 4

4 medium Honeycrisp apples

⅓ cup (37 g) crushed pecans

⅓ cup (75 g) coconut sugar or dark brown sugar

½ cup (75 g) raisins

2 tsp (5 g) ground cinnamon

Pinch of sea salt

4 tbsp (55 g) butter, cut into 4 equal pieces

¾ cup (160 ml) water

2 cups (280 g) vanilla ice cream (optional)

Core each apple from the top, removing a lot of the inside, leaving about ¼ inch (6 mm) around the sides and at the bottom.

In a medium bowl, mix together the pecans, coconut sugar, raisins, cinnamon and salt. Fill the cavity of each apple with the mixture. Top with a slice of butter.

Pour the water into the Instant Pot. Place the apples in the pot side by side, filled cavity up.

Secure the lid with the steam vent in the sealed position. Select manual or pressure, and cook on high pressure for 3 minutes.

Use a quick release, then remove the apples, using tongs.

Serve hot with vanilla ice cream (if using).

LEFTOVER GLAZED DOUGHNUT-APPLE CRISP

My kids love doughnuts. Who am I kidding? I love doughnuts! The only problem is that my kids leave doughnuts behind and I save them just in case they change their mind. I feel guilty throwing them out. So, I tossed them into a sticky and sweet Instant Pot apple crisp. It doesn't get a crunchy top like traditional apple crisp. But fear not; the apple cinnamon flavor is spot on and those cut-up doughnuts absorb all that melted ice cream you will inevitably scoop on top. **SB**

SERVES: 4 to 6

6 Honeycrisp apples, partially peeled

½ cup (115 g) brown sugar, divided

1 tsp ground cinnamon

½ tsp pure vanilla extract

1 cup (237 ml) water

½ cup (40 g) old-fashioned rolled oats

3 tbsp (43 g) unsalted butter

¼ cup (30 g) all-purpose flour

3 leftover glazed doughnuts, cut into 1" (2.5-cm) pieces

Vanilla ice cream, for topping

Cut each apple into 4 wedges, around the seeds (discard the seeds). Cut those wedges in half; you should have 8 pieces. Place the apples, ¼ cup (58 g) of the brown sugar, and the cinnamon, vanilla and water in the Instant Pot.

Secure the lid with the steam vent in the sealed position. Press pressure cook until the display light is beneath high pressure. Use the plus and minus buttons to adjust the time until the display reads "1 minute."

When the timer sounds, quick release the pressure. Remove the lid.

In a small bowl, mix together the remaining brown sugar and the oats, butter and flour.

Stir the doughnuts into the apple mixture.

Press sauté. Use your hands to crumble the oat mixture over the apple mixture. Let the crisp bubble away for 2 minutes.

Press cancel. Let the crisp cool for 5 minutes before spooning into bowls and topping with vanilla ice cream.

PEAR & CRANBERRY CRISP

Tart cranberries and sweetened pears go perfectly together in this simple crisp. This recipe is so hands off and easy, and perfect for the holidays! Serve with an optional scoop of vanilla ice cream. **AR**

SERVES: 6

3 large Anjou pears, peeled, cored and diced

1 cup (100 g) fresh cranberries

1 tbsp (13 g) granulated sugar

2 tsp (5 g) ground cinnamon

½ tsp ground nutmeg

½ cup (120 ml) water

1 tbsp (15 ml) pure maple syrup

6 tbsp (90 g) unsalted butter, melted

1 cup (80 g) old-fashioned rolled oats

⅓ cup (75 g) dark brown sugar

¼ cup (30 g) all-purpose flour

½ tsp sea salt

½ cup (50 g) pecans, toasted (optional)

Vanilla ice cream, for serving (optional)

In the Instant Pot, combine the pears and cranberries and sprinkle with the granulated sugar. Let sit for a few minutes, then sprinkle with the cinnamon and nutmeg. Pour the water and maple syrup on top.

In a medium bowl, stir together the melted butter, oats, brown sugar, flour and salt.

Spoon the mixture on the fruit in the Instant Pot.

Secure the lid with the steam vent in the sealed position. Select manual or pressure, and cook on high pressure for 5 minutes. Use a quick release.

Spoon into individual bowls and serve hot. Top with pecans and vanilla ice cream (if using).

GF
GLUTEN-FREE
GRAIN-FREE

RASPBERRY-LEMON CURD

Oh, the possibilities with this deliciously easy lemon curd! This citrus and raspberry concoction makes a delightful addition to a springtime dessert or brunch. It's silky, smooth and made with just a few classic ingredients and minimal cook time. Serve over ice cream, a cheesecake, yogurt or even cookies. Store for future use or even as a thoughtful homemade gift in a jar. **AR**

MAKES: Approximately 1½ cups (340 g)

12 oz (340 g) fresh raspberries
¾ cup (150 g) sugar
2 tbsp (30 ml) fresh lemon juice
1 tsp lemon zest
2 large egg yolks
2 tbsp (28 g) unsalted butter

In the Instant Pot, combine the raspberries, sugar and lemon juice and zest.

Secure the lid with the steam vent in the sealed position. Select manual or pressure, and cook on high pressure for 1 minute.

Use a natural release for at least 10 minutes. Release any remaining steam.

Remove the lid. Use an immersion blender or transfer the mixture to a blender and pulse until smooth. If removed, place the mixture back inside the Instant Pot and select sauté.

Meanwhile, in a small bowl, whisk together the egg yolks. Slowly fold them into the raspberry mixture. Continue to stir while the mixture comes to a boil, then select cancel. Add the butter.

Transfer to a glass or other airtight, heatproof container and let cool to room temperature. Refrigerate until the curd is completely set. Serve chilled.

Store this recipe in the fridge for up to 2 weeks.

GLUTEN-FREE   GRAIN-FREE   PALEO

HONEY-SWEETENED LEMON CURD

Rich, thick, tangy and sweet, this heavenly lemon curd is such a treat! Serve it with fresh fruit such as seasonal berries, spread some on a scone or muffin, add it to a dessert tart, top it with homemade whipped cream or simply enjoy every bite by the spoonful. It is so easy to make with the help of the Instant Pot, too! **ESV**

MAKES: 1½ to 2 cups (340 to 455 g)

4 large eggs

⅓ cup (80 ml) honey

Zest of 3 lemons

½ cup (120 ml) fresh lemon juice

7 tbsp (99 g) grass-fed butter, melted and cooled

1 cup (237 ml) water

In a blender, combine the eggs, honey, lemon zest and juice and melted butter and process on low speed for 30 seconds until fully blended.

Pour the lemon mixture into a 1½-quart (1.5-L) casserole dish that fits inside the Instant Pot; cover the casserole dish with its glass lid. If your casserole dish doesn't have a glass lid, you can cover the top of the dish with unbleached parchment paper, then top it with foil and secure it around the edges.

Pour the water into the Instant Pot and insert the steam trivet. Carefully set the covered casserole dish on the trivet.

Secure the lid with the steam vent in the sealed position. Press manual and set on high pressure for 5 minutes.

Once the timer sounds, press keep warm/cancel. Allow the Instant Pot to release pressure naturally for 15 minutes. Using an oven mitt, do a quick release. If there is any steam left over, allow it to release until the silver dial drops, then carefully open the lid.

Using an oven mitt, carefully remove the casserole dish from the Instant Pot, then remove the glass lid. Use a whisk to whisk the curd constantly until the mixture becomes completely smooth, then pour into your choice of half-pint (250-ml) glass jars, ramekins or a single glass airtight container or simply leave in the casserole dish. Transfer the lemon curd to the refrigerator to set.

Let chill for a minimum of 5 hours, or until fully chilled. Serve chilled.

NOTE: Use a lighter-colored honey such as clover, not a wildflower honey, which tends to be too overpowering in flavor.

DAIRY-FREE OPTION · **GF GLUTEN-FREE** · **GRAIN-FREE** · **PALEO** · **V VEGAN OPTION**

FROM-SCRATCH SPICED APPLE– CRANBERRY CIDER

Although hot chocolate may be the most traditional warming drink for the colder months, I think spiced cider deserves a chance for first place. This naturally sweetened dessert version isn't your average store-bought cider—this is the legit, real-deal, made from whole food ingredients, perfectly spiced hot drink to sip on, made even more special when topped with ice cream! It's such a fun sweet treat, you're going to want to make this special drink throughout fall and winter! **ESV**

MAKES: 5 cups (1.2 L)

6 apples, peeled, cored and quartered

2½ cups (590 ml) filtered water, plus more as needed

3 cups (300 g) frozen or fresh cranberries

Zest and juice of 2 medium oranges

⅓ cup (80 ml) honey or pure maple syrup

1 (1" [2.5-cm]) piece fresh ginger, peeled and sliced

3 cinnamon sticks

13 whole cloves

Vanilla ice cream, for serving (optional)

In a high-powered blender, combine the apples and water and process until fully blended and liquefied.

Pour the apple juice through a fine-mesh strainer into the Instant Pot.

Add the cranberries, orange zest and juice, natural sweetener of your choice, ginger, cinnamon sticks and cloves. If the liquid volume does not reach the "5 cup" mark on the inside of the Instant Pot, add more filtered water until it does.

Press sauté and bring the mixture to a boil. When the cider starts to boil, turn off the Instant Pot by pressing keep warm/cancel.

Secure the lid with the steam vent in the sealed position. Press manual and set on high pressure for 10 minutes.

Once the timer sounds, press keep warm/cancel. Allow the Instant Pot to release pressure naturally for 15 minutes. Using an oven mitt, do a quick release. If there is any steam left over, allow it to release until the silver dial drops, then carefully open the lid.

Using an oven mitt, very carefully ladle or pour the superhot spiced cider through a fine-mesh strainer into a very large bowl or large heatproof pitcher. Repeat the straining one more time to remove all the fruit pulp, if necessary.

Serve immediately in your favorite mug, topped with a scoop of vanilla ice cream for extra decadence (if using).

If you're not ready to drink the spiced cider right away and would like to keep it hot, place it back in the pot after straining and turn on the Instant Pot's warming setting by pressing keep warm/cancel.

CONDIME
AND
SAUCES

HEARTY BOLOGNESE SAUCE

This classic and simple meat-based ragout sauce is brimming with hearty ground beef, bacon, tons of crushed tomatoes, lots of garlic and vibrant Italian herbs. It's absolutely delicious topped with a bunch of freshly grated Parmesan over a bed of cooked grain-free or gluten-free pasta, or spaghetti squash. **ESV**

SERVES: 6

3 tbsp (43 g) grass-fed butter, ghee or avocado oil

1 large yellow onion, diced

8 oz (225 g) white button or cremini mushrooms, thinly sliced

2 large celery ribs, thinly sliced

1 large carrot, peeled and diced

7 cloves garlic, finely minced or grated

2 lb (905 g) grass-fed ground beef

¼ cup (60 ml) good-quality dry red wine

¾ cup (175 ml) chicken or beef stock

1½ cups (270 g) crushed tomatoes

¼ cup (10 g) finely chopped fresh basil

¼ cup (15 g) finely chopped fresh flat-leaf parsley

½ tsp dried oregano

1 tsp sea salt

Zest of 1 lemon

¾ cup (175 ml) milk

6 oz (170 g) precooked bacon, crumbled

Cooked grain-free or gluten-free pasta, or spaghetti squash, for serving

½ cup (40 g) shredded Parmesan cheese, for garnish

Place your healthy fat of choice in the Instant Pot and press sauté. Once the fat has melted, add the onion and mushrooms and sauté, stirring occasionally, for 7 minutes, or until caramelized. Then, add the celery, carrot and garlic and sauté for 3 minutes, stirring occasionally. Add the ground beef, breaking it up with a wooden spoon, and cook until it's browned, 5 to 7 minutes. Add the wine and deglaze the pot, scraping up any browned bits with a wooden spoon. Add the stock, tomatoes, basil, parsley, oregano, salt and lemon zest, giving it all a stir. Press keep warm/cancel.

Secure the lid with the steam vent in the sealed position. Press manual and set on high pressure for 15 minutes.

Once the timer sounds, press keep warm/cancel. Using an oven mitt, do a quick release. When the steam venting stops and the silver dial drops, carefully open the lid.

Press sauté, give the sauce a stir, then add the milk and crumbled bacon. Allow the sauce to come to a simmer and stir until the milk is fully mixed in. Simmer for about 5 minutes, or until the sauce slightly thickens. Press keep warm/cancel. Allow the sauce to rest for 10 minutes.

Serve immediately over cooked grain-free or gluten-free pasta or cooked spaghetti squash, topped with shredded Parmesan cheese.

FIRE-ROASTED TOMATO & BUTTERNUT SQUASH SAUCE

Any parents out there still struggling to get their kids to eat more veggies? I am raising my hand with you in solidarity. I tried cauliflower—too stinky. I tried kale, spinach, arugula—too green. After a lot of trial and error, I figured it out: butternut squash! When tomatoes and squash come together, you can hardly taste it; the squash is just like a hint of sweetness in the background. It also helps thicken the sauce. I have been making this for my kids for some time and they are none the wiser. **SB**

SERVES: 4 to 6

2 (14.5-oz [411-g]) cans fire-roasted diced tomatoes

1 cup (237 ml) water

1 yellow onion, diced

3 cloves garlic, chopped

3 cups (420 g) peeled, seeded and cubed butternut squash

1 tsp salt, plus more to taste

1 tsp pure maple syrup

1 tbsp (15 ml) balsamic vinegar

1 tsp dried oregano

1 tsp dried thyme

Pinch of crushed red pepper flakes

½ tsp freshly ground black pepper, plus more to taste

3 tbsp (48 g) tomato paste

In the Instant Pot, combine all the ingredients, except the tomato paste, and mix well.

Secure the lid with the steam vent in the sealed position. Press pressure cook until the display light is beneath high pressure. Use the plus and minus buttons to adjust the time until the display reads "10 minutes."

When the timer sounds, quick release the pressure. Remove the lid.

Stir in the tomato paste. Use an immersion blender to puree the sauce until smooth. Adjust the salt and pepper, if needed.

DAIRY-FREE OPTION   GLUTEN-FREE

GRAIN-FREE   PALEO   VEGAN OPTION

NOURISHING MUSHROOM GRAVY

There's just something about gravy that satisfies the palate. This luscious, savory sauce goes so perfectly with mashed potatoes, meat dishes, stuffing (page 387) and roasted veggies. This easy Instant Pot version is packed with the woodsy flavor of caramelized mushrooms and has hints of fresh herbs and bacon. **ESV**

MAKES: 3 cups (710 ml)

3 tbsp (43 g) grass-fed butter, ghee or avocado oil

2 yellow onions, sliced

8 oz (225 g) white or cremini mushrooms, cleaned and halved

3 cloves garlic, chopped

1½ tsp (1 g) chopped fresh sage

1½ tsp (2 g) chopped fresh thyme

1 tsp sea salt

2 pieces precooked organic bacon (optional)

3 cups (710 ml) chicken or vegetable stock, or bone broth

Place your healthy fat of choice in the Instant Pot and press sauté. Once the fat has melted, add the onions and sauté, stirring occasionally, for 5 minutes. Add the mushrooms and continue to sauté, stirring occasionally, for 7 minutes, or until the onions and mushrooms are light golden brown and caramelized. Add the garlic and sauté, stirring with a wooden spoon, for 1 minute or until fragrant, making sure to scrape up any browned bits at the bottom of the pot. Press keep warm/cancel and add the sage, thyme, salt, bacon (if using) and stock.

Secure the lid with the steam vent in the sealed position. Press manual and set on high pressure for 3 minutes.

Once the timer sounds, press keep warm/cancel. Using an oven mitt, do a quick release. When the steam venting stops and the silver dial drops, carefully open the lid.

Carefully transfer the hot gravy into a blender, making sure to leave at least 3 inches (7.5 cm) of headspace as hot liquids expand in the blender. Cover with the blender lid and, wearing an oven mitt while holding the lid closed, blend on low speed until completely pureed, about 30 seconds.

Transfer the gravy back into the Instant Pot, then press sauté and allow the gravy to simmer for 10 minutes to thicken. Once thickened, allow the gravy to sit and rest in the Instant Pot for about 15 minutes before serving.

Once the gravy has rested, it can be served immediately or stored for later use in an airtight glass container, such as a Mason jar, for up to 3 days.

NOTE: If you have roasted chicken drippings or turkey drippings and/or leftover roasted crispy chicken skin (from 1 chicken thigh), add these to the Instant Pot when you add the precooked bacon. Both of these add an extra-special layer of flavor to the gravy.

GF GLUTEN-FREE · GRAIN-FREE · PALEO

CARAMELIZED ONION COMPOTE

There is nothing like a good caramelized onion compote. When cooked with this method, the onions become so buttery with a sweet caramel flavor. This compote is so good served as a condiment alongside savory dishes and it's extra special served as an appetizer on a charcuterie board full of meats, cheeses, pâté, cured olives, pickled veggies, dried fruits, crackers and crostini. **ESV**

MAKES: 2 to 3 cups (640 to 960 g)

3 tbsp (43 g) grass-fed butter or ghee

7 large yellow onions, thickly sliced

3 cloves garlic, minced

1 tsp sea salt

1 tsp finely chopped fresh thyme leaves

¼ cup (60 ml) filtered water

Place your healthy fat of choice in the Instant Pot and press sauté. Once the fat has melted, add the onions, stirring occasionally for 7 minutes until the onions are light golden brown. Add the garlic, salt and thyme and sauté, stirring with a wooden spoon, for 1 minute, or until fragrant, making sure to scrape up any browned bits at the bottom of the pot. Press keep warm/cancel. Add the water and give it a quick stir.

Secure the lid with the steam vent in the sealed position. Press manual and set on high pressure for 7 minutes.

Once the timer sounds, press keep warm/cancel. Allow the Instant Pot to release pressure naturally for 5 minutes. Using an oven mitt, do a quick release. If there is any steam left over, allow it to release until the silver dial drops, then carefully open the lid.

Press sauté and, using a wooden spoon, stir occasionally for 5 minutes, or until all moisture has evaporated and the onions are a caramelized light brown color.

Use an immersion blender or transfer the onions to a food processor or high-powered blender and pulse just until they become a rustic mash, 5 to 7 seconds, do not overmix. You may need to do this in batches if you're using a blender.

Pour the onion compote into a serving dish or jar. Serve immediately as a condiment or serve slightly cooled off or at room temperature as a spread with appetizers.

NOTE: Store the leftovers in an airtight container (preferably a heatproof glass container, such as a Mason jar) and store in the refrigerator for up to 2 days.

DAIRY-FREE GLUTEN-FREE

GRAIN-FREE PALEO VEGAN

CRANBERRY KETCHUP

Ketchup is one of those condiments that is a favorite for so many people. The tomato version is great, but there's an extra-special version that is just as good, if not better! Because my husband and I do better without tomatoes, I love to make this super yummy version for us to enjoy instead. We love to serve it with homemade sweet potato fries, on burgers and so much more. **ESV**

MAKES: 2 cups (554 g)

2 cups (554 g) blended Cranberry Sauce (page 495)

¼ cup (60 ml) cider vinegar

½ tsp onion powder

½ tsp mustard powder

½ tsp ground cinnamon

½ tsp ground allspice

¼ tsp ground cloves

¼ tsp garlic powder

¼ tsp ground ginger

½ tsp sea salt

In the Instant Pot, combine all the ingredients and give everything a stir.

Secure the lid with the steam vent in the sealed position. Press manual and set on high pressure for 1 minute.

Once the timer sounds, press keep warm/cancel. Using an oven mitt, do a quick release. When the steam venting stops and the silver dial drops, carefully open the lid.

If the ketchup is too liquidy, press sauté and allow to come to a simmer and cook, stirring constantly, for 1 to 2 minutes, or until thickened.

Pour the ketchup into an airtight container (preferably a heatproof glass container, such as a Mason jar) and place in the refrigerator to fully chill. Serve cold as a dipping sauce or condiment.

CRANBERRY SAUCE

I look forward to making this special homemade cranberry sauce every year when cranberries are in season and especially for the holidays. Let the Instant Pot help you out during the busy season and cook this delicious, spiced-cherry-citrus, naturally sweetened, well-loved condiment for you. **ESV**

MAKES: 3 cups (831 g)

10 oz (280 g) frozen or fresh cranberries

1 cup (155 g) frozen cherries

2 apples, peeled, cored and halved

Zest and juice of 1 medium orange

1 tsp ground cinnamon

½ cup (120 ml) honey or pure maple syrup

In the Instant Pot, combine all the ingredients.

Secure the lid with the steam vent in the sealed position. Press manual and set on high pressure for 2 minutes.

Once the timer sounds, press keep warm/cancel. Allow the Instant Pot to release pressure naturally for 10 minutes. Using an oven mitt, do a quick release. If there is any steam left over, allow it to release until the silver dial drops, then carefully open the lid.

Option 1: For a chunkier cranberry sauce, press sauté, then allow to simmer, stirring constantly, for about 5 minutes, or until thickened.

Option 2: For a smashed cranberry sauce, use a potato masher and gently smash the fruit until it reaches your desired consistency, then press sauté and allow to simmer, stirring constantly, for about 5 minutes, or until thickened.

Option 3: For a blended cranberry sauce, using caution, carefully pour the cranberry sauce into a blender, cover and puree on low speed until smooth, about 7 seconds. Alternatively, use an immersion blender to puree the cranberry sauce. Pour the cranberry sauce back into the Instant Pot, press sauté and allow to simmer, stirring constantly, for about 5 minutes, or until thickened.

Serve the cranberry sauce immediately if you prefer it warm; otherwise, store it in an airtight container (preferably a glass container, such as a Mason jar) in the refrigerator for up to 3 days and serve chilled.

NOTE: If you're used to and prefer a supersweet cranberry sauce, feel free to add more sweetener of your choice to the cranberry sauce after the cook time. Give it a taste test and see whether the sweetness is to your liking, and if you prefer, add more sweetener.

DAIRY-FREE GLUTEN-FREE

GRAIN-FREE VEGAN

PUMPKIN PUREE

All of those times we purchased canned pumpkin, who knew that pumpkin puree would be so easy? And so much tastier than the canned version! This simple puree can be swapped in for canned for baked goods and desserts, and in savory pumpkin recipes as well. Store for a week in the fridge, or freeze for later use. **AR**

MAKES: 2 to 3 cups (490 to 735 g) puree

1 (2-lb [905-g]) pie pumpkin
1 cup (237 ml) water

Slice the pumpkin in half along its equator; remove the stem and seeds.

Pour the water into the Instant Pot and insert the steam trivet. Place the pumpkin, cut side down, on top of the trivet.

Secure the lid with the steam vent in the sealed position. Select manual or pressure, and cook on high pressure for 10 minutes.

Use a quick release, and make sure all the steam is released before taking off the lid. Using pot holders or tongs, carefully remove the pumpkin.

Gently scoop the flesh into a large bowl or food processor. Using an immersion blender or the food processor, pulse until smooth.

Store in the refrigerator for up to 1 week.

SALTED CARAMEL SAUCE

The perfect condiment to any dessert—ice cream, cheesecake, cookies, brownies or as a dipping sauce for fruit—this salted caramel is fun to keep on hand. While it may go without saying that this particular caramel sauce can also be made on the stovetop, sometimes the Instant Pot helps us in a pinch. I also love the depth of an Instant Pot, making it easier to make caramel without having to keep a close eye while cooking. **AR**

MAKES: 1½ cups (340 g) sauce

1 (13.5-oz [400-ml]) can full-fat coconut milk

⅔ cup (150 g) coconut sugar

½ tsp sea salt

1 tsp pure vanilla extract

Select sauté on the Instant Pot, set to "high" if possible. Combine the coconut milk and coconut sugar in the pot and give the mixture a quick stir.

Let the mixture bubble and begin to brown for at least 10 minutes, and up to 15 (depending on how your pot is; for a medium sauté, it will take up to 15 minutes). Select cancel, then add the salt and vanilla.

Allow the caramel to cool and thicken for another 20 minutes. Remove from the pot and store in a glass container.

NOTE: Recipe can be stored in the fridge for up to 2 weeks. Reheat when ready to use and serve hot!

GF GLUTEN-FREE · GRAIN-FREE · PALEO

SPICED APPLE BUTTER

This scrumptious condiment is commonly slathered on muffins, bread, toast, scones, muffins and more. It's also served as a side dish along savory meals, and of course, you can eat it by the spoonful, too. Traditionally there is no butter in apple butter because the apples slow cook for hours to form a thick consistency, but this Instant Pot version cooks in minutes and butter is added for that silky, traditional taste. **ESV**

MAKES: 1 quart (1.1 kg)

12 apples, peeled, cored and quartered

5 tbsp (70 g) grass-fed butter

¼ cup (60 ml) filtered water

4 tsp (9 g) ground cinnamon

½ tsp ground cloves

½ tsp ground allspice

In the Instant Pot, combine all the ingredients.

Secure the lid with the steam vent in the sealed position. Press manual and set on high pressure for 3 minutes.

Once the timer sounds, press keep warm/cancel. Allow the Instant Pot to release pressure naturally for 15 minutes. Using an oven mitt, do a quick release. If there is any steam left over, allow it to release until the silver dial drops, then carefully open the lid.

Using a slotted spoon, ladle the mixture into a blender or food processor, making sure to leave at least a few inches (about 10 cm) of headspace and not fill it to the top, as the hot steam will need room to escape. If a lot of excess liquid remains in the Instant Pot, use only if needed to blend; otherwise, discard. Pulse just until fully combined and smooth—you may need to do this in batches if you're using a blender.

Pour the apple butter in a heatproof airtight container, such as a glass Mason jar, and place in the refrigerator until fully cooled. Serve chilled. Store in the refrigerator for up to 2 days.

NOTES: I prefer to use a 50/50 ratio of sweet apples (e.g., Honeycrisp) and tart apples (e.g., Granny Smith), although it's just as good with 12 sweet apples.

If possible, use organic apples since apples are on the EWG's "Shopper's Guide to Pesticides in Produce" Dirty Dozen list.

RASPBERRY-CHIA JAM

Nothing better than a good slather of jam on toast with butter. Jam on crackers with a cheese board isn't too shabby, either. I guess I'm saying I pretty much just love jam. Jam with added protein is even better. Little chia seeds thicken this sweet and tart raspberry jam as it cooks and cools. With this inventive jam, you'll be as big a fan of jam as Joey from Friends. **SB**

SERVES: 4

12 oz (340 g) frozen raspberries
⅓ cup (80 ml) water
⅓ cup (80 ml) plus 1 tbsp (15 ml) honey
2 heaping tbsp (25 g) chia seeds

In the Instant Pot, mix together all the ingredients.

Secure the lid with the steam vent in the sealed position. Press pressure cook until the display light is beneath high pressure. Use the plus and minus buttons to adjust the time until the display reads "2 minutes."

Quick release the pressure and remove the lid.

Let the jam cool in the pot for 10 minutes and then transfer to lidded Mason jars. Store in the fridge for up to 2 weeks.

DAIRY-FREE GLUTEN-FREE GRAIN-FREE VEGAN OPTION

STRAWBERRY JAM

Turn fresh berries into a delicious, fresh, homemade jam! The real stuff contains only the best ingredients, and without being overly sweet like the store-bought jars. It's so easy to make, and the perfect topping to so many things. Feel free to swap out for your personal favorite berry! **AR**

MAKES: Approximately 2 cups (640 g)

1 lb (455 g) strawberries

⅔ cup (133 g) sugar

1 tbsp (15 ml) fresh orange juice

1 tsp orange zest

2 to 3 tbsp (30 to 45 ml) honey (optional)

In the Instant Pot, combine the strawberries and sugar. Let sit for up to 1 hour to bring out some of the natural juices, an important step in ensuring the recipe comes to pressure.

Add the orange juice and zest. Select sauté on the Instant Pot and bring the mixture to a boil. Boil for 2 to 3 minutes, then select cancel.

Secure the lid with the steam vent in the sealed position. Select manual or pressure, and cook on high pressure for 6 minutes.

Use a quick release, and remove the lid once all the steam has been released.

Select sauté on the Instant Pot and boil for another 3 to 4 minutes, or until the jam reaches the gel point. Add the honey if you would like additional sweetener. Select cancel.

Mash the strawberries, if desired, and let it cool to room temperature. Transfer to an airtight container and refrigerate until completely set.

The jam can be stored in the refrigerator for up to 3 weeks, or the freezer for 6 months.

ABOUT THE AUTHORS

KRISTY BERNARDO is the author of *Cooking from Frozen in Your Instant Pot®* and *Weeknight Cooking in your Instant Pot®*. She's also the creator of The Wicked Noodle, a cooking blog that features simple cooking. Kristy teaches cooking classes, speaks at conferences and events and appears on local TV and radio cooking shows. She lives in Ashburn, Virginia.

EMILY SUNWELL-VIDAURRI is the author of *Amazing Mexican Favorites with Your Instant Pot®*, *The Art of Great Cooking with Your Instant Pot®* and *Low-Carb Cooking with Your Instant Pot®*, and the founder of the gluten-free cooking blog Recipes to Nourish. She lives with her husband and children in Sacramento, California.

AMY RAINS is the author of *One-Pot Gluten-Free Cooking* and the founder of Wholesomelicious. She has been featured by *Country Living*, Real Simple and BuzzFeed, among others. She lives in Williamsburg, Virginia.

STEFANIE BUNDALO is the author of *Quick Prep Cooking with Your Instant Pot®* and the founder of Sarcastic Cooking. Her recipes have been featured on Self.com, and she's worked with a number of liquor companies such as Wave Vodka and Buffalo Trace Distillery to produce recipes that highlight their products. She lives in Homer Glen, Illinois.

INDEX